HOW TO SELL YOURSELF

HOW

Joe Girard

with Robert Casemore

TO SELL YOURSELF

WARNER BOOKS

A Time Warner Company

This Warner Books Edition is published by arrangement with
Simon & Schuster, Inc.

Warner Books, Inc., 666 Fifth Avenue, New York, N.Y. 10103

W A Time Warner Company

Printed in the United States of America

First printing: March 1981

20   19   18   17   16   15   14   13   12   11

Book design by Irving Perkins

Cover design by Gene Light

Cover photo by Sigrid Estrada

Library of Congress Cataloging in Publication Data

Girard, Joe.
    How to sell yourself.

        1. Success. 2. Conduct of life. I. Casemore,
    Robert, joint author. II. Title.
    BJ1611.2.G55 1981   158'.1   80-20802
    ISBN 0-446-38367-8 (U.S.A.)

June, my pal, my wife, may this book inspire others to reach for success, as you inspired me.

Contents

10 CONTENTS

Introduction

A WELL-WRITTEN motivational book produced out of the experience of a successful person can be of inestimable help to any reader who really wants to do more with his life. Such a book has power—the power to communicate innovative ideas, the power to change attitudes and the power to stimulate the will to personal achievement.

America has produced more successful men and women than any other nation in history, and one reason for this phenomenon is that Americans read more motivational books than any other people anywhere. And this book, *How to Sell Yourself*, by Joe Girard, is one of the best books in this field. In my opinion, it will become a classic in the success literature of our time.

I once asked one of our outstanding book distributors, "What is the chief important factor in the value of a book?" His quick answer was, "The person who wrote it. Does he or she have something to say and the ability to say it well? But more important, is the author a living example of the ideas developed in the book?" On the basis of that standard, this is an outstanding book, for the author, one of those rare dynamic, enthusi-astic and highly competent men developed in the American free-enterprise system, is listed, not without cause, in the *Guinness Book of World Records* as the world's greatest salesman. The spirit, the skills and the personality that made him top salesman come through on every page of this book. In the book he shares openly and gladly the experience and learning that lifted him from the bottom—and a very low bottom, at that—to the su-preme apex of the selling profession.

But it is more than skilled salesmanship that comes through to the reader. It is the presence of an alive and vital person who transmits dynamic energy. The joy of life itself springs from the pages of the book. And with it comes the impression that a friend is writing to you, a friend who believes that you can do what he has done. He tells you that you have within you a great potential for achievement. He believes in you because he learned out of great adversity to believe in himself.

Joe Girard is a sincere man. He writes only what he believes; indeed, only what he knows; for what he tells about has hap-pened to him personally. He is convinced that similar great things can happen to you also. He is like a coach telling you what you can do and how to do it. Then he stands with you, helping you on the upward climb.

The central thrust of the book is that we must learn to sell ourselves. People will buy from a salesman because they are convinced that the salesman is a right person. The buyer likes him and trusts him. That being so, his product must likewise be right. Salesmanship actually is a process of persuasion in which an individual is induced to walk a road of agreement with the seller. And the chief element in the process of persuasion is a man or woman who is trustworthy, who wants to help, who desires to serve. This has made Joe Girard Number One Sales-man of the World. It can help you too, in whatever your job may be, to move right up there to the top.

I like this book because I like Joe Girard. He is one of my

most inspiring friends. When I am with him in person I get remotivated. And as I read the manuscript of this book, I felt the same motivation to get out there and do a better job.

But I like this book also because it is packed full of positive thinking. It contains all kinds of workable ideas for self-improvement. It's an interesting, different, innovative book. It will make you like yourself more than you do. It will sell you to yourself. And only the person who has a humble yet realistic belief in himself ever makes something great of himself. Joe Girard can help you. I know, for he has helped me.

NORMAN VINCENT PEALE

CHAPTER ONE

Selling Yourself on You

MY NAME is Joe Girard.

I grew up in the motor capital of the United States, Detroit, Michigan, the city that put the whole world on wheels.

I suppose it was natural that I, like so many others from this dynamic city, would become a part of the automobile business. Not making cars, but selling them. As a matter of record I am the *World's Number-One New Car Salesman*.

In case you think I hung that tag on myself, let me set you straight. The title was given to me by the *Guinness Book of World Records*. I still hold it, and I'm still in the book. As of this writing, no one has successfully challenged me—no one has beaten my record of 1,425 new cars sold in one year alone. They were not fleet sales; all were individual units sold at retail, belly to belly.

What the *Guinness Book of World Records* doesn't mention

is that I really sell the World's Number-One Product—which is not an automobile at all: It's me, Joe Girard. I sell Joe Girard, I always have, I always will, and no one can sell *me* better than *myself*.

Now, let me bowl you over. The World's Number-One Product is also *you*, and no one can sell *you* better than *yourself*—when you know how. That's what this book is all about: how to sell yourself. Read it carefully, soak it in, commit parts of it to memory.

At the end of each chapter I'm going to tell you some things to do *now*, as you read along, each day—things that will make you the World's Number-One Salesperson of Yourself. Do those things and you'll be a winner. I guarantee it!

Sell *myself*, you ask? Certainly, because we are all salespeople from the time we can reason effectively to the end of our days. I once heard Father Clement Kern, of Most Holy Trinity Church, now retired, one of our city's most beloved Roman Catholic priests, say to this effect: Even *after* the end of our days we'll probably be doing our level best to sell St. Peter on ourselves.

We're All Salespeople

The kid who is trying to talk his mother into letting him stay up an extra hour to watch TV is selling.

The girl who hints to her boyfriend that she'd rather see a romantic movie than a hockey game is selling. And when he tries to talk her out of the idea and get her on the edge of the ice, *he's* selling.

The teenager who wants the old man's car for Saturday night is selling.

And the guy who steps up the voltage as he says good night at his girlfriend's door is selling.

Anybody who has ever asked the boss for a raise is selling.

The mother who talks up the virtues (if any) of broccoli to her child is selling.

Whoever you are, wherever you are, whatever you do and wherever you do it, you're busy selling. You may not have been aware of this, but it's true.

Who, then, is more qualified to show you how to do a better job of selling yourself than someone who climaxed a career in selling by being crowned the World's Number-One Salesman?

But first things first.

You Must Be Sold on Yourself

Before you can sell yourself successfully to others—and thus sell your ideas, your wishes, your needs, your ambitions, your skills, your experience, your products and services—you must be absolutely sold on yourself: 100 percent.

You must believe in yourself, have faith in yourself and have confidence in yourself. In short, you must be totally aware of your own self-worth.

It was my mother, Grace Girard, who instilled in me an awareness of self-worth, who helped teach me self-respect. God knows, she had formidable opposition in my father.

To this day, as I bounce over the half-century mark, and as I hang up my gloves as a new-car salesman, I still remember vividly the conflicts I had with my father. I could do nothing right. For reasons I have never been able to understand, he spent most of his life assuring me that I would never amount to anything. As a Sicilian kid who sold newspapers and shined shoes in bars, I seemed to have nothing going for me but the street smarts I was learning. I began to believe my father. My self-respect nose-dived through my teen years until one day I found myself staring at the prospect of reform school. Close call, but my mother, thank the good Lord, wasn't buying what my father was selling.

Mother spent most of her life assuring me that I could be Number One. She always stressed to me the importance of selling myself, of thinking of myself as worthy. In her own way she was saying what my friend Dr. Norman Vincent Peale told me years later: "Joe, you are what you believe, you are what you *think* you are."

It all begins with how you think about yourself. Just *who* are you, anyway?

There Is Only One You

I remember my mother smiling and holding my hand and saying, "Joey, there is no one else in the world like you." Thank God, most of us have mothers who think about us that way. Mine was something special, and because I had so much love for her, I believed what she told me. And besides, I didn't have a twin brother, so who could be like me?

However, I did grow up with twin brothers in my neighborhood, Eugene and John LoVasco, and I remember them well. They were absolute look-alikes. I can still hear their mother telling mine that she couldn't tell the boys apart. It was true. Everyone knew that Eugene and John were twins, and identical twins to boot. But were they? Years later, when I had moved away, I happened to mention them to an FBI friend, and he told me that there is no such thing as identical twins.

Consider this: The FBI has files of fingerprints numbering in the millions, maybe even billions. And we've all been told that no two of those sets of fingerprints on file are alike. No two people since the beginning of time have had identical fingerprints. No two people yet to be born will have fingertips or even palms that will coincide.

But that's not all. My FBI friend also told me that voiceprints can be made of words whispered, spoken, sung or shouted, and that these are what are now used in positive identification. As with fingerprints, no two people ever had or will have exactly the same voice. The human ear might not be able to detect a difference, but a voiceprint can.

It's an indisputable fact. No two people have identical personalities. On the surface, so-called identical twins may look alike, so much so that their own parents might have difficulty in telling them apart, but if you were to try to match the right half of one's face to the left half of the other's, they simply wouldn't go together.

There is only one *you*. There is no one in the entire world to equal you, to match your fingerprints, to match your voice, to match your features or to match your personality. You are an original in the fullest sense of the word. You are *number one*. And now that you know it, your job is to reinforce that fact in your conscious and subconscious mind every day.

How to Show You're Number One

I wear a gold lapel pin that says *No. 1*. I'm never without it. I used to wear it because I'm the Number-One Salesman. Even though I've stopped selling cars and lead a whirlwind life of lecturing before business and industry groups and on college campuses, and writing what I've learned so that others may benefit from it, I still wear that pin because it reaffirms my belief in myself. *I'm sold on myself*, and that pin says so out loud.

You wouldn't believe the number of people who ask me, "What does your lapel pin mean?" Strangers on planes, people with whom I share a lecture platform or a television camera, even men and women in elevators who usually stare straight ahead and say nothing—they all ask me that question or a variation of it.

I tell them, *"It means I'm the number-one person in my life."*

Sound selfish? Egotistical? Not at all. *Looking Out for Number One* is a book that enjoyed a status for some time as a runaway best seller. Some readers regarded it as putting forth an extremely self-centered viewpoint. Others, more charitable, saw it as a handbook on enlightened self-interest. I believe that each of those reactions missed the point. The message I came away with was this: *If you don't believe you're number one, no one else will.* What you must look out for is that *belief*.

Now, you do this: Go to your nearest good-sized jewelry store or the jewelry department of any large retail establishment. There you will find that you can buy yourself a similar Number-One symbol. Most jewelers have it. I've even seen it in mail-order catalogs. The symbol might be a pin like mine, or it might be a necklace, a bracelet, a charm or a ring. Wherever you wear it and whenever you do, it will flash in the sun or glisten in the light of the room. It will throw a spark back to your eye and remind you constantly that you are number one. It's part of what's called psyching yourself up, selling yourself on *you*.

Muhammad Ali: Psyching Yourself Up

Not since Joe Louis, the Brown Bomber who came pounding his way out of the same Detroit ghetto that I did to become heavyweight champion of the world in 1937, has there been a champ with the guts and drive and class of Muhammad Ali. He changed his name along the way, remember? (I'm going to be telling you some more things about Joe Louis later on, but for now let's consider Ali.) He won the championship first in 1964, when he was Cassius Clay, and he won it again as Muhammad Ali in 1974.

Ali told everyone who would listen—in person, in the locker room, in the ring, in front of radio microphones and TV and movie cameras, in newspapers and magazines—that he was number one. His words became a trademark. *I am the greatest!*

You better believe it. I've watched Ali before a fight as he starts to sell himself. He tells the press, in poetry yet, "I'm going to knock him down in five/He's going to take a dive/I'm going to sting him like a bee/So he won't see." Ali liked to call the round. What was he really doing? Simply selling himself. He turned on all the valves to get the adrenaline, the juices, flowing. What happened? His opponent heard this or read this and started *unselling* himself. To top it off, in the ring, while the referee was citing the rules, Ali would look at his opponent and tell him what he was going to do to him. It's all part of selling himself.

The first time he fought Leon Spinks is the only time he did not go through this normal psyching-up process, and the world saw Muhammad Ali go down to defeat. He failed to sell himself on himself, failed to reaffirm that he was number one. The second time he fought Spinks he didn't forget, and the world saw him regain his title, heavyweight champ of the world. He is the greatest!

You have all kinds of opponents, all kinds of obstacles, in life. You're in the ring every day. You can win or you can go down for the count. Why not be a winner? It's more exciting, it's more rewarding, it's more downright fun!

A fellow I know, John Kennedy, who scouts for the Toronto Argonauts, quotes this to-the-point saying among athletes: "Winning is what counts in a game. Coming in second is like kissing your sister."

You don't have to be on the muscle about it, you don't have to tell your opponents, your obstacles, what you're going to do to them. Just be positive and tell yourself that you are the greatest. Do it right now. Say it out loud as you look up from this book: *I am the greatest!* Say it again. If you're all alone, shout it a couple of times. Make the walls shake. Sounds good, doesn't it? Now go back to reading this chapter.

All people who sell themselves successfully are first sold on themselves. Selling yourself on you can take a lot of forms, but most of them add up to this: Learn to like yourself. How?

George Romney: Three Steps for Liking Yourself

George Romney—former president of American Motors, former governor of my state, former Secretary of Housing and Urban Development and a man widely known for his integrity, his ability and his spirituality—once presented these thoughts, I'm told, in a speech he gave before the members of his Mormon Church.

1. Never do anything, anywhere, that you would be ashamed of.
2. Don't be afraid to give yourself a pat on the back now and then.
3. So live that you'd be glad to have yourself for a friend.

I think it's a terrific three-step formula for liking yourself, and Romney surely must follow his own advice. As I've observed him through the years, as I've seen him give freely of his skills and experience to his fellow citizens, I can tell that not only is he genuinely sold on others—he is also thoroughly sold on himself.

But don't think he hasn't faced obstacles. I recall when he first decided to run for governor of the State of Michigan and he mentioned honestly that he had prayed in order to reach a decision. You may or may not know of the jeers, the laughter that he received at the hands of some of the media. Another time, he mentioned just as honestly that he had been "brainwashed" concerning certain aspects of military and foreign affairs. Again, the media and many people hurled the word back in his face. But he went on to use those obstacles as stepping-stones.

Turning Catcalls into Compliments

If you just keep selling yourself on yourself, you'll have an easier time of getting to be and remaining number one. There will be many obstacles, and you must be prepared for them. Early in life my mother warned me that the years ahead would be full of problems, but she cautioned me never to dwell on them. To do so, she pointed out, is to set yourself up for getting caught in a trap of negativism. This can happen, and it nearly did to me.

The year I first became the Number One New Car Salesman, I was honored at a banquet given by the automobile company whose cars I sold. It was known as the Legion of Leaders banquet. I received a lot of heady applause that first time, but little did I know or even suspect the image-shattering obstacles that were in store for me.

The next year I was back again—the Legion of Leaders—and the applause lessened. The third year at the banquet I received not applause, but boos.

I stood there at the speaker's table and I was stunned. I was so shocked and dumbfounded that I was literally paralyzed. I looked down toward the end of the table and saw my late wife, June, in tears. I looked out over the audience of other salespeople and I could feel their reactions—of I don't know what —as if they were giant obstacles suddenly shoved in my path toward success.

As I stood there listening to the jeers and catcalls of my fellow salespeople—those who were not number one in selling, but the twos and threes—I suddenly gained some courage by remembering another who had suffered the boos of the crowd. In my book he is one of the greatest ballplayers of his time, a man who batted .406: Ted Williams. I remembered that every time the stadium echoed with boos for Williams, his average went up. At that moment in my life, I learned from him how to turn off the catcalls and get on with the job.

So at the banquet that night, I tossed aside my prepared speech. I asked the people who had booed me to stand up so that I could look at them, see what they were like and thank them. *Yes, thank them.*

I said, "Thank you. I'll be back again next year." I put a number-one smile on my face. "You have given me the right to come back. You have fueled my tank to keep my motor going."

Then I went over to my wife. She sat there with mascara running down her cheeks. I asked her why she was crying, and she told me that she was ashamed and embarrassed by the people booing me. She was shedding tears of sympathy for me and tears of anger for the others.

I took her hand. "June," I said, "the day they quit booing me is the day I'm no longer number one. They've paid me a compliment."

I came back the next year and the next, and the same thing happened each time. And each time I would turn their bad manners, their catcalls, 180 degrees into compliments.

After eight years in which I had consistently remained the number-one car salesman, NBC-TV came out to the Legion of Leaders banquet to tape this phenomenon for a national newscast. NBC had heard how the World's Number-One Salesman was being booed by his peers. They had read about it in the press—*Automotive News* and *Newsweek*—and in the wire services, United Press International and Associated Press.

Once again, before the camera and on national TV, the same thing happened. I still smiled and said, "Thanks, I'll be back next year."

During those years, in the quiet of my room at night, I tried to understand why I had been booed. Was it envy? Jealousy? Was it that they did not want to work as hard as I had worked? Maybe they didn't want to meet the price of being number one, didn't want to pay their dues.

I determined then that if I wanted to keep selling myself successfully I would police those things out of my life. Envy, jealousy, a willingness to settle for second best, a willingness to just give up. I suddenly realized what had been happening at all those banquets. *Those who are number two and number three in life are not content until they pull the number ones down to their level.*

That was the trap my mother had warned me about.

Three Kinds of People

There are three kinds of people in this world.

There are the number ones. You can tell them easily. Those are the people who have sold themselves on themselves. Those are the achievers. They are always enthused, they never complain, they wear a number-one smile. They are positive proof that what you get out of life is what you put into it. They are winners. And they have the ability to charge your battery with their enthusiasm. *Those are the people you want to emulate.*

Then, there are the number twos. There's one in every office, every department, every shop, every classroom, every locker room. They are the people who are always looking for a shoulder to cry on, for someone to tell their troubles to. They are the gripers in life. They are the losers, *the people to stay away from.* They are put-downers and puller-downers. Run from them to avoid any danger of becoming like them.

And there are the number threes. They are the people who have copped-out of life, who have simply given up. Their attitude is "What's the use?" They are the ones who say, "Let George do it." In a way they are even more pitiful losers than the number twos because they've never even made an effort. *Shun them.*

The Road to Winning

You can only win in the business of selling yourself by believing you are number one and acting like it. By reminding yourself every day—verbally or by some visible sign—that you are number one. Just as plants need fertilizing, so does your mind. Put a little card up where you can see it every day, a card that says *I am Number One*. Look in the mirror every morning and tell yourself *I am my own best salesperson*. As Dr. Norman Vincent Peale—minister of the Marble Collegiate Church in New York and best-selling author of *The Power of Positive Thinking*—counsels, say it and say it and say it again. You are what you think you are.

It's a matter of image. Robert L. Shook, the noted businessman-author, states in his book *Winning Images*: "If you want a winning image with others, your first concern must be a winning *self*-image."

My friend Lowell Thomas wrote to me recently and said, "I wish I could start all over again and follow in your footsteps." This, coming from a man who is himself the world's number-one adventurer, the world's number-one newscaster, is one of the finest compliments ever paid me. It proved to me that, in my own way, I had sold myself successfully to him.

And, in your own way, you can sell yourself just as successfully to others. The number-one rule is to have faith in yourself, the greatest product in the world, an individual who has no counterpart anywhere.

You are Number One!

Do These Things NOW!

- Buy a small numeral *1* lapel pin (or ring, necklace or bracelet) and wear it proudly every day.
- Tape a three-by-five file card with *I Am Number One*

printed on it to your bathroom mirror where you can see it first thing every morning. Read it and smile.

- Keep a similar card in your office or shop or kitchen or locker. Put another on the sun visor of your car.
- Repeat this statement ten times every morning upon arising: *I Am My Own Best Salesperson.*
- Repeat this statement ten times every night before going to bed: *I Am the Number-One Person in My Life.*
- Associate with others who know how to sell themselves, who are winners.
- Avoid the losers from now on.
- Put negative thoughts—envy, jealousy, greed, hate—out of your life.
- Determine that you'll take every "catcall" in life from now on as a compliment and build on it.
- Give yourself a pat on the back at least once every day.

CHAPTER TWO

Selling Yourself to Others

NOTHING IS ever sold without a buyer, not even you. So, put yourself in a buyer's shoes for a moment and ask yourself, would anyone want to buy you?

Since you are always selling yourself in some way at some time, to some person or group of persons, you want to stand out. You can't afford to be brand X. Brand X doesn't sell.

In order to sell yourself successfully to others you must make yourself into a most-wanted package. You are trying to get people to do something your way, or see something as you see it. You want them to change their viewpoints, to make them like you or love you.

I mentioned some of the occasions in Chapter One, yet there are many others: Trying to get yourself a date for Saturday night is selling. Asking the boss for a raise, or a promotion, or a transfer, or a few extra days vacation, is selling. Any kid wanting to get out of homework is selling. Begging the coach to take you off the bench and put you in the game is selling. Dentists, doctors, lawyers, teachers—all are constantly selling themselves. So are cops. Frequently they do a lousy job.

A few years ago, policemen across the country began to lose the respect of youth, and the word *cop* changed to *fuzz* and *pig*. Sometimes the label was obscene. Why do you suppose this happened? One reason was that law-enforcement officers had ceased to sell themselves as friends to young people. They appeared to be the enemy of jeans, long hair and beads. Whether it was true or not, they associated dress and life styles with marijuana and the entire drug scene. They often seemed the foe rather than the defender of the right to dissent. A bust for possession of a joint often carried a greater penalty than a bust for embezzlement. Teen rebellion swept the nation.

It has taken a lot of hard work, understanding and reaching out on the police officers' part to reverse their image to one of friend and protector. For example, and this is only one of many, they have done a good job in my city, Detroit, with the Police Athletic League for kids. It's no accident that the words spell PAL. Who will quarrel that *pal* is not a better package than *pig*?

Think of the package you present to others, both as to contents and wrapping.

The Importance of a Salable Package

You can't be an unknown quantity and sell yourself. Millions of dollars have been spent by manufacturers, advertising agencies, market research people and retailers to decide just how to package a product to make it more salable. Size, shape, color and design have been mulled over for weeks and months or maybe longer. The packages that represent the food you purchase, the shirts, the cosmetics, the liquor, the travel tours, are designed with two things in mind—*eye* appeal and *buy* appeal.

Few people are even rarely tempted to buy a grab bag item, and when they do they are usually disappointed. Most always the contents amount to nothing, and nothing inspires nothing. The grab bag itself can't hide the fact of nothingness.

Ideally, contents and wrapping should go hand in hand.

The contents are what you are inside. The personality that shines through your eyes, the smile on your face, the words that express your thoughts and ideas, your readiness to listen, your enthusiasm, your attitudes and outlook.

The wrapping is your outward appearance: your cleanliness, your grooming, your complexion, your weight, the clothes you wear and the way you wear them, the posture you assume, the shoes you walk in.

The emphasis in this book about selling yourself is on the inner contents of your package and how to develop them to such a fine point that putting yourself over becomes ever easier. For now, however, let's consider some things about your wrapping. After all, that's the first thing others see. The sale of yourself begins there. It can be won or lost because of the wrapping.

How often have you received a package that has been carelessly handled in shipment? The package has been dropped perhaps, or it is soiled, the paper may be torn and the twine loosened. The moment you received such a package you probably started to worry about the condition of the contents.

It's the same with people. Our exterior image must reflect positively the qualities we wish to sell to others. If the outside wrapping causes others to worry about us and what we are, we can begin to say goodbye to the sale.

Eight Rules for Body Care

1. *Shower or bathe daily.* You'll look better and you'll feel better. Use a cologne but make sure it isn't overpowering.
2. *Take care of your hair.* Shampoo it regularly. Don't date yourself, style it in the current fashion. Keep it well combed and brushed. Never allow dandruff to mar your appearance.

3. *Use makeup sparingly* if you're a woman. Apply it carefully to emphasize your best features. War paint is out. Your desire is to influence, not conquer.
4. *Shave as often as necessary* if you're a man—twice a day if you must. There is no excuse for five-o'clock shadow. It does not make you look macho, it only makes you look unshaven. Keep an extra razor or electric shaver at your office or shop or locker. Use a good after-shave.
5. *Manicure your nails regularly* if you're a woman. Choose a nail polish that compliments your hands, not one that calls undue attention to them. Black, flaming red, are headlights.
6. *Keep nails clean and trimmed* if you're a man. A manicure is a matter of personal choice. Watch out for nicotine stains. (That goes double for women.)
7. *Keep physically trim.* Get those extra pounds off if you need to. (It can be done, as you'll learn later in this chapter.) Start an exercise program now.
8. *Check your posture.* Stand tall, walk tall. Hold yourself erect, shoulders back, belly in. You are number one. Number-one people never slouch, standing or seated.

Now, a word about clothing.

Remember, *what* you wear is an indication to many people of what you are. "Clothes make the man" is a phrase that carries a great deal of truth. *When* and *where* you wear them are also decisive factors. An evening dress and furs are beautiful when worn by a woman to a restaurant or a theater; they are ridiculous at a morning business meeting. Farfetched? Not at all, I've seen it happen.

I know a man who is a guidance counselor, a practicing psychologist, who, when at work, is the most conservative of dressers. He has to be, in order to inspire confidence in his counsel. However, at night, when partying, he changes his entire personality and image by wearing casual jeans or leather, a necklace and zodiac pendant, and even a small gold earring in his left ear. It does not bother him at all to be mistaken sometimes for a member of the gay community, which he is not.

But, can you imagine what the effect would be if he dressed on the job as he does during his leisure hours? His counsel would most likely go unheeded.

One of the pioneers in the creation of sales training materials, especially those for selling cars, is Jamison Handy who, at this writing, is in his mid-nineties and still active in the audio-visual field of communications. I've been told he makes it a point to wear specially designed suits without a breast pocket. He maintains that such pockets are a distraction to people with whom he talks, because the pockets usually are stuffed with a handkerchief, or an array of pens and pencils, or cigarettes or cigars. He feels people's eyes are caught by these objects and their minds stray from the speaker's message.

But, this is a quirk. As much as I learned from him about selling at retail, I think that in his particular eccentricity he makes a mistake. I know of many people who are just as distracted by the fact that his suits have no breast pocket. They find themselves staring at that vacant spot beside his lapel, and while they do so his words are momentarily lost.

There is nothing so fleeting as fashion. One year it is wide lapels and wide neckties, the next year it's back to narrow ties. Single-breasted suits or double-breasted—it's your choice. Vests? They can be matching or contrasted. Hemlines? They move up and down like elevators. Hats and caps, they come and go. Jeans are worn around the world. In short, style is always a matter of personal taste and preference. With so many choices at your fingertips, here's some advice:

Eight Rules Concerning Clothing

1. *Buy the best clothing you can afford.* Don't stint. Quality tells and quality clothing will look better on you and wear longer. Make sure that what you buy—suits, dresses, hats, shoes—fits you well.
2. *Build a complete wardrobe.* Choose clothing for business, for

work, for evening wear, for travel and leisure. Be selective. Often items can do double duty. Mix or match may be the perfect answer for you.

3. *Dress for the occasion.* Always wear clothing suitable for the situation. You would not call on a bank president in blue jeans, nor would you wear a three-piece pinstripe worsted to play a game of touch football.

4. *Hang your clothing properly.* Care in hanging suits, dresses, sweaters and slacks will assure their keeping their shape. Treat what you buy with respect.

5. *Have your clothing cleaned and pressed regularly.* Stains and spots and wrinkles will do nothing for you when it comes to selling yourself, but they sure can work against you. Proper cleaning, too, will help them wear better and last longer.

6. *Choose accessories that compliment, not distract.* Loud neckties on a man are a distraction. So are large dangling earrings on a woman. So are oversized belt buckles and overloaded charm bracelets. A shirt with stripes and a suit with plaid might simply make one dizzy.

7. *Match your shoes to your wardrobe.* Keep them to basic browns and blacks, and choose separate footwear for business, for dress-up occasions, for leisure and for sports.

8. *Take care of your footwear.* Shoe trees will help them keep their shape. Keep shoes well shined, watch for scuffs and don't let the heels wear down. The only man I know of who could get away with a hole in the sole, as seen by millions on TV, was the late Adlai Stevenson. Remember, he lost the election.

In short, do everything you can to make yourself the most buyable package possible. As a final test ask yourself this question: *Would I buy me?*

Know What You're Selling

Each time I set out consciously to sell myself I ask myself what is the purpose of the sale? Do I want to coax my daughter, who says she can't cook, to try her mother's recipe for my favorite dinner—pasta, with a sauce that paints a picture of sunny Sicily?

Do I intend to convince the general sales manager of a foreign-make automobile that selling principles are the same the world over, and that my long association with an American-make car is no handicap?

Do I wish to persuade a marine dealer that his boat sales-people will benefit just as much as car salespeople from the eight-week course in selling offered by the Joe Girard Sales Training School?

Or, do I simply want the paperboy in our neighborhood to be convinced that I'm the nicest customer on his route? Insurance, really, that he won't overshoot my front steps by a country mile as he pedals by on his bike.

Once I have a clear idea of the purpose of the sale, I next ask myself, what can I do to assure success?

I could never convince the general sales manager of the foreign-make car that I was his man if I kept telling him about what I did for American-made car sales instead of what I can and will do for the foreign make. He is not interested in my past, he is only interested in his future, in *what I can do for him*. That is what I'm really selling.

And, I must emphasize selling principles to the marine dealer rather than how to sell automobiles if I want him to send his boat salespeople aboard my school. *Tested sales procedures* are what I'm really selling. Recently I taught some basic principles of qualifying and closing to a boat salesman, the only one in a group of thirty-nine automobile salespeople. By the end of the second week of the school, the car salespeople were showing improvement, but so was the boat salesman. A man with a completely different product was able to use the principles just as effectively.

And, just as the paperboy on my block has to sell himself to me, so must I sell myself to him. Good-delivery insurance I call it. I'll be the nicest customer on his route for sure, if I pay promptly when he collects, if I show him that I appreciate his service—a *dry* paper on rainy or snowy days, and placed on my porch within easy reach of the front door.

*If you want to sell yourself successfully
make sure you know what you've got to sell!*

Day after day people are making an effort to sell themselves, and too many are failing because they're selling what they are *not* instead of what they *are*.

The Golf Pro

A few months ago I witnessed an unfortunate violation of that principle. I was a guest promoting one of my books on a non-network radio talk show. I knew there were two things I needed to sell: first, myself, and then the book. Since the book was about selling, it would have been wasteful of the air time allotted to me to try to sell my viewpoints on such matters as sex education in the public schools, recognition of Red China or the surgeon general's warning on cigarette smoking. That was not what I was there for.

I spent my few minutes speaking of my background in sales and, more important, how and why I came to write the book in question. Those minutes were sales oriented and nothing else.

I shared the radio time with a young man from the Midwest. He was a local golf pro and, for all I know, a good one. He had recently won an eighteen-hole "open" sponsored by a popular motion picture star. Now he was slated to enter another professional golf tournament within weeks, and his chances of taking home a large prize looked good.

Here was an ideal time to sell himself and the country club where he was the pro, but, he blew it. Instead, he talked about the local discotheque as if he had to sell *it*. He talked about the current fishing prospects for coho salmon. He talked, so help me, about prospects for peace in the Middle East.

All interesting subjects, to be sure, and it proved that he was well-rounded—but that wasn't why he was there. He was there to talk golf. In the short time given him I don't think he spent more than a minute talking about his career and the game. He neglected to sell his *real* product, himself.

It's important to know what we have to sell and display it at the right time to the right people. That calls for taking inventory, knowing what we have on hand to work with. Let me give you another example of taking inventory, making sure the outer wrapping is right, so that people will accept what is inside the package. In this case, *me*.

Oral Roberts: Achiever

Not long ago I was invited to speak to over five thousand students at the fall opening of Oral Roberts University in Tulsa, Oklahoma.

Oral Roberts is a man of faith and a man of achievement. Your religion may differ from his, as mine does, but that does not lessen his achievements. Most of his life he and his family have bucked great obstacles and organized opposition. But, he did not let opposition deter him. Using the main principles of selling himself that I am advocating, he brought a healing influence to all who would listen. He brought his message to millions over radio and television, he founded and developed a growing university that is sending forth thousands of fine young people into the world, and he now stands at the threshold of a mighty hospital in Tulsa dedicated to healing through both the miracle of medicine and the miracle of faith.

Oral Roberts—Mr. Achievement—a man who knows how to sell himself and is continuously doing so. Before this speaking engagement, President Roberts had listened to me on a tape sent to him by my friend Lowell Thomas. Afterwards he said, "This man greatly changed my life." I felt very humble.

Oral Roberts is an achiever and achievement was what he

wanted me to talk about as I faced those fine young men and women. There they were, thousands of college students, and there was I, a guy who was a high school dropout.

If the occasion had been some three years earlier, regardless of my selling achievements, I wonder if I would have been asked to speak. Why? Because of the wrapping. *I was a fat slob.* There is no more honest way of putting it. I had been just as busy stuffing myself throughout my life as I had been selling automobiles.

There is a rule at Oral Roberts University that every student must observe. It can be summed up best as "shape up or ship out." Harsh, perhaps, but true. A student at ORU cannot go around with extra pounds on his or her frame. He or she is given an opportunity to get the lard off, but if it doesn't happen, out the student goes.

You may disagree with such a policy, but after all it is a private school. On the one hand you may say the policy is high-handed. On the other you can say the student, health-wise, will be far better off when his or her weight is held to normal. With a policy like that at ORU can you conceive of them asking a fat slob to speak? It would have been very difficult to have sold myself.

Fortunately, however, when the time came to speak I was in good physical shape to do so. I talked about a number of things in my life that day and one of them was weight. Without mentioning the ORU no-fat policy, I told them that the 156-pound man who stood before them had been, a little more than a year earlier, a 207-pound blob, with a waist size I was too embarrassed to mention. I also told those in that chapel that if any of them needed to lose weight they could do so—that if I could do it, they could do it too.

I'll tell you now what I did not have time to tell them then. How I did it. I owe it all to one of the finest specimens on God's earth, my friend Jack La Lanne.

Jack La Lanne: Challenger

I first met Jack in the summer of 1975, along with a number of prominent businessmen, when we were given the Golden Plate Award for outstanding achievement during the year. Mine was for retail selling, Jack's was for preaching the gospel of physical fitness. Jack's body was all muscle, mine was all polyunsaturated fat.

After the banquet, at which I ate more than I should have, Jack spoke to me. "Joe, I admire your philosophy," he said. "I like what I see from your neck up. But, frankly, I can't stand what I see from your neck down." He looked with disdain at my larded belly. "You are the world's greatest salesman," he continued, "but here's a sale I'll bet you can't make to yourself, one that you can't close successfully."

Then he challenged me, challenged me to take off that weight and keep it off. What's more, he told me how to do it. He outlined some sensible eating habits. He told me to cut down on starches and increase my intake of protein and fruit. He suggested a daily breakfast of bran and fasting one day a week (my busiest day when I would have less time to think of food). He also cautioned me, as I must you, to see a doctor before beginning any weight-reduction program.

Three Exercises for Keeping Fit

Then Jack La Lanne gave me a program of three simple exercises. He told me to work up to them gradually until I was doing each of them forty-two times. Why forty-two? Perhaps he took an eyeball check of my waistline and settled on that. The three exercises were:

1. 42 situps, morning and night.
2. 42 pushups, morning and night, from a position resting on my knees.
3. 42 bicycle-pedaling kicks while lying flat on my back, morning and night.

I went home and promptly decided to "do it later."

You see, my slob of a body was telling my mind what to do instead of my mind controlling my body. (More about that in the next chapter.)

Three months went by and then one morning, in the fall of 1975, as I came out of the shower I looked at my body. Ugh! That glob! I looked like that creature emerging from the lagoon. I hated what I saw. I hated it so much that right then and there I determined, with the good Lord's help, that I would take on Jack La Lanne's challenge.

I had a physical checkup. I started to eat sensibly, and every time I was tempted to overeat and overdrink I made my body obey my mind. I fasted one day a week, and every time I was tempted to skip the fast I made my body obey my mind. I began to work up to the 42-42-42 exercises, and every time my aching muscles begged me to stop I made my body obey my mind.

The results one year later? 156 pounds—51 pounds of lost blubber—a flat, hard belly and a thirty-four-inch waist. I dashed off a letter to Jack telling him he'd lost the bet. Back came a new challenge. "But, can you *keep* it off?" Again, one year later it was still off and it's off right now.

So, I had earned the right to speak about losing fat to those five thousand students in the chapel at Oral Roberts University. What I could do they could do, too, if they needed to. I sold myself.

Thank you, Jack La Lanne!

Selling yourself always involves taking inventory.

A chiropractic association asked me to speak to them. How could I sell myself to those doctors, me an ex-car salesman?

What they wanted me to sell them were techniques on how they could sell themselves to the public. They were tired of being referred to as bone crushers and slipped-disk jockeys. In a one-hour version I told them what I'm telling you in this book.

A commander in the United States Navy asked me to speak to naval recruiters. Theirs was the job of signing up young American men and women. What could I say to them? I felt totally unsuited to the job. I told the commander that I wasn't their man. He said to me, "Mr. Girard, I'll bet you a dollar you'd speak if you knew who else was going to be at the speaker's table."

"Who?"

"How about the President of the United States, Gerald Ford?"

I said, "Where do you want me to send the buck and when do you want me to show up?"

Perhaps the wrong motivation, but with that incentive I set to work to take inventory. I knew that naval recruiters had a good product to sell: government service, an excellent retirement program, a chance to learn a trade, even go on to college and build a career. There was a great deal more to navy recruiting than "Anchors Aweigh" and "a girl in every port." Once again the simple truth hit me. The first job of the navy recruiter is to sell himself as someone in whom young Americans could put their confidence. They, too, got the one-hour version of this book.

You are selling yourself to others every waking moment of the day. That is something you already know. What you may need to know is how to do it better. The remainder of this book shows you how.

Do These Things NOW!

- Every morning upon arising ask yourself *would I buy me*? Don't stop until you can say yes.
- Make sure the wrapping of your package makes people want to know what's inside. Be buyable.

- Check your grooming daily. Body bathed, face scrubbed, clean shaven if you're a man, attractively made up if you're a woman.
- Stand tall. Put your shoulders back as a number-one person should. If you've got any lard, get it off! 42-42-42.
- Check your wardrobe. Clothes cleaned and pressed? Shoes shined? Suit, shirt and tie coordinated? Dresses, blouses, skirts and suits in simple good taste?
- Dress right for the occasion—no more beads and chains for the meeting with the boss.

CHAPTER THREE

Building Self-Confidence and Courage

THERE IS no such thing as *no confidence*. Everyone has confidence in something.

If you are depressed and admit it, it shows that you have a certain measure of confidence in your depression. Your confidence will never fail you. What can fail you are those things in which you place your confidence.

In selling yourself successfully, absolute confidence in yourself is a must, plus a confidence that you will not fail in the sale. Confidence in turn breeds courage. This being true, we must make sure that our *self*-confidence goes to work for us because, in selling ourselves we are putting our confidence in ourselves.

We had better do so, because if we haven't got confidence in ourselves, how in the world can we expect anyone else to have confidence in us.

I call this important factor *building* self-confidence because, so often, like children's building blocks, we find ourselves knocked down and we have to *build* ourselves back up all over again.

It's happened to me many times. I would be ashamed to talk about it if I had not learned from the experience and gained greater self-confidence and courage from it.

Let me tell you of a time when my self-confidence nearly failed me. In the early part of 1976 I received a telephone call from Dr. Norman Vincent Peale. He is the foremost spokesman on the subject of confident attitudes. He has helped countless thousands find their way from despair to victory over fear. And he is my friend. I have spoken of him before and I will again, not only because I admire him as a person, but because he has taught me some of the greatest lessons in life. He has called me the World's Number-One Positive Thinker. If I am, it is because of him.

The phone call went something like this:

"Joe, I want you and your wife to come to New York, to my church. Please, both of you come."

I knew Dr. Peale well enough to suspect that, along with a social visit, he must have another reason for this invitation. I waited.

"Joe, I want you to come to New York and pray with me."

Pray with him! Can you imagine the impact those words had on Joe Girard? Who was I to pray with Norman Vincent Peale, probably the best-known minister in the United States? Who was I to even imagine that I had something I could offer him, when his entire life has been built on helping countless others.

My confidence in myself began to fade like a summer tan. I found myself, April 4, 1976, sitting in the front row of the church and hanging on to every word.

The Most Powerful Words in the World

"I want to tell you about the two most powerful words in the world," Dr. Peale said. "The first has only five letters, but it has the strength to move mountains." The sentence seemed to roll like thunder from his lips. "That word is called *faith*." He spelled it. "Faith in yourself, faith in others, faith in your abilities, faith in today, faith in your future. If *you* don't have it, who will have it in you?"

Then he spoke of the second of the two most powerful words in the world. So powerful that, if you let it, it can wipe out faith. "That word," he said, in tones that showed his contempt for it, "is a four-letter word called *fear*." Again, he spelled it. "Fear that you can't be or do something, fear of the past and its consequences, fear of tomorrow for what tomorrow might bring, fear that you might fail."

I thought to myself, if that four-letter word isn't a dirty word, it ought to be. But, I didn't have much time for further thoughts because I realized suddenly that Dr. Peale was speaking about me. To demonstrate *faith* and *fear* he was talking about me. I was dumbstruck. He had pointed me out—June and myself—sitting there in the front row. By then my self-confidence was completely shattered as I felt all eyes of that congregation riveted on the back of my neck.

Fear and faith. Failure and success. The story of my life. My mind raced along with his words as he recalled my days in the ghetto of Detroit, my father's constant reminders that I would never amount to anything, and my mother's equally constant reassurances that I could overcome any obstacle if only I put my mind to it.

Here is the substance of what Dr. Peale spoke about that April Sunday morning.

I had arrived at what I thought was a successful career of

building custom-designed homes. I had a happy marriage, a wonderful wife and two fine children, Joe Jr. and Grace. Then, after what seemed like a series of events that added up to a nightmare, I found my construction career in a shambles. I had overextended, I had relied on false promises and I was suddenly, deeply, $60,000 in debt. Process servers with a sheriff's warrant were ready to dispossess me from my home. The bank was ready to pounce and take away my car. Worse, within a very short period of time there was literally no food remaining in the house and no money with which to support my family.

Overnight, *fear* became the ruling factor in my life. I parked my car several blocks down the street from my home so that the man from the bank wouldn't spot it. I sneaked into my home through a window at the rear to avoid the repossessor out in front. Sneaking! Me, Joe Girard!

I played a dishonest game with my kids because I was scared to death the process server would find a way into my home and so be able to hand me a summons. I told Joey and Gracie that we were in a contest with our next-door neighbors and those across the street—a game that involved *not* opening the front or back doors. I told them that whoever opened the doors first lost the game.

Of course, none of those tactics worked. Games were not the answer. I soon lost my home, my car and my self-respect just as I knew I would. I had to learn the hard way that you can never build back self-confidence by hiding behind walls and doors.

Fear grew even stronger when the day came that my wife told me that all the food was gone. Suddenly the future took shape only as a bag of groceries that I must get at all costs. Yet I had little confidence that I could get it.

I got down on my knees and asked the Lord to give me my confidence back. What so often happens, happened. The Lord and my wife worked together.

When I was at my lowest, June took me in her arms and said,

"Joe, we had nothing when we were first married. Then, for a while, we had everything. Now, we have nothing again. I had faith in you then and I have faith in you now. You can become successful once more. I believe in you." What a wonderful woman! Throughout her short life, right up until she passed away in early 1979, she never once tore me down, never once complained, never once lost her faith in me. I learned at that moment this important truth:

> *One of the best ways to build faith and confidence in yourself is to accept it from others.*

Dr. Peale's words that April Sunday brought the memories flooding back.

I started all over again, traveling the building-block road of building confidence. I called on one of Detroit's leading car dealerships and asked for a job selling wheels. The sales manager, the man who gave me a chance, Don Haley, was reluctant at first.

"Have you ever sold cars?"

"No."

"What makes you think you can?" (Dr. Peale's own counsel, *you can if you think you can*, brought Don Haley's question back to my thoughts.)

"Well, I've sold other things—newspapers, shoeshines, homes, produce. But, what people really bought was *me*. I sell myself, Mr. Haley."

Already I was building back enough self-confidence to forget that I was thirty-five and that selling was considered by some as a very young man's game.

He smiled. "It's the dead of winter, Girard. Sales are slow. If I put you on I risk a mutiny by the other salesmen. There just aren't enough walk-ins for everyone to handle."

With June's faith making mine stronger I said, "Mr. Haley, if you don't hire me you'll be making the biggest mistake of your life. I won't go after walk-ins, just give me a desk and a phone.

In two months I'll beat your best salesman's record. That's a promise."

Haley gave me a dusty desk in an upstairs corner, hooked up a phone that had been disconnected and I was off to a new career.

The first sale of the day is always the hardest, but, once made, the rest of the day looks like your oyster. It was then that I learned another great truth:

Confidence Breeds Confidence

It works in every area of life, not just in selling cars. As I had told Don Haley, I was selling *myself*. The first sale of yourself each day becomes the pacesetter for the balance of the day.

That was the beginning of my climb back to the top. From a dusty desk and a phone book to sale after sale after sale. Haley couldn't believe it. In two months I did exactly what I'd said I'd do. I beat the record of every other salesman in the place.

I bought back my self-respect by repaying the $60,000 debts —to lumber companies, plasterers, bricklayers, earth movers— dollar for dollar, not ten cents on the buck. A wonderful thing happened after that and it sent my sales soaring. Those people I repaid were the people who first bought cars from me in the beginning years of my sales career. In turn, their confidence in me built greater confidence in myself. Confidence breeds confidence. From my first sale—to 1,425 new cars in one year. From down for the count to the World's Number-One Retail Automobile Salesman.

That was the sermon Dr. Peale was giving about me, the story of how I had discovered some important truths, some principles concerning self-confidence and courage.

Now, if I can pass those principles on to you, and if you put them to work as I know you can, then I will have truly sold myself to you.

Fear and Faith

As a kid it seemed I always had my dad, on the one hand, filling me with negative thoughts: You'll never amount to anything . . . you'll always be a failure . . . you're no good. He was always drilling principles of fear into me.

And it seemed I always had my mother, on the other hand, filling me with positive thoughts: Have confidence in yourself . . . you'll be a winner . . . you can be what you want to be. She was always instilling in me the principles of faith.

I always thought of fear and faith in terms of my parents. Actually, we all have the same whisperings of fear and faith, however sparked, to a greater or lesser degree.

Fear whispering at one side: You can't do this . . . you won't succeed in selling yourself . . . it's too big a job . . . you haven't got the guts . . .

Faith whispering on the other side: You can do anything if you think you can . . . you have more courage than you know . . . people will respect you and have confidence in you because you are worthy of respect and confidence . . .

What can you do about those fear-faith whisperings? Here's what I did. I was driving down an expressway one day when I decided that a good way to build self-confidence and courage would be to simply tune out the whisperings of fear, just play hard-of-hearing, and refuse to listen to every negative thought or word that came my way.

Also, as I was driving along I realized that I, a 156-pound human being was in complete control of a 4,000-pound vehicle. I was its master. As long as I remained in control, remained its master, we—the car and I—would arrive safely at our destination. But, if I were to let the vehicle get out of control, then chaos would result.

A friend of mine, an eminent brain surgeon, once told me

that there are two "people" walking around in each suit of clothes, each dress. The *mind* and the *body*. The part of the mind that you might call the captain of your ship is about the size of an eraser. Yet, small as it is, when mind is exercised over matter, powerful changes can occur. Unfortunately, as my friend the surgeon pointed out, only about 5 percent of the people let themselves be controlled by their minds. The other 95 percent are controlled by their bodies. In the same way, too few of us are guided by *faith*, while too many of us are led by *fear*.

The mind says, "Go ahead, be confident, you can do it, do it *now*." That's faith speaking, the first of the two most powerful words in the world.

The body says, "Hold back, you might fail, you can't do it, do it later." That's fear in your ear.

In building confidence in yourself there is no such thing as "do it later." There's a sign in a Detroit Greektown restaurant that is a favorite eating spot of mine, with the best lamb chops this side of Athens. The sign reads: "You can have all the credit you want—tomorrow!"

A safe offer because there is no such thing as tomorrow. Today decides what you're going to be tomorrow. Today is what counts. Put out of your mind the fears, weaknesses and confidence-destroying thoughts of a week ago, a month ago, a year ago. Today is the day you must decide you'll let that eraser-sized portion of your mind—faith—control your body. Today is the day you banish fear forever. But, you ask, how?

Five Rules to Get Rid of Fear

Here are five rules to help banish fear and replace it with self-confidence and courage. They work for me and they will work for you.

1. Believe in yourself.
2. Associate with confident people.
3. Tune up your confidence machine.
4. Be master of your ship.
5. Keep busy.

Let's consider each:

First, *believe in yourself.* Self-confidence starts with belief in yourself. Remember those seven powerful words: *You can if you think you can.* Do this: Put another card on your bathroom mirror and one on the sun visor of your car with those seven confidence-building words. Look at them every day. Repeat them aloud. Let them soak into your system. Then, do this: Add just two more words below them—and these are from my own experience—*I will.* You will if you think you will.

I grew up in a very tough neighborhood. The minute a kid left his house he'd have to fight his way up the street. I had to become a scrapper, a street fighter, in order to survive. I had to lick every bully on the block. My mother's advice again lent me self-confidence. "You can do it, Joey, if you think you can." After a while the self-confidence showed and I found I no longer had to lick somebody to survive in my neighborhood. My self-confidence had been matched by respect from others.

Second, *associate with confident people.* Stay away from negative, fearful people. I remember a few years back when there was an oil embargo facing the United States and the fueling of a car loomed as a potential problem in selling a vehicle. People stopped buying. Some salesmen in my dealership lost their confidence and quit their jobs. I made it a rule to associate only with those salesmen who did not fear the future, who still had confidence in their ability to sell, oil embargo or no oil embargo. By doing so I reinforced my own self-confidence. Remember, confidence breeds confidence.

Third, *tune up your confidence machine.* A widely acclaimed lecturer, who speaks frequently before sales clinics and seminars, was once looking for a theme with which to inspire people so that they might build their self-confidence to a higher level. While driving to his speaking engagement in Ohio he saw a billboard advertising a well-known additive, a detergent to put in your gas tank when you filled it up. This additive promised to clean your carburetor and give you more miles to the gallon. Bingo! There was his theme for his talks. "Clean out the carburetor of your confidence machine with the additive faith." He is right. Your confidence machine will only keep working if you keep it cleaned, fueled, oiled and finely tuned.

Fourth, *be the master of your ship.* Brigham Young, the famous Mormon pioneer trailblazer, led his people from the Mississippi Valley to Utah. They found a wilderness which, through faith and hard work, they turned into a thriving, prosperous metropolis, Salt Lake City. Mormons are encouraged not to use tobacco. Brigham Young feared that he might not be able to overcome his natural liking for it, so he always carried with him a plug of chewing tobacco. I remember a scene from a movie about Brigham Young showing that whenever old Brig felt tempted, he would take the plug from his pocket, squint at it squarely and say, "Am I bigger than this plug of chewing tobacco or is it bigger than me?" Knowing he was bigger, back would go the plug into his pocket and not into his mouth. Faith over fear, mind over body.

Henry Ford said that all confident people gained their courage by facing their fears instead of running away from them. You must learn to do the same. Face your self-doubts squarely and say, "Am I bigger than they are or are they bigger than I?" Then jam them back in your pocket. Be the captain of your ship.

Fifth, *keep busy.* In a busy person fear and self-doubt can find little room to dwell. In 1974 the automobile dealerships of metropolitan Detroit went from a six-day week to a five-day week. It was the only area in the United States in which car salesmen then found themselves working only Monday through Friday.

Because Saturdays were my biggest days, I saw nothing but a slump ahead, that is, until I started to listen only to the whisperings of faith in my right ear. I fueled my confidence machine, cleaned its carburetor and buckled down to work. I told myself that the market was still there and that people still needed cars. I simply knew I must do the same amount of work in five days that I used to do in six.

I was so busy that I had no time to think whether or not I could succeed. The results of keeping busy? That first year I sold nearly as much in a five-day week as I had formerly done in a six-day week. In fact, my total was only forty-nine cars fewer than that of the year before.

On a recent vacation trip I took time now and then to shoot some pictures with a brand-new Instamatic camera my wife had given me. Her words at the time seem to fit the subject of this chapter. She said, "Joe, they tell me this camera does all the work for you. You can take pictures with confidence. You don't have to worry about exposure or focus or have any fears about the result."

She was right. But that Instamatic did more for me than simply take good pictures. I wanted to know how such a pocket-sized marvel came to be. I found the answer in B.C. Forbes's *Men Who Made America Great*. Here was a fantastic story of overcoming fears and building self-confidence and courage. Nobody needed it more than a young inventor from New York who, in time, would turn America into a nation of photographers. Only a strong belief in himself saved him from poverty and despair, taught him how to banish fear and set him on the road to making the taking and printing of images so simple that everyone could do it.

George Eastman and the Brownie

As a kid, George Eastman moved to Rochester, New York, where he grew up as a tinkerer and inventor. He was an amateur mechanic, and tools seemed to fit his hand as easily as mittens. Of course, George Eastman didn't invent photography; pictures were being taken even at the time of his birth in the 1850s—in fact, some of the greatest pictures we have today were "shot" by Matthew Brady in the days of Abraham Lincoln. Photography in Eastman's youth was done by a wet-plate process which was cumbersome. So, George set out to invent a portable outfit and, later on, to improve the new method, the gelatin dry-plate process.

His success and prosperity grew, he began to manufacture dry plates and he could barely keep up with the demand. Then suddenly, without any warning at all, disaster! People stopped buying his dry plates, retailers began returning them to Eastman's small factory in job lots, complaints poured in from all over—the chief complaint being that the plates had lost their sensitivity. In short, the pictures were lousy.

George Eastman had to start all over again, even as I did when the bottom fell out of my construction career. He had to sell himself to retailers, photographers and the general public. Panic gripped him. His self-confidence in his ability slipped away, fear that he could not produce the kind of film plate photographers wanted haunted him around the clock. His was a story of going from success to the specter of poverty, from confidence to self-doubt.

He tried again and again to learn what was wrong. He made trips to England where, reportedly, the dry-plate process seemed to be working successfully, but even with newer formulas which he learned in Great Britain, success eluded him. When it seemed impossible to gain capital because selling himself was becoming increasingly difficult, Eastman was about to give up.

He was to say, later, that all the troubles of his later life were as nothing compared to what he went through at that time.

His partner, one Henry Strong, had faith in him and, as with my wife, June, expressed that faith and urged George on. He began to put to work the steps needed to get rid of fear and build back, block by block, his self-confidence.

He renewed his belief in himself. He lectured himself sternly, reminding himself that he had an active brain, an abnormal curiosity and a storehouse full of ambition.

He made up his mind to associate only with people who were self-confident and who still had confidence in him. One such person was Bill Walker who had put the dry-plate business behind him and who urged George, with his inventiveness, to bend his efforts toward a flexible material that would take images. And George bent to the task, creating with Walker the first roll film. He became more confident, and confidence breeds confidence.

He tuned up his confidence machine with growing faith in the future of roll film and a growing faith, too, that his future might lie not just in the creation of film but, more important, something to use it in. He ceased to be, as he had been in his early days, a rudderless ship. He started to become the captain of his ship. He faced his former fears squarely and, one by one, began to banish them.

Wiping them out became easier because he found little time to dwell on them. He worked night and day. He was so busy he found himself sleeping at the factory at night in order to find time to do the things that needed to be done.

Then, ultimately, new success. Faith and self-confidence evolved into the Kodak, a name which meant absolutely nothing but which sounded nice. The box Brownie swept the country. Even a child could operate this wonderful, highly portable picture-taker that used simple roll film. The famous Eastman slogan *You Press the Button, We Do the Rest* caught on like a brushfire.

And, here I was, on vacation, with my Instamatic, still pressing the button knowing I could take pictures with the rest of them. With confidence. The real button to press is our *confidence button*. No one learned that truth better than George Eastman who sold himself so successfully through the rebuilding of his self-confidence and courage.

The world is full of achievers, people who found success because of their confidence in themselves. They used confidence to overcome all manner of obstacles. Consider:

Recently, balloonist Maxie Anderson and two companions crossed the Atlantic in a balloon when all others before them had tried and failed. These winners expressed this thought in unison upon landing in France, *we never doubted that we could make it!*

Eleanor Roosevelt used self-confidence to overcome her own lack of beauty and went on to inspire a polio-crippled president and an entire nation.

Shirley MacLaine went on to prove that she could be as fine a writer as she is an actress because she had confidence in herself that she could do it. Even the title of one of her best sellers expressed that confidence: *You Can Get There from Here*. The keyword is *can*.

Charles "Boss" Kettering self-confidently proceeded to invent a self-starter for combustion engines when everyone else in the industry said it couldn't be done. It was launched on a Cadillac.

There are many many more, and every one of them who sold himself or herself successfully in the world of business or politics or show business or writing is a *can-do* person.

You can turn weaknesses into strengths. You can develop courage to meet any situation in which you are selling yourself. You can turn self-doubts to self-confidence.

James K. Van Fleet counsels in his book *Miracle People Power* to act as if it were impossible to fail and do the thing you fear to do. Go to it!

Do These Things NOW!

- Believe in yourself. Put cards up in your home, your car, your office, your shop, your locker, with the words *I Believe in Myself.*
- Repeat those words ten times each day.
- Repeat the words *I will* ten times each day.
- Refuse to listen to the whisperings of fear—turn up the volume on the whisperings of faith.
- Associate with confident people from now on. Borrow confidence from others.
- Tune up your confidence machine. You'll get more courage to the gallon when you put in the additive of faith, those whisperings that come in your right ear.
- Keep busy. Self-doubts can't live with busy people.
- Every morning, on arising, say, *I am the captain of my ship.* Act like it the rest of the day.
- No matter what happens each day to raise your fears, *do* that thing you fear to do.
- Act as if you can't fail—and you won't.

CHAPTER FOUR

Developing Positive Attitudes

SELLING YOURSELF successfully depends a great deal upon your attitude toward others. In turn, your attitude toward others depends a great deal on your attitude toward yourself.

Several months ago, after one of my talks on selling, a young man (I'll call him Larry) approached me during the coffee break. He tapped me on the shoulder and asked, "Mr. Girard, why did you tell me earlier this morning that I don't sell sports equipment and accessories when you know I do? I sell the finest line of athletic equipment, the best skis made in the world." There was pride in his voice and I smiled at his youthful enthusiasm.

He was referring to that particular moment in my talk when I usually ask some of the members of the audience to stand up, introduce themselves and sketch in some of their sales experiences. Some people are hesitant, some are not, but there has rarely been a time, audience after audience, when the pattern varies.

Each salesperson would stand up, face the class, give his or her name and firm, and, without fail, mention a product or service.

"I sell furniture."

"I sell cars and trucks."

"I sell insurance."

"I sell TV and stereo."

Larry, who stood by me now after the lecture, coffee and Danish in hand, had said, "I sell ski equipment, skis, boots, bindings, poles, parkas."

And to each volunteer, including Larry, I had stated bluntly, "No, you don't!" (Of course they do, but I was trying to instill in them a larger view of their profession, selling.) Larry, who had now challenged my comment, waited impatiently for an answer.

"Larry," I asked, "how are sales?"

He hesitated. "I'm getting by."

"Getting by! Hey, that's not what a winner does. That's a negative attitude. A winner's attitude is 'I'm forging ahead!' "

Larry looked troubled.

"I meant what I said, Larry. Skis, boots, bindings—the whole package for fun in the snow—are not your *real* product. Your real product is *you*. That's the attitude you must develop and always hold. It's positive and it's an attitude that keeps your work in proper perspective."

"I never looked at it that way," he said thoughtfully.

A problem with most new salespeople, and some long-time ones as well, is that their attitude toward themselves, instead of toward their products or services, needs to become much more positive and broader in nature.

Larry needed to take a different bearing toward his job, his product, himself and probably even his life. He could continue in his present course, certainly, but he would be missing the deeper satisfaction that comes from selling oneself more successfully.

Possibly, unlike Larry, you're not even remotely connected with sales. Whatever you are—doctor, lawyer, merchant, chief, first-class mechanic, first-class secretary, first-class wife and mother—whatever you do at the day-in-and-day-out necessity of earning a living or keeping a home, the same factor of positive attitude applies. What are your attitudes about yourself? Are you a positive-thinking person? Are you cheerful, optimistic, proud without being overbearing, humble without being submissive? Or, are your attitudes negative, defeatist, pessimistic?

For the moment, put on your consumer's hat and consider this situation: Suppose you need and decide to buy a new set of wheels. You're going to shop around, that's expected. Let's say, then, that you've narrowed your choices down to one. You've picked a make and model, you've settled on the options and you've got a pretty good idea of the ballpark price.

Enter the factor of attitude. Two different salespeople offer you comparable deals. Would you be more inclined to buy from the one who sells you *only* a vehicle, some additional-price equipment, some safety features and horsepower? And, who leaves himself *out of the sale*? Or, would you buy from the one who, on top of all those product advantages, is also warm and friendly, self-assured, helpful and considerate. One who sells you more than just a product, *one who sells himself*?

Who would you most likely buy from? I know the answer and so do you. You'd buy from the one who has not only product knowledge but a viewpoint about himself as well, an attitude that he makes a part of the sale.

My young friend Larry needed to change his attitude slightly. So did the others, but it was Larry who put the question directly to me. Larry hadn't bothered to sell himself, he was simply selling skis. Well, during that coffee break, Larry told me he'd give it a try—a real try. He'd put himself into each sale, think of himself as his number-one product and regard himself as the best. I ran across him again, some weeks later. I was as excited as he was to learn that his sales had leaped upward 40 percent. To hear him talk you'd think he was single-handedly keeping all the ski lifts in America going. A simple change in his attitude from *I'm getting by* selling skis (negative) to *I'm going to be a winner* selling myself (positive) did the trick. It is almost unbelievable what such a change can do. I've kept track of Larry's career these past months. It's booming. He has become a success in selling sports equipment because he sold himself. He just needed a kick in his attitude.

To sell yourself more successfully maybe you need to change your attitudes, too. As with everything else in life there are recognizable opposites in attitude: positive and negative, constructive and destructive, broad and narrow, cheerful and despairing. In sports it's heart versus give-up. In music it's upbeat versus downbeat. The secret you must learn and master is how to develop more positive attitudes toward yourself. This in turn will lead to more positive attitudes toward others. And, that will make it easier to sell yourself to others regardless of who you are trying to influence or for what purpose.

There are three basic rules to follow in order to develop more positive attitudes:

Three Rules for Positive Attitudes

1.   Widen your outlook.
2.   Turn yourself around.
3.   Use your think-power.

Let's consider each.

First, *widen your outlook.* We all look at life through some kind of mental glasses, beyond the ones we may actually wear to correct vision problems. Some people, as we all know, look through rose-colored glasses, and what they see is usually overly optimistic and entirely unrealistic. My mother once told me that when she was a girl one of the favorite books of her generation, widely sold, was called *Pollyanna*, and subtitled *The Glad Girl*. She was so golly-gee *glad* that she drove most realistic people up the wall. She wore rose-colored glasses.

Some people wear mental frames that pinch, and they go through life with a constant headache—a headache to themselves and a headache to everyone else.

And some people wear mental contact lenses, invisible, but which like all contact lenses need to be removed periodically. For them, part of the time, life is always out of focus.

Outlook! The way we look at life and through what glasses. The song some people sing with their distorted vision is "Dear me, the sky is falling" while others sing "Everything's coming up roses."

How you look at life is the way you look to others. One of the first steps in selling yourself to others, in finding success in every endeavor, is to *widen* your outlook toward people, places and events. The only kind of glasses you need to do this is your own set of binoculars.

The Man Who Searched the Heavens

I've frequently told this story in lectures and in my writing to dramatize the point. A father, an Italian like myself, once gave his young son a telescope on the occasion of his tenth birthday —one of those kind that extends, the kind that sailors used to use. I saw a movie some time ago about Captain Horatio Hornblower, and he was using one just like it. The boy's father was of a generation which referred to such a simple instrument as a spyglass. This is fitting because with it the lad spied a valuable lesson and took it to heart.

One day the boy was using his spyglass when he complained, "Father, this is useless. I can see better without it. Everything is too small." The father smiled. Of course, the boy was looking through the wrong end. He wasn't getting the big picture at all, not of his toys, not of the big tower that leaned in the city, not of life. He had the narrow outlook through the glass. The father gently turned the little telescope around.

Now, the father had widened the son's outlook, and how fortunate that he did. The boy grew up and improved the primitive telescope and with it discovered the moons of Jupiter, the rings of Saturn and the mountains on our own moon. He became the world's foremost astronomer of his day. His name was Galileo.

The secret Galileo learned from his father is one we need to discover as well: that to see things in proper perspective we must widen our outlook. When you look at life, at others, at objects, at events, at your job, at your family, do you see the whole picture or only part? Do you examine both sides of a question? Are you fair or are you judgmental? Are your perceptions bigoted and colored? Do you keep an open mind? Perhaps you are standing in the way of yourself. Do prejudices either for or against something or someone throw the picture out of focus? Do you fail, as has been so often said, but wisely, to see the forest for the trees?

Outlook means exactly what it says. Looking outward not inward, embracing others and ceasing to be self-centered. Start to see life as larger than yourself. Like Larry, start to see your product as being really *you*. See *yourself* as what you're really selling.

The right outlook toward people, family, business associates, friends, ideas and products and services can work wonders in creating a new *you*—a person everyone wants to know, enjoy, share with and, yes, even love.

How to Widen Your Outlook

Each time you catch yourself looking at people or events or institutions with a narrow, perhaps even bigoted, viewpoint, say to yourself, "There are two sides to every coin, every question, every idea." Then ask yourself, "Am I looking at both sides? Do I mostly see the little picture and rarely the big picture? Have I made an effort to understand all the viewpoints, all the shadings?"

Then, picture yourself as holding a telescope to your eye the right way, as Galileo's father showed him, and watch the situation enlarge and come into focus. You'll be surprised that, as the picture widens, your outlook widens as well. That widened outlook is a necessary step in developing positive attitudes that will help you sell yourself to others.

Second, *turn yourself around*. As you can see, this involves a degree of action, more than a degree, actually 180 degrees. A reversal of any previous negative attitudes. A complete turn-about. It's one thing to think positively, it's another to rid yourself of previous bad thinking habits. Unlearning what might have been years of negative viewpoints takes time and effort.

Before I changed my own negative attitudes, I was anything but a success—financially or otherwise. It took a 180-degree turn on my part before I changed the course of my life. I was flat broke, deeply in debt, afraid of the future and shamed before my family because of financial reverses. I turned away when my kids raised their faces toward me; I didn't want them to see the tears in their old man's eyes. I was bitter and resentful. I was sick of being up against the ropes. I was negative with a capital *N*.

Then one day my wife said to me, "Joe, stop wiping your shoes on yourself! To me you're the most important guy in the world and I won't have it." She forced me to do some thinking. It was her way of putting a "turn around" sign in front of me. I tried to take a new look at myself from every angle, trying to see myself again as number one and not low man on the totem pole. I soon discovered, at her prodding, that just any angle wouldn't do. *It has to be a 180-degree angle on your compass of life.* Angles smaller or larger set you off in all directions.

Only a "180" heads you completely in the opposite direction of your negativism and defeatism. Just as it is necessary when your car is stuck in mud or sand, or your wheels are spinning on ice and snow, to back up slowly in order to get a fresh start forward, so too must we reverse a wrong course from time to time in order to go forward. That's what I did and I went from failure to success.

If you have been negative, it's time—as the song goes—to "accentuate the positive and eliminate the negative." If you're down in the dumps, turn around and climb out. If your shoulders are drooping, do a "180" and straighten them. If you've been holding grudges, harboring resentments, "broom them away" as my mother used to put it. If you see yourself in danger of becoming a number-two or, God forbid, a number-three person, shift gears to reverse the process and get back to being number one.

Just how do you take a "180"? It's a mental action, of course, but I've always found it helpful to link mental actions to physical ones. I've spelled out this technique for building positive attitudes to people in every walk of life. Recently I passed along the idea to several young automobile salesmen, new in the business, without a lot of bad habits to unlearn. Yet it was just as important to them to build positive attitudes from the start. They've tried it and it works. I received this enthusiastic letter from their boss, Joseph Lunghamer, vice-president and general manager of Stadium Chevrolet in Pontiac, Michigan. He states, in part: "Our two salesmen work at keeping a positive mental attitude no matter what is going on around them. Our industry needs more training like yours to lead us to professionalism."

Here's the physical action tip:

I have what I call a "pace space" in my office. I use it for pacing while thinking and for getting up to take a seventh-inning stretch. I also use it for a "180." You're welcome to copy mine right down to its dimensions and features if you wish. It's three feet wide and eight feet long and it happens to run east-west. But, north-south will do just as well and so will any room in your office, home or shop. At the west end of mine there is a small table with a wastebasket beneath it. At the east end is a wall on which I have hung a calendar, one with room enough to jot things down under the daily dates.

Now, whenever I have a negative thought or find I'm in a negative mood I write it down on a slip of paper. I go over to that west end table and drop the paper, tightly wadded, in the wastebasket. Then, unless I walk backward, I have to turn 180 degrees in order to walk my "pace space" to the end wall with its calendar. Next, I write on the calendar the affirmative action I need to take in order to wipe out the negative one. I've taken three physical actions. I've eliminated the negative in the wastebasket, I've taken a "180" turnaround and I've accentuated the positive by pinning the thing to be done to day and date. It may be today, it may be tomorrow, it may be next week. But, I do give myself a deadline. Don't laugh at the "pace space," it works. Because what I've really done in the turnaround is *make a commitment*.

You'd be surprised at the negative thoughts I've tossed in the wastebasket: impossible to find the kind of instructor I need to send to Chicago . . . nothing I can say of value to the dental association . . . can't market the San Francisco videotapes . . . can't stand the mayor of Detroit . . .

Then, after my turnaround, my calendar notes show the difference this attitude builder can make: advertise for an instructor in Chicago, not Detroit . . . don't talk dentistry, tell dentists how to sell themselves . . . sell video rights to someone else and let him market the tapes . . . go down to city hall and find out what makes the mayor tick, you may like him . . .

Those are the positive actions. Of course, I use a Girard shorthand to put them on the calendar. Whether you know shorthand or not, link your mental actions to physical ones. Turn yourself around to develop positive attitudes.

Third, *Use your think-power*. How many times have you chuckled at signs in offices and other public places, even on bumper stickers, that read, *Think Thin* or *Think Summer* or *Think Snow*? Tom Watson, the genius behind the success of IBM, shortened it to a one-word challenge that faced every one of his computer and business machine employees. The sign simply blazed, *Think*! Of course, it wasn't long before some wag with a sense of humor created his own cockeyed version spelled or rather misspelled *Thimk*. Even then that gag sign put forth a positive message. You were caught by it, smiled at the intentional error and carried away the idea.

Those signs, as well as the scores that are similar, are asking you to use your *think power* in order to bring about a desired end. Each one is asking you to put your thinking machine in gear. Think-power is powerful stuff, and one of the secrets of developing positive attitudes, of selling yourself more success-fully, lies in using that power to the highest degree.

I'm not what you'd call a regular theater-goer and I certainly haven't brushed up very much on my William Shakespeare, but I know that he wrote about a young, hotheaded prince named Hamlet and, in the play about him, old Will comes up with a powerhouse idea: "There is nothing either good or bad, but *thinking* makes it so." You can fill your head with discourage-ment by thinking negative thoughts, or you can change your whole attitude about yourself and others by thinking positive thoughts.

Some years before I was born, a positive thinker put forth a theory that shortly became popular. His name was Emile Coué and he wrote a small but dynamite-laden book called *Self-Mastery Through Conscious Autosuggestion*. A mouthful, so let me give it a Girard simplification.

Coué was a French doctor and although his theory was first put to the test by his patients, it wasn't long before thousands of Europeans and Americans were starting each morning by saying Coué's magic words, "Day by day in every way I'm getting better and better." His idea was *think* it and you'll *be* it. It was as simple as that. Each day—each 1,440 minutes—was a new day to *think yourself* into a new you.

Think-power! Of course other thousands snickered, but the French doctor was absolutely right. He was not only right, he was the forerunner of all the others to come who would preach the power of positive thinking: Norman Vincent Peale, Bishop Fulton J. Sheen, Bruce Barton and Elmer Wheeler—they all swam in Emile Coué's wake.

Think for a moment about what can happen. Let us say you wish to be accepted by the people who belong to a club you've just joined, or a church or a lodge or a bowling team or a union. Whatever the organization, acceptance really hinges on selling yourself. If, upon joining, you think of yourself as un-equal to the others in some way—lacking in social graces, per-haps, or strong faith, or leadership ability, or a bowling score that's not up there where you'd like it—then, that's the kind of image you'll project. If the song you sing is, "Poor me, I'm a nobody, friendless and unappreciated," that's the way others will sing it, too.

On the other hand, if you think of yourself as a fairly nice person, someone others would enjoy knowing, you're pretty certain to come across that way. If, in your mind's eye, you think of yourself as a friendly guy or girl, chances are that's the way you'll act.

Again, poetry is not my dish, but I'm told Robert Burns wished for the power to "see ourselves as others see us." My answer to Bobbie is, "no problem." The truth is *others see us as we see ourselves—and think ourselves to be.*

How do you use think-power? By exercising it. Like any physical exercise designed to develop a muscle, these mental exercises must be done daily. Make this your mental "daily dozen" every morning, first thing upon arising.

The Think-Power Daily Dozen

1. Think of yourself as successful.
2. Think of yourself as loving.
3. Think of yourself as attractive.
4. Think of yourself as friendly.
5. Think of yourself as helpful.
6. Think of yourself as generous.
7. Think of yourself as in control.
8. Think of yourself as strong.
9. Think of yourself as courageous.
10. Think of yourself as optimistic.
11. Think of yourself as affluent.
12. Think of yourself as having peace of mind.

Take each think-power exercise one at a time. *Don't rush.* To give yourself ample time get up ten to twelve minutes earlier than has been your habit. Choose a place where you can be alone and without distractions. Stand relaxed, shut your eyes and grip the back of a chair lightly for support. Allow about a minute for each think-power, self-image attitude to sink into your mind. Keep your eyes closed throughout. You will be using your conscious mind to tell your subconscious to take over. After a few weeks of this stimulating exercise, each powerful thought will be deep in your inner consciousness, always there to guide you.

For example, with the first exercise, think of the things you know you must do that day, and picture yourself as being successful in each task. Mentally wipe out any thought of failure.

With the third, for example, picture yourself as pleasing in appearance and appealing to others (not necessarily in a sexual sense, although there is no reason not to think so). However, wipe out any thoughts of vanity.

With the fourth, see yourself as the warm and friendly person you want to be. Think of the first person outside of your family you expect to see that day, then mentally give that person a smile and a handshake. Later on extend your hand and offer the smile for real. You won't be able to help yourself.

And so on throughout the list. After each exercise take a deep breath, inhaling slowly, then let the breath out just as slowly. Soon, as psychologists and behavior scientists have discovered, a miraculous change will begin to take place within you. That is because, as with all truths, this particular one becomes self-evident: *You become what you think*. Even the Bible reminds us, "As a person thinketh, so he is."

You can picture the effects of this mental daily dozen just by reading through the list. For example, a first step in becoming successful is to think of yourself as successful (think-power exercise number one). Thinking yourself thin is a powerful motivating force for sticking to your diet and controlling your appetite (think-power exercises number three and number seven).

Make up your mind *now* that from here on you are going to paint mental pictures of yourself that are successful, attractive, positive, the world's number-one product. Then, use your think-power every time you're out to sell others on *you*.

The Man Who Opened the Heavens

One of the most dramatic examples I know of where think-power meant the difference between success and failure in selling oneself is the life of the late Dr. Wernher von Braun, the father of the American space program. I've shared a speaker's platform with him, I've been privileged to enjoy his wisdom and common sense, I've been proud to call him a friend.

Think of his background, his beginnings in Germany with the Nazis in power under Hitler, the use of his skills in perfecting the rocketry that almost brought Great Britain to her knees, his arrival in America as a man coming from a crushed and defeated nation. What could possibly lie ahead for him when his image had been forged from goose-stepping storm troopers who overran country after country? It is even said that he was the model for the infamous Dr. Strangelove of the movies.

Wernher von Braun had much to offer, but first he knew that he would have to sell himself to our government, our people and our business and industrial complex if the exploration of space was to happen. He put the principles of think-power to work, although he never particularly thought of them as a daily dozen.

He pictured himself as successful in winning a new and positive role for himself in America, he refused to think of himself in any other way, he refused to look at life as a defeating force. He was in a country foreign to him, an alien, and he went out of his way to be friendly and helpful to all with whom he came in contact. He was cheerful and optimistic despite setbacks in our space program and he was bold and courageous in putting forth his ideas. He told me he had to think of himself in that manner before he could act. Most important, thinking in terms of peace, not war, led to a new peace of mind for him.

Think-power on the part of Wernher von Braun led men to soar upstairs to the stars. Think-power led to that "one small step for man, one giant step for mankind."

Believe me, attitudes can be changed. Start thinking positively. Have faith in yourself. Believe that good is going to come your way. Regard yourself as the best. It won't be long before you'll find that others are now sharing those same positive attitudes about you, about what you do and about what you stand for.

Then you will know that you have made the sale.

Do These Things NOW!

- Widen your outlook by looking at all sides of a question.
- Toss out your prejudices no matter how deeply you may have clung to them in the past.

- Keep your telescope on life in focus and always look through the proper end.
- Make a "pace space" where you can write down and throw away negative thoughts at one end, turn around, and then write positive actions with deadlines on a calendar.
- Decide now to exercise your think-power.
- Each morning upon arising and each evening before retiring say aloud, "Day by day in every way I'm getting better and better." (The idea is not mine nor is it the idea of others who followed Coué, but I use the technique regularly and there is no reason why you shouldn't. Doctor Coué would be pleased.)
- Say to yourself at least three times each day, "Others see me as I see myself and think myself to be."
- Use your think-power by doing the think-power daily dozen. Do them every morning, relaxed, eyes closed and with deep, full breathing between each mental exercise.

CHAPTER FIVE

Exercising Enthusiasm

A HUMAN whirlwind! That's what Lowell Thomas calls me. Since he has had no rivals in hitting the high trails of adventure, no competition in keeping a score of irons in the fire (from radio broadcasting to motion pictures, from lecturing to reporting and making news), his comment is no small praise.

Thomas is really talking about the Joe Girard brand of enthusiasm. Enthusiasm is like a whirlwind. It is a dynamic quality. And it can be acquired. You can make yourself enthusiastic, you can build enthusiasm into your personality by the never-fail method of exercise.

Exercising enthusiasm! It's just as important as your daily physical workout. Just as you can keep your body in tune, so can you tune up your enthusiasm machine until it's purring like a well-oiled engine.

How excited are you about selling yourself? Putting yourself over? Getting that contract? Making that team? Talking your husband into that Mediterranean cruise?

Do you want success so badly you can taste it, smell it? Do you really desire to make people like you, respect you and recognize you as a leader? The difference between achieving those goals and failure to achieve them often hinges on that one single factor, enthusiasm.

In his book *Enthusiasm Makes the Difference* Dr. Norman Vincent Peale cautions against holding back. He talks about giving your whole mind and self to whatever your goal may be. In short, he preaches, and I second the motion, that we should throw ourselves into life with vigor. What a brisk, exciting, full-of-pep word that is—vigor! It's the way the late Robert Kennedy played touch football. The way Joe Louis came out fighting. The way I put my heart and soul and body into it whenever I lecture.

Golden Gloves

There was a time in America when every young kid who was handy with his fists and fast on his feet worked up a storm of enthusiasm over a figurative set of boxing gloves, all gold. Traveling the road of the Golden Gloves tournaments was as magical as traveling the yellow brick road to Oz. No one was ever more excited about the Golden Gloves than Joe Jouis.

I grew up in the same neighborhood as Joe Louis. Folks call it a ghetto now, only we didn't know it was that. I watched Joe with a kid's wide-eyed wonder. I saw him box his way up from Golden Gloves to world's heavyweight champ. I cheered at his victories and I knew he earned every bit of his acclaim. But even I couldn't match the enthusiasm Joe put into every bout back in those Golden Gloves days and afterwards. Sports writers said the Brown Bomber moved and acted like a man on fire. And that's what Joe was—on fire to make something of himself, to *be* somebody.

I also know about Joe's disappointments, his discouragements, his hurts. Often he had to sleep in hotels for blacks only, keep to himself, keep out of "white folks'" territory. He was on the receiving end of all the obscene words that stood for black. After all, Joe came before we started to realize that black is beautiful and that to become color blind is the first step toward some kind of brotherhood of man.

Despite the ups and downs of his career, despite the shameful exploitation of a decent man, despite his right to be bitter, Joe never let it show. He was the most enthusiastic person around. He always looked forward to training. He was excited about every match in the ring. How did Joe get to be such an enthusiastic person? By exercise. He exercised his enthusiasm until it was as muscular as his body.

In his early days, as he moved up from the preliminaries to the main bout, you could see that exercise taking place. Tell him a match was in the offing and he would think about it for a moment, then his eyes would light up, then his face would break into a grin and then he'd let out a whoop. You could see him get worked up, see him get excited, see each spark within him set off another spark. He exercised his enthusiasm because to him exercise was a way of life.

He was as energetic and as conscientious about exercising enthusiasm as he was about selecting sparring partners, working out at the punching bag, skipping rope and doing roadwork. The more he shaped up his enthusiasm muscles, the more he got excited about things, the more his enthusiasm grew. All who were around Joe Louis caught his spark. Those who are around him now catch it. And there are still a lot of sparks. Can you imagine Joe's enthusiasm upon learning that the city of Detroit remembers him in a big way, that a beautiful new sports complex and arena on the riverfront will be named after and dedicated to him?

Although his health has failed, his enthusiasm for life, for people, for things has never failed. Not even a stroke could put a damper on it. He's still on fire and he still kindles one in others. That's because enthusiasm is as contagious as a head cold, only more enjoyable.

Joe Louis did not become heavyweight champion of the world on enthusiasm alone, of course, and he would be the first to tell you that enthusiasm is no substitute for training and experience. You can be the most enthusiastic person in creation when it comes to selling yourself, but if you haven't got anything to sell, your enthusiasm won't carry you very far. Enthusiasm alone never got the champ's crown for Joe. Enthusiasm alone never got the ball past the one-yard line and over the goal. It takes strategy and know-how.

You're selling the world's number-one product—*you*. And you never want to be without that flavorful ingredient—enthusiasm. Let's put it to work. Let's exercise it. How?

I've already told you about my three-step physical fitness program of exercise: (1) forty-two situps, (2) forty-two push-ups and (3) forty-two bicycle-pedaling kicks. I also follow a four-step enthusiasm exercise program which I guarantee can help you become one of the most enthusiastic people around, someone others will enjoy being near, someone who gives off sparks. Here it is:

Four-Step Enthusiasm Exercise

1. Care about something deeply.
2. Get excited out loud.
3. Use a battery charger.
4. See life as a kid.

Let's dig into the program.

First, *care about something deeply*. Always have something to be enthusiastic about, a goal, an idea, a project, a plan, another person, a family. Caring about something is very important. People sense this at once and it's a terrific boost in the job of selling yourself. Caring about something is the great warm-up exercise in developing enthusiasm.

How many times have you said to your wife or husband or to a friend, "Hey, let's go for a ride or a walk." And, you start out, but with no planned destination. You ride or walk along awhile in silence, and then you look at each other and say, "Let's go home." What has happened is that you had nothing in mind, nothing that you really cared about as you set out—no goal, no aim, no special objective, not even something as simple as scenery or the changing color of the leaves in autumn.

On the other hand, you know how it is when something like this happens. You can be taking that same ride or walk, when, luckily, your attention is caught and held. Perhaps it's by a fine sunset, or maybe a parade, or possibly a city's skyline, or sometimes a beautiful animal. All at once find yourself caring about what burst into view and, with caring, your excitement quickens and your enthusiasm grows. You find yourself fairly bubbling with it. But you could have enjoyed that enthusiasm much earlier if you had planned to see that sunset or head for that parade. There's a great deal of truth in that saying, "Planning is half the fun of getting there." Although I suppose something can be said for the aimless stroll or the play-it-by-ear ride, there's a great deal more to be said for the one that's planned. A brisk walk or journey to go *someplace* or see *something* gets the enthusiasm juices flowing. An aimless trip is, mostly, tiring.

I remember the first time I drove the family to Disneyland. As we drew closer to it our anticipation became keener. Then we saw the first sign: *Disneyland 535 Miles.* We looked at one another and smiled. Then we saw another sign: *Disneyland 350 Miles.* We really began to get enthusiastic. Then, *Disneyland 125 Miles*—and, finally, we were there. We had cared about Disneyland and because we did so our enthusiasm was being exercised every mile of the way.

That tired old statement "I couldn't care less" is 180 degrees opposite from enthusiasm. The unfortunate thing is that a couldn't-care-less attitude is also contagious. If you couldn't care less it isn't very long before the person you're trying to sell yourself to, to influence in a positive way, couldn't care less either.

Enthusiasm grows with achieving the goal, the aim, the plan you care about. I always have some kind of long-term goal in my sights—a mountain to climb, if you will. The family trip to Disneyland was such a goal and, when we rounded the corner and there it was, the family's excitement could hardly be held in check. Now, from where I live you can't drive to Disneyland in one day, so we made the trip over several days.

In the same way I break each of my long-term goals into a series of short-term goals—maybe for the day ahead or the week to come. Smaller hills to climb on the way to the mountaintop. I find that as I reach each short-term goal my enthusiasm grows. Each new accomplishment feeds on the previous one.

Try this sometime: Stop a number of people on the street or in your neighborhood or where you work or where you play and ask them, "What are you going to do today?"

Believe it or not, nine out of ten—maybe ten out of ten— will reply, "I don't know."

Ask them, "What do you want to achieve?"

"I don't know."

Ask them, "Where are you going in life?"

"I don't know."

If you don't know what you want to do or what you wish to achieve, how can you get excited about it? How can you get enthusiastic about something you don't care about? But when you care, that's a different story.

Make It a Fun Goal

For years, Charles Drummond was one of the top shoe salesmen east of the Mississippi River. He still would be except he's now hung up his order blanks and retired—with distinction and enviable sales records because he was a man who knew how to sell himself *enthusiastically*.

"Bulldog" Drummond, as he was called both in the shoe business and on the baseball diamond where he once played pro ball in eastern leagues, didn't work in a shoe store. He represented Queen Quality shoes and he traveled nearly every state in the union, but with concentration in the Midwest and South. He sold women's shoes to retail outlets of every kind. If a shoe store didn't exist in an open point, he'd get one started. Many a shoe department in some of the country's largest department stores owe their beginnings to "Bulldog" Drummond.

He sold to buyers from a hotel or motel sample room but he would also head out for some of the remotest hamlets if a buyer couldn't come to him. To keep his enthusiasm for selling shoes exercised at all times, he would set himself goals, usually based on the new spring and fall lines. He would say: "If I get my line in eighty shoe stores during January, February and March, I'll treat myself and my wife to a trip to Hollywood. Now, "Bulldog" is like most people. He found it a lot easier to get enthusiastic about a pleasure trip to California to see the footprints of the stars in front of that Hollywood Boulevard theater than to get excited about days on the road and nights in hotels. The first was fun, the second was work.

So, what he really did was set himself a *fun* goal. He put a California label on the three months. Then, he found that an amazing thing always happened. As he worked harder to sell shoes in order to treat himself to a trip, he found his enthusiasm beginning to spill over from the thought of Hollywood to the job at hand. Suddenly selling shoes became fun, too. He grew more and more excited as the weeks ticked off. He grew more enthusiastic than ever, if that was possible. He looked forward to each day of selling, each mile of travel. To tell the truth, by the time he had earned the Hollywood trip for himself and Mrs. "Bulldog," it was almost an anticlimax to three months of enthusiastic selling.

Set that goal, have something to care about, and make it a *fun* thing. Charlie Drummond did and he achieved amazing success because he sold himself by always exercising enthusiasm. I've learned to walk in that guy's shoes.

What having something to care about boils down to is this: *Give yourself an enthusiasm incentive*, one that makes each day exciting. But here's a tip to go along with that advice. If you don't achieve what you set out to do today or this week or this month, don't dwell on it. Just keep your eye and heart set on the goal and it will be reached. You get back what you put out, and that's cause for enthusiasm itself.

Consider the farmer. What he sows today he reaps tomorrow. He doesn't get paid for what he does today, instead he gets paid in the fall, when his crop comes in. That's what he's enthusiastic about. He just keeps busy every day, turning over the dirt, cultivating and visualizing his crop. His enthusiasm grows as he sees his planting grow, his crop sprouting and becoming ever bigger.

Second, get *excited out loud*. I start exercising enthusiasm first thing in the morning in the shower. There is something about a shower, water and soap that sets me singing. My wife would grow a little irritated with me and she chided me for years. Her frequent morning comment was, "Who do you think you are, your fellow *paesano* Enrico Caruso?"

I can't help it. As soon as I wake up I tell myself, "Be happy!" and I'm happy. God has given me a wonderful gift, another 1,440 minutes, another 24 hours, another day—*today*, the first day of the rest of my life as someone has said. Today is the day that counts and I'm going to make today better than yesterday. Yesterday is gone—you can't relive it. And tomorrow is another day to be lived in turn as it dawns.

That's why I sing. I show my enthusiasm for the 1,440 out loud. You can do the same, and don't worry if you can't carry a tune even with a handle on it.

The Split-Week Booking Success

Let me tell you the story of Mr. Enthusiasm himself, a man who sold himself in the business world by getting so excited out loud that he made everybody's rafters ring—more important, the rafters of a very large appliance manufacturer in Ohio. This gentleman sold himself right into the enviable position of heading up the company's training program and product announcement meetings.

Since I sold cars made by a sister division of this appliance company—or if not a sister division at least a first cousin—I heard about this enthusiastic guy from friends who attended cross-over sales rallies and announcement meetings of the corporation's automotive and home-appliance products. His fame in the industry was widespread and his life was becoming something of a legend by the time I became acquainted with him. At one time he had been a touring member of a vaudeville-lecture circuit (I believe such a circuit was called Chautauqua) which booked speakers, comedy acts, musical performers and all kinds of entertainment into the grass-root areas of the country. This gentleman's talents lay in music.

On one occasion he was playing what is called a "split week" in this Ohio town where the appliance company has its world headquarters. I understand that a "split week" is simply half of a full week's engagement. Attendance was nowhere near what *Variety* likes to call "boffo" and so my musician acquaintance looked up an old friend in town.

"Why don't you come to work at my company?" the friend urged. "The work is steady, the pay is good, the people are swell and you'd like this neck of the woods."

"But, I like what I'm doing. Music is my work."

"You can put your musical talent and all your pep to work selling iceboxes and stoves."

The showman thought about it briefly, then made a decision. "Sounds like a good booking."

He dropped around just at the time a sales rally was being held. He felt it was the most dismal event he had ever seen, more like a wake than a rally is the way he put it. He saw his chance for a spot with the company because he also saw the need his friend spoke about, a need which he knew he could enthusiastically fulfill.

He began to sell himself into a spot which up to then did not exist—a spot where he could put some life into training, some pep in rallies, some show-biz in product announcement meetings. He became so enthusiastic about his ideas that he began to sing before the startled management group, all the more astonishing because he wasn't that hot as a singer. Grinning, they agreed to put him on.

The results were startling. Appliance salesmen began to perk up at training meetings, dealers started giving standing ovations at product announcement time. One of his achievements was to help organize a robust male chorus of employees which sang rousing marching songs from operettas at sales rally after sales rally. The salesmen became as enthusiastic as the students at Heidelberg and the Canadian Northwest Mounties of whom they sang. His sales rallies and announcement shows became productions which were talked about for months as dealers and salesmen caught the enthusiasm and carried it into the field. If ever a man sold himself to success in a totally different field, it was this "music man" who let his enthusiasm show out loud.

Try it. As you start on your way to work, tell yourself how happy you are to be able to get out and do what you're doing, to be going where you're going. Champ at the bit. Tell yourself you can't wait to get where you're headed for—success. And, while you are headed that way, hang around with other enthusiastic people. Look around you, keep your eyes open for them, notice the achievers, the number-one people, and borrow their qualities.

Actually, the best way to do that is not just to borrow, but to trade. Notice that when you smile at someone you're likely to get a smile back, and if you make an enthusiastic comment to someone it will probably spark a similar comment in return. You know it works. Ever notice that when you yawn it isn't very long before others are yawning, too. But, smile and sing and they'll do the same. When you show your enthusiasm out loud it crackles like electricity.

Third, *use a battery charger*. Let me tell you about Ed Start. He was so enthusiastic at the beginning of each day I used to call him "Head Start." Ed sells cars and trucks and he had an office next to mine. I would have been lost without him. I like to say that I didn't sell cars, I sold myself. With Ed you might say he didn't sell cars and trucks either, he sold enthusiasm. He was a charged-up battery and in that way he sold himself every day. His enthusiasm level was always ready to flow over. He always seemed to be *up*. He could get excited about practically everything. He was fun to be around. He still is.

If and when I found myself in an unenthusiastic frame of mind, and I sometimes did, I'd mosey over to Ed's office and get a battery charge, just as when your twelve-volt isn't putting out and you ask a friend or a passing motorist if he has jumper cables. Whenever I felt my enthusiasm muscles getting soft, I could count on Ed's battery to come through. He'd say something like this: "Joe, I watched you on the floor yesterday when you were selling that family a station wagon and you were *terrific!*" Or, "Joe, the way you smoothed the feathers on that ruffled service customer was pure genius." Ed had a way of exaggerating, but when one's spirits were low it sounded great. He was a picker-upper. Whether it was a verbal compliment or a pat on the back, Ed knew just how to get you out of the pit and back on the track. Before long my excitement was in high gear again; Ed had started my enthusiasm engine in short order.

One day Ed surprised me. It never occurred to me that maybe sometimes he needed a charge, too. That sly fox would come to me and borrow the jumper cables. I learned from Ed that battery charging is a give-and-take proposition. The more I help someone exercise enthusiasm muscles the more I'm exercising my own. The truth is, as I've said, *sparks set off sparks.*

Get yourself someone you can count on to recharge your batteries. Make sure that person is a winner, a number-one person like yourself, to give you a charge when you need it. And, just as important, be a battery charger yourself.

Fourth, *see life as a kid.* Look at the world, no matter how old you are, with wide-eyed wonder. Have an attitude always of expectation.

When I was a kid we were super poor. We were on what was then called relief. Practically every family in the neighborhood was on relief and my teacher would check to make sure, because she was taking a report to give to the Goodfellows. This was an organization of old newsboys who sold special editions of Detroit newspapers at Christmas in order to raise money so that every poor kid would have a present at the holiday season.

As Christmas neared, the Goodfellows would work the neighborhood block by block. As they got closer to my street I could hardly wait to get my hands on that Christmas box. It was always the same gift each season and I knew what was inside, but that didn't dampen my enthusiasm. There would be a pair of long johns, the kind with the flap in the back, a small box of candy from Sanders, a coupon that would be exchanged later for a pair of shoes and, if you were a boy there would be a game and if you were a girl there would be a doll.

Four such boxes came to my house—I had an older brother and two younger sisters—and my mother would wrap the Goodfellows' gifts and put them under a very small tree which she managed to scrounge. By Christmas morning my brother and sisters and I would simply burst with enthusiasm as we anticipated opening those boxes. We were wide-eyed with excitement. But, that's the way kids are. Kids look at the world around them with awe and wonder, as something rich with surprise and suspense. Each day is an adventure—the first day of school, the last day of school, teacher getting sick, a birthday, a holiday. Kids *anticipate the day*. And that's a pretty good rule for adults to follow, too. Adults must capture the enthusiasm of kids and learn to anticipate the day.

There you have them—four steps to help you develop enthusiastic qualities, to help you become an exciting person, to help you sell yourself more successfully: (1) Care about something deeply; (2) get excited out loud; (3) use a battery charger; and (4) see life as a kid.

You know this too: Without exercise your muscles will soon get soft and flabby. It's the same with enthusiasm. Without exercise your excitement muscles will get flabby. So, just as I do my 42-42-42 physical exercises every day, morning and night, I also do my enthusiasm exercises every day—all day long. And so have all successful people throughout history.

The Niña, the Pinta and the Santa Maria

Did you know it was really *enthusiasm* that discovered America? Enthusiasm for trade, for spices, for lush merchandise from the East, even for a corner on the market. And there's nothing wrong with that.

Christopher Columbus had a crazy notion that the world was round, not flat, and being so it ought to be easier to get to the wealth of the Indies by sailing west instead of the long way around, east and south around Africa.

Trouble was that nobody had ever sailed west before to go east and so nobody was particularly enthusiastic about the idea. It was as hard then as it is now to get excited about the unknown. But explorers do, and Columbus had adventure in his blood. Besides, he was a darned good sailor. Columbus cared about something. His dream was something to get enthusiastic about even though he met rebuffs all along the way. Unfortunately, Italy, his own home, wouldn't give him the time of day, so he went to Spain instead. Spain was a seafaring nation, and the ships of Queen Isabella and King Ferdinand roamed far and wide.

To get what he wanted from someone he knew could give it to him, Columbus now knew that first he had to sell himself. He presented his credentials and they were impressive. But, more important, he added that extra flavor of enthusiasm. He painted an exciting picture of wealth and prestige that could be Spain's. His enthusiasm grew as he talked because, being an adventurer, he looked at the world with awe and wonder. He was so *up* that he literally hopped around and his voice grew more charged. He showed his enthusiasm out loud right in front of the king and queen and all the court. And, as always, his sparks set off sparks. Columbus got what he wanted by selling himself—three ships and a crew for each. Spain would never be the same again. In her name he found the New World.

Enthusiasm is what discovered America, and aren't you glad it did? Think, then, what enthusiasm can discover for you as you set sail to sell yourself.

Do These Things NOW!

- Get excited about yourself. You should—you're the world's number-one product.
- Throw yourself into life with enthusiasm and vigor. Hang in there.
- Start the four-step program for exercising enthusiasm.
- (1) Care about something deeply. Give yourself an enthusiasm incentive.
- (2) Get excited out loud. Sparks set off sparks.
- (3) Use a battery charger. Be one yourself.
- (4) See life as a kid. Anticipate each day.
- Associate with enthusiastic people, with achievers, with winners.
- Each morning upon arising say three times, "I'm going to make today even better than yesterday."

CHAPTER SIX

Learning to Listen

GOD GAVE every one of us two ears and one mouth. Perhaps He was trying to tell us something. And, as is the case with many of us, we aren't listening.

I have a framed sign in my office to remind me to keep my ears open. I don't know who first came up with it. It reads: "I know that you believe that you understand what you think I said. But, I am not sure you realize that what you heard is not what I meant."

How's that again? you ask. Let's unscramble it in this chapter and discover the fine art of listening. Learning to listen is something every person needs to master if he wants to sell himself successfully.

Learn to listen is the best advice I can give a young salesperson just starting out. And it's also good advice for those who have made a lifetime career of selling. More important, it is good advice for everyone who is selling *himself* in so many ways all the time. Let's make a list of people who, along with all their other qualifications, need to be good listeners if they wish to be successful.

- Salespeople
- Counselors
- Psychiatrists
- Clergy
- Parents
- Teachers
- Doctors
- Nurses
- Dentists
- Lawyers
- Pilots
- Politicians

Those are just a few. With a little thought you could probably come up with twenty more in five minutes. Why do they need to be good listeners? Why do *you*, wherever you may fit in the list?

Consider *salespeople*. If you sell a product or service you still must keep in mind that what you are really selling is *you*. You are the world's number-one product. I earned my title as the World's Number-One Salesman through hard work and learning more about my product. The hard work consisted of putting in long hours on the job. Learning more about my product meant I boned up on myself—not cars. I kept trying to learn more about me. *Who* I was and *what* I was.

In so doing I made an amazing discovery. I found out that if I spent more time listening than I did talking I would learn a great deal about me.

People would tell me this. Prospects would tell me. Owners would tell me. Coworkers would tell me. I learned that to one customer I was practically a father confessor. I learned that if I just let him pour out all his troubles of the past week on my shoulder, I was on my way to a sale. When I failed to heed that lesson I was in danger of losing the sale. In fact I lost a memorable one. Here's the story.

My Son, the Doctor

This lost sale hurt. A well-known contractor came in to see me. He was a self-made man, with little formal education, who with hard work and goal setting had become quite affluent. I presented the product, a top-of-the-line model with all the luxury options and accessories. I took him for a demo ride. I handed him the pen and order blank—and I blew it.

At the end of the day I like to meditate on the day's successes. That night I could only think about the big failure. I spent all evening trying to figure out what went wrong. Finally, as the evening wore on I could stand it no longer. I picked up the phone and called the guy.

I said, "Look, I tried to sell you a car today, in fact I thought I had, and you walked out."

"That's right," he said.

"What happened?" I asked.

"Are you kidding?" I could almost see him over the phone as he looked at his watch. "It's eleven o'clock at night."

"I know it. I apologize. But, I want to be a better salesman than I was this afternoon. Would you tell me what I did wrong?"

"You're serious?"

"You bet."

"All right. Are you listening?"

"I'm all ears."

"Well, you weren't this afternoon." He then went on to tell me how he had just about made up his mind to buy from me and he was in that period of last-minute hesitation before signing. To ease his own mind—after all, he was shelling out ten grand—he had started to tell me about his son, Jimmy, who was going to the University of Michigan and studying to be a doctor. He was proud of his son and he mentioned all of the boy's achievements, his grades, the dean's list, his athletic ability, his ambitions. As he told me about them that evening, in all honesty I couldn't remember that he had said it in the afternoon. I hadn't been listening.

He told me that night that I hadn't seemed to care, that I showed no interest, that my mind seemed to wander once I thought I had the sale clinched. He told me that I had been actually straining to hear some joke another salesman was telling outside my office door.

That was why he lost interest in me—because I had showed no interest in him other than as a guy with a checkbook. How could I? I hadn't listened to him other than when I had qualified him as to his wants and needs. But he had greater needs than just transportation—he had a need to be complimented on a son who was his pride and joy.

That's why he didn't buy *me*. It may seem strange that since what he had come in for was a new car and since my product, a good car, fitted *that* need, he still hadn't bought. What difference did it make if I listened to his kid's achievements or not?

Not strange at all—and a whale of a difference. Since I claimed that what I really sold was *myself* it follows that what he was really buying along with the car was *me*. Frankly, I didn't measure up that afternoon as an attractive product.

This time I heard him out. When he was finished I said, "Thank you for helping me. You've taught me a lot. I'm sorry I wasn't listening this afternoon." I told him I was proud, too, to hear how well his son was doing, and that I knew with a dad like he had the boy would be a success. I said, "Perhaps the next time you'll give me a second chance and buy from me."

What did I learn from that call at nearly midnight? Two things. First, I learned the importance of listening carefully and how failure to do so meant a lost sale. Second, that if I took the lesson to heart I could recapture the sale the next time when he came back.

There was a next time and he did buy, but in the meantime he had pounded home a lesson I've never forgotten.

Salespeople, listen to me! There are other ways, too, that you can lose a sale by not keeping your ears open. Every salesperson has learned somewhere along the line that by *talking too much* he has bought the product back in five minutes. Most people are presold through advertising or other means. What they've really come in to see you about is some kind of reassurance that they're making the right decision. And again, remember, most people aren't buying *things*—they're buying what those things will do for them: give them prestige, a sense of power, comfort, safety, economy, respect. But, how in heaven's name will you know that if you don't keep your ears open? Half the time people are busy telling you what they want, while the inexperienced salesperson keeps telling them what he thinks they should have.

One of the hardest things in the world to do is to shut up. That's as blunt as I can put it. More people fail to sell themselves because they are too busy talking.

Let's move on down the list. Consider psychiatrists. I once sold a car to a psychiatrist who was very good-natured about being thought of as a "shrink." During the course of the presentation he said he envied me because I had a tangible product to sell—an automobile or a truck, while he had nothing to offer. I knew he didn't mean that literally, he was simply trying to make a comparison between bucket seats and a couch. I told him he was selling himself short, that he had a pair of good ears to offer and, most important, the ability to listen. He didn't tell people what to do, he listened and let them discover for themselves. A psychiatrist is like a sounding board.

Next, the *clergy*. I remember Father Bill, the priest of my parish in east-side Detroit. He was the most successful priest there—if you can measure success, as I do, by being respected and loved. All the members of the parish wanted to have Father Bill listen to their confessions. Listen is right, and without interrupting, because Father Bill's secret wasn't in telling them what to do for penance, but to hear them out and then gently ask them what they thought they should do. Father Bill, too, was a good sounding board.

What about *parents*? How many fathers and mothers really listen to their kids. My father never did, and the memory still smarts. My mother did, and I will never forget it. How many kids have gone wrong because their parents gave them a deaf ear? The kid who has a parent who *listens* is the luckiest kid in the world. And a parent needs to listen between the lines. A son may be saying, "I don't care what time you say I have to be in tonight." What he may really be saying is, "Let me know how far I can go—put limitations on me." If you haven't heard that plea you'll find he's the kid who says later, "Boy, does my old man tune me out!"

Teachers need to listen to their students, *counselors* need to listen to the career-conscious, *doctors* need to listen to the patient in order to arrive at a correct diagnosis, *nurses* need to listen to the worried, the frightened, the lonely in hospitals. *Lawyers* need to listen to prepare a brief that might have a decent chance to win in court. *Politicians* need to listen more to the voice of the people and learn from it, rather than spouting off on their platforms. And, where would a *pilot* be who is being "talked in" for a landing when the ceiling is zero if he didn't listen? He'd shortly have a different set of wings.

Listening Is a Fine Art

A friend of mine stood for two hours at Fifth Avenue and Forty-ninth Street, waiting in vain to meet his wife, because he wasn't listening when she said Madison and Forty-ninth. And I missed a flight to Des Moines recently because I wasn't listening when they announced that passengers were boarding.

We assume that because a person has two ears attached to his head he knows how to listen. Not so. Most of us with two ears are so busy thinking about what we're going to say next that what the other fellow is saying falls on deaf ears.

And, that's the problem. Everybody loves a good listener. Jazz bands, after-dinner speakers, a misunderstood husband, the guy who's telling the jokes at the office party. The answer to the problem then is not to be thinking of what you're going to say next, but make an honest effort to listen attentively to the other person. Besides, you might learn something. As the old saying goes, listening is the greater part of learning.

Surveys indicate that we hear about only 50 percent of what is said. How, then, can a person who wants to sell himself or herself more successfully tune in on the other 50 percent?

You'd be amazed how many people have had something to say about it. It's even covered in the Good Book. The Bible says, "Be swift to hear, slow to speak." In other words, ease off. Let the other person have his turn at bat. One of the great truths of all times is that it's hard to hear when the tongue is busy. So try sitting for a while with clenched teeth, hold your tongue and let your ears do the work. Make a special effort to refrain from talking so that you can give the other person the stage.

Soon that old law of compensation goes into high gear. The other person, aware that he's been holding forth at some length, will pause and turn the floor back to you. And when you're invited to speak you've sold yourself.

Another thing, as you've so often heard, actions speak louder than words. Good listening involves active participation on your part. Involvement. You may be holding your tongue, but it doesn't mean that you have to crawl into a hole. What can you do? Smile when the other person smiles. Frown in agreement if he frowns. Use facial expressions that show you are listening. Believe me, it will be appreciated.

An insurance salesman, a tremendous success at selling himself, John LoVasco (and more about him later), once told me his secret of holding his tongue. He follows this advice: "Least said, soonest mended." To him, that meant don't interrupt. Or, if you must interrupt, do it as few times as possible. Interruptions breed irritation. Hear the person out. People who are successful find that if they just keep listening any negative feelings others might have about them simply melt away.

One of this century's great statesmen, Winston Churchill, said: "Speech is silver while silence is golden." There is great value in silence when communicating. Silence can be healing. Silence can signify understanding. Silence on your part allows you to not only hear clearly what the other is saying, but it lets you listen between the lines as well.

I know the advice may sound puzzling at first, but if you want to be heard, keep quiet. It's one of the best ways I know of selling yourself successfully. I know. It helped make me the world's number-one salesman. And what I can do, you can do.

The Park Bench Listener

Bernard Baruch was one of the greatest listeners of all times. Of course, he was a lot more, too. He was one of the greatest financiers in the United States and a true statesman. After he made a fortune in a brokerage house, selling stocks and bonds and *himself*, he went on into government service. His career was enviable. He was an advisor to three administrations. Under Woodrow Wilson he was chairman of the War Industries Board, and he served on the peace delegation that met in Paris at the close of World War I. Under Franklin D. Roosevelt he served as a consultant. He advised the president on how to take the profit out of war in order to assure a better chance of peace. And under Harry Truman he authored the Baruch Plan of atomic energy control.

But it was as a listener that he gained his greatest fame. In his later years he seemed to make his office a friendly park bench and there he would sit daily and feed the pigeons and provide a broad shoulder to all who stopped by to talk. He offered willing, open ears. And many people did stop by, the ordinary people of the city, the little people, the great and the near-great. Mayors, governors, senators, presidents sought out that "park bench," if not literally then by extension through asking Baruch to come to Washington. And most of the time the little people, the great and the near-great didn't seek Baruch out for advice, they sought him out as a man they could talk to, a man who would let them get things off their chests.

Bernard Baruch sold himself to businessmen and generals, to kings and commoners, to cabinet members and presidents because, above all, he had learned to listen.

How can you learn to be a good listener?

Get set for another daily dozen.

Twelve Rules for Learning to Listen

1. *Keep your mouth shut* so your ears will stay open.
2. *Listen with all your senses.* Listen first with the ears. Keep them wide awake. Don't settle for just 50 percent, get the whole story.
3. *Listen with your eyes.* Maintain eye contact, it shows you're hanging on to every word. We've all heard the expression "in one ear and out the other." No one has ever heard, however, "in one eye and out the other."
4. *Listen with your body.* Use body language for total awareness. Sit up straight, don't slouch. Lean forward to be more attentive. Present an alert appearance.
5. *Be a mirror.* Smile when the other person smiles, frown when he or she frowns, nod when the other nods.
6. *Don't interrupt.* That breaks the speaker's train of thought. It breeds irritation.
7. *Avoid outside interruptions.* If you're in an office and have enough clout, ask your secretary to hold all calls. Or, try

to go someplace where interruptions are less likely to occur.

8. *Avoid sound distractions.* Turn off the radio or TV or background music. Nothing "background" should compete with the person you're listening to.

9. *Avoid sight distractions.* Don't let an outside view or an inside view of office, shop or work activity blind you to listening with your eyes.

10. *Concentrate.* Pay attention to the other person at all times. This is no time to glance at your watch, trim your fingernails, yawn or light a cigarette or pipe. In fact, don't smoke. Just handling a cigarette can break your concentration.

11. *Listen between the lines.* Try to hear the "fine print." Often what a person *doesn't* say turns out to be more important than what he or she does say. A tone of voice, an offhand expression, a shading, an embarrassed cough—all are tipoffs that the person is saying something, but not in words.

12. *Don't be an ATANA.* An ATANA is what I call people who are All Talk And No Action. Make your action one of *listening carefully.* I've watched the ATANA people. They hang around water coolers and the coffee machine. They gossip, they tell jokes. I call 'em the dope ring; they're dopes and they're a drug on the market.

There they are: twelve good rules for learning to be a better listener and in doing so gaining a far better chance to sell yourself successfully.

Just think how lost you'd be if you couldn't listen. Someone once posed this question: If you had to lose one of your five senses—sight, hearing, speech, touch and smell—which one would you pick? Most people immediately say hearing. They say they'd rather be deaf. But research indicates that that is not so. People adjust to blindness far easier than they do to deafness. Those who are sightless seem to learn a different way to "see." In fact, their hearing becomes far more acute. They "see" with an inner eye and often "see" far more than we can imagine. But being without hearing is to live in a total world of silence—the deaf are completely tuned out of the world of sound. Being unable to listen is a far greater burden than being unable to see.

Not long ago I attended a theatrical performance, a musical, in which a young man with a splendid baritone voice, had the lead role. He sang song after song to the great delight of the audience. Someone pointed out his parents who were seated in the front row, basking in the applause their son received.

Later, I talked to the director of the production, a friend of mine. I said, in passing, that the lead singer's parents had been present. I remarked how proud they must have been to hear that glorious voice. Then the director told me. "His parents are totally deaf and always have been. Never once have they heard that God-given voice and they never will." The director continued, "When I first learned that I cried on the way home from rehearsal."

Think about it. Aren't you glad *you* can listen?

Things to Do NOW!

- Add the daily dozen listening rules to your exercise list and do them every day.
- Make sure you don't buy back the sale of yourself with your big mouth.
- Remember, the other person isn't interested in what *you* have to say until *he's* had his say.
- Write this on a three-by-five file card and put it up where you can see it every day: "Often to say nothing at all is better than saying a mouthful."

CHAPTER SEVEN

Speaking Another Language

WE HAVE all heard stories by returning travelers from abroad who had found themselves in difficulty at airports and railroad stations, at hotels and restaurants, and at service stations and border crossings, simply because they lacked knowledge of a particular foreign language.

The lost traveler in Madrid is baffled when he seeks directions. The relatively easy purchase of a bus ticket in Munich can be frustrating if your only knowledge of German is *ja* or *nein*. Some Americans even find it impossible to understand English—so the joke goes—when it is spoken by a London cabbie.

When we don't understand another person's language, or when that person doesn't understand ours, then a breakdown in communication takes place. Misunderstanding, confusion, even hostility can be the result.

Yet, look at the wonderful effect a knowledge of the other person's language can have on individuals and on groups. Recently, after centuries of tradition, the first non-Italian pope was selected by the assembled cardinals of the Roman Catholic Church in Rome. When the signal smoke arose above the Vatican, a surprised and stunned world learned that the Church had chosen John Paul II, a Pole, to sit on the throne of Peter. To thousands upon thousands of Italians it seemed unthinkable. Not to have a *Pàpa*, one of their own, could have alienated many of the faithful in Italy. But, at his first appearance before the crowded St. Peter's Square, this Polish pope spoke his first words in Italian and instantly won the hearts of millions. He knew instinctively that in order to sell himself successfully to this prayerful yet troubled crowd, and to millions of others within the sound of his broadcast voice, he must speak "another language," which in this case was *theirs* not *his*. The love and affection and good wishes that came pouring back to him because of that simple little truth are beyond measure.

Become Bilingual in English

Speaking the other person's language, however, goes far beyond what we normally think of as the ability to master another tongue, to be fluent perhaps in French, Spanish, Italian or Russian.

The other person's language that I'm referring to is the same language as our own. It doesn't matter what your native tongue is—it may not be English—but *how* you use it and *when* you use it often spells the difference between good communication and failure to communicate.

Failure to communicate is, for many people, the single largest reason for their failure to sell themselves. It isn't that we don't know the words or that we lack a suitable vocabulary, it's usually because we don't know how to use the right words at the right time.

Buck Rodgers and the Right Words

Most readers of my generation recall Buck Rogers as a space adventurer in the twenty-first century, long before we as a nation heard about UFO's and before we walked in space and before *Star Wars* filled movie theater seats like no other picture. Those of you who are younger have at least heard of Buck Rogers. As a hero of the comic strips and Saturday afternoon serials, Buck was daring, fearless and completely at home in a world of scientific marvels and futuristic technical advances.

But he's *not* the Buck I'm talking about.

I want to tell you about another man, a real one, who, in his field, is as daring and fearless and adventurous as the other Buck ever was—and, who lives in a world of space-age technology more complex and advanced than the other Buck ever dreamed about.

I'm talking about Francis G. "Buck" Rodgers, vice-president of marketing at IBM, which some people consider the most important company in all history. His career is proof that solid reward can be found in the world of business, and he spends a great deal of time lecturing and telling everyone who will listen —especially young people—about the satisfaction that can be found in private enterprise.

He is selling himself every day of the year. As a lecturer he knows the importance of the right word at the right time. As a salesperson in the fullest sense of the term he has learned the secret of talking the other person's language. Buck's world is one of highly sophisticated computers, electronic circuits, interfacing units, memory banks, data processing and printouts. It includes even a lot more that I don't pretend to understand. It's a highly sophisticated language that he knows and speaks. He also knows it is *not* the language of most of the people who need and want IBM's services in some way or another. *His* professional language is not normally *theirs*.

IBM has a sales force worldwide. It numbers in the thousands, and Buck's job, as vice-president in charge of marketing, covers the sale of everything from recording tapes and data-processing systems to duplicating systems and office machines. While I don't live in a world of computers, I do have some first-hand knowledge of IBM's product—I have two of their electric typewriters in my office. Buck didn't sell them to me personally, but I wish he had. He's a success and I like to meet successes.

But, how much of a success would he be if he hadn't mastered the technique of speaking the other person's language, along with the many other rules he has put to use personally in the art of selling himself?

Imagine the baffled reaction of many businesspeople if Buck or any one of his trained salespeople were to make an appointment, come in and say: "I'd like to sell you a transistorized electronic system of interconnected units, capable of being programmed with over ten thousand input factors, ranging from inventory control to invoicing and everything in between, with memory-bank storage facilities, instant readout, and interface capabilities with all your field satellites. The entire computerized operation will function under controlled humidity conditions and in ambient air which has been electrostatically scrubbed."

Sounds impressive, but I don't understand it and I don't pretend to. It isn't my language and it isn't the language of most business managers with whom I'm acquainted. More important, it's not the sales language that has made Francis G. "Buck" Rodgers the great salesman he is.

Here's what Buck has to say about it, as quoted in Robert L. Shook's book *Ten Greatest Salespersons—What They Say About Selling*: "Many are under the impression that there's a certain mystique about a computer, IBM's most widely recognized product. That's a fallacy. We simply supply a solution to our customers' problems."

Buck goes on to emphasize that he is not selling a computer as such but what a computer will *do*. Every salesperson who is successful knows this to be true. You don't sell a *thing*, you sell the *benefits* of the thing. Elmer Wheeler, who has become famous as the father of "sizzlemanship" in selling, pointed out that one should sell the sizzle and not the steak. It's the sizzle that makes people's mouths water. And a good salesperson uses mouth-watering words to do it.

So does Buck Rodgers as he uses the other person's language. Quoting again from Shook's book, Rodgers states: "I've got something that's going to *make your job easier*, it's going to *reduce your cost*, and it's a way to allow you to *give better service to your customers.*" (The italics are mine.) Those key words, italicized, are the other person's language, the words he understands, the words that quicken his interest.

There are a number of reasons why Buck Rodgers has become an outstanding business success; being bilingual in his native tongue—being able to speak the other person's language —numbers high among those reasons.

But it's not just in selling a product and service (more about those in later chapters) that this ability is important. Its real importance lies in its proven ability to help you sell *yourself*. Here are eight suggestions on how to do it—methods that I find invaluable.

"Other Language" Tips

1. Use "move forward" words.
2. Drop the "hold back" words.
3. Use simple words.
4. Don't wave "red flag" words.
5. Go easy on the slang.
6. Say what you mean.
7. Mean what you say.
8. Forget the profanity.

Let's consider those do's and don'ts.

First, *use "move forward" words*. I call them that because they move you right along in your relationships with others. People like to hear them, they make others feel good about you, they tend to make others respond to you. Here are some of the "move forward" words that can work wonders for you because every one of them is in the other person's language and he or she will be quick to recognize them: (Of course there are many more like them.)

You, yourself, yours
We
Our, ourselves
Sorry
Promise
Please
Thank you
Excuse me

I know of a major communications company that has made it a corporate rule that all letters going out under its letterhead, regardless of who writes them, from the president on down, cannot be mailed if they contain the word *I*. The letters are carefully checked by supervisors—in fact, secretaries have become so efficient at discreetly rewriting their bosses' letters that further editing is hardly ever necessary.

The first person singular has simply been struck from this corporation's vocabulary. But the words *you* and *yours* really get a workout. "*You* will receive within a few days . . ." Or, "*Your* shipment was sent yesterday . . ." This company knows that whomever it deals with will warm to such personal words. One of their public relations men who adopted the rule even in his personal correspondence and who has achieved great success with it told me, "Joe, to change the words of the old song a bit, it's a sin to tell an *I*."

The words *you* and *yours* and *yourself* are always attention-getting words. The moment you say them, the people you are talking to, or writing to, become more alert, more responsive. Next to their own names, those words have the sweetest sound. They can cause wonderful things to happen. For example, because you have spoken or written to them in words they relate to, *their* language, if you will, they suddenly become more interested in *you* and what you have to say to them.

Here's that quote again by Buck Rodgers: "I've got something that's going to make *your* job easier, it's going to reduce *your* cost, and it's a way to allow *you* to give better service to *your* customers." (Again, the italics are mine.) You will notice that Buck sinned with the first word, but he repented with four other "move ahead" words.

I was talking with a successful furniture salesman a short while ago, and he said that he learned that talking his customers' language with its frequent use of the word *you* helped him sell more sofas than pushing a manufacturer's name, well-built springs or price. "The customer expects the first two," he said, smiling, "and hopes for the best on the third." He's found that a simple sentence in the other person's language—like "from what *you've* said about the color scheme of *your* walls and carpeting, this sofa in beige velvet will certainly make *your* family room something special"—will sell more furniture in the long run than, "There's a sale price on these—10 percent off."

A jewelry clerk from whom I bought a pin for my wife once asked, "Joe, how did *you* get to be the world's number-one salesman?" The moment he asked, he had me. He aroused my interest. He had used that magic word *you* right from the start, right after the other word I love best, my name, Joe. Notice, he didn't say, "Tell *me* how *I* can get to be a better salesman."

Both my friend in furniture and my friend in jewelry are very successful because they've mastered the technique of using the other person's language.

When you decide that words such as *you* and *yours* are going to become an important part of your vocabulary, and when you put those words to use, shortly another wonderful word will work itself into your speech and writing—wonderful because it helps you sell yourself better. As every professional salesperson knows, as every husband and wife appreciate, as every boy and girl in love soon learn—the word is *we*. There is a gentle couple in my neighborhood who just celebrated their golden wedding anniversary. They told me one thing they discovered from fifty years of happiness together is that the word *we* is the most beautiful word in the world.

We and *our* are words that share with or include the person, so use them often, too. They show that you've really become bilingual.

What about some of the other words? It is always difficult to apologize for something to someone. However, to say you're *sorry* and mean it always makes you grow in the other person's eyes. The word *promise* is full of promise. Whenever you promise something and keep that promise (more about that in another chapter) you grow in the other person's eyes. *Please, thank you* and *excuse me* are all "move forward" words that go a long way toward helping you sell yourself.

Second, *drop the "hold back" words*. I call them that because their use is like a checkrein on yourself whenever you are selling your most important product, you. After all, that's what you're doing most of your waking day. When people hear these checkrein words they tend to turn away from you. They may not understand exactly why they do, but they do all the same. When you're talking the other person's language avoid as much as possible these "hold back" words or ones like them:

I, me
My, myself
Later
Maybe

Those words usually indicate that you are communicating on *your* terms, not on the other person's. There is this big difference—the point of view. Speaking the other person's language shows that you see things from his or her viewpoint. That's what is liked and appreciated. So the secret is always to try and communicate with other people on *their* terms. That doesn't mean to give in to their demands, or to give up your convictions or to sell out (more about that, too, in another chapter). It does mean that by your words you are putting yourself in the other person's shoes and under the other person's hat and seeing things through the other person's eyes. When you do that, you're on your way to greater personal, social and business success than you ever dreamed possible.

There are other words, too, that are "hold back" words. When you use the word *later* from the other person's viewpoint, for example, he or she may tend to cool off toward you immediately. On the other hand, the use of the word *now* will raise you in the other person's esteem. Other people like you to do things for them *now* not *later*. So, words like *now, right away, certainly, of course,* etc. move you forward again. Words like *maybe, sometime, in a minute,* etc. are "hold backs" to be avoided.

Perhaps at this point, you're saying, "hold on, Girard! You're saying that *I* is a 'hold back' word. But, aren't you going around telling everybody 'I am the greatest?' " The answer to that is no. I don't tell that to anyone else; I tell it only to Joe Girard. Remember, I called it a psyching-up process. I tell myself that I am number one, that I am the greatest. I'm speaking only to *me*. Were I to tell others that it would be a turn-off. It would sound as if I were only traveling through life on an ego trip. When I wear a numeral *1* pin, I use it to tell others, if they ask, that I am the number-one person in *my* life, not theirs. They are number one in *their* life and that is the point I try to drive home. In all honesty it must be said that when Muhammad Ali, whom I mentioned earlier, tells the whole world that he is the greatest, he is psyching himself up, yes, but he also turns a great number of people off—including fans as well as sports writers. And no amount of Ali's poetry can change that fact.

Third, *use simple words*. I don't mean basic English or basic whatever your native tongue is, and I don't mean every word has to be one syllable. But my advice is to get rid of the big words, the tongue twisters, the hard to understand words. Why? Because chances are good that they're not in the other person's language. If you want to sell yourself better, then it's highly important that you're understood.

No one knew that better than Winston Churchill, who led England through its "finest hour." Winston Churchill understood that when Britons needed to rally to their country's defense, he must talk to them in their language, in words that would spur them to fight "on the seas and oceans . . . in the air . . . (and) on the beaches." He did not give them double-talk, he told them in words they understood, "I have nothing to offer but blood, toil, tears and sweat."

Churchill shared what he had learned when he wrote, "All my life I have earned my living by words that I write and words that I speak. If I have learned about the use of words, what I know best and what counts most is this: of all the words I know the short words are of most use. They are the words others know. They are the words that bring other men to know. And they are the words which move men."

I prize that advice so much I have Churchill's words framed and hanging near my desk. I urge you to copy them, too.

You cannot sell yourself well—in fact you're dead—if you need an interpreter. Consider this memo which an insurance adjustor sent to the main office handling claims: "The pressure involved in getting depositions from on-site witnesses for both the claimant and the disputing party has made it necessary to revise the suspense date set for arbitration of the findings upwards of three days with no slippage foreseen." I read it and shook my head, bewildered. Translation: "The full report will be on your desk Thursday, no later." Remember the rule, keep it simple.

Along with that, fit your words to the occasion. Good car salespeople know that you talk style and beauty and comfort and safety to a woman, not horsepower and compression ratios. If you're with a doctor, remember that his language includes medical terms but your language probably doesn't. Don't tell him some high-sounding words you read in a medical book or column. Keep it simple. Tell him you have a stomach ache or that it hurts when you breathe. He'll understand. Doctors already know the rule. Unless they're talking to another doctor, when they'll use each other's language, they talk in terms the patient can understand. No doctor has ever said (at least I don't think so), "Take ten grains of the acetyl derivative of salicylic acid and retire." We've all smiled, instead, at the "other language" advice, "Take two aspirins and go to bed."

Fourth, *don't wave "red flag" words*. These are warning words that usually get the other person's defenses up, maybe even lower his boiling point. Say *Republican* to a *Democrat* and sometimes it can be like waving a red flag in front of a bull. At the same time, *tax* and *spend* are "red flag" words to a Republican.

The best way to tell a red flag word is to ask yourself what are the words that get your back up? If I were to make a list here it would really reflect only those words that get my back up. Many of them might not bother you at all. In truth, you can only know what are red flag words to a person after you've come to know the person himself. From then on, you use caution. It is always a possibility that you will use such words when you talk to strangers simply because you do not know them. However, there are some general *categories* of words which often can be red flag words to some people. Those categories are:

Religion
Politics
Race
Ethnic Background
Family
Economics

I know that seems to cover the waterfront. So what it boils down to is this. *Know your person, then avoid words in the above categories that you sense will rub him the wrong way.*

You must feel your way through these yourself. You must be wise enough to know that you will run into little trouble talking about religious matters if the other person shares your religious beliefs or value system. But, you won't sell yourself if you beat the drums for birth control when the person you're talking to is a devout Roman Catholic. And you won't sell yourself if you support socialized medicine and you're talking to a doctor. Red flag words either heat up the room or create a distinct chill. Again, don't sell out your principles (if you believe in socialized medicine, for example), just watch the words you use. Believe it or not, when you do watch the words you use, you can talk socialized medicine with a doctor and never once raise his temperature. The key word is *tact*.

Fifth, *go easy on the slang*. There is nothing wrong with slang expressions. They find their beginnings in work life, in military service, on college campuses and in ethnic communities. They are strong expressions and often are valuable to make a specific point. They also tend to date quickly, to be replaced with a newer word or phrase. Further, they rarely serve you as well as the straightforward expression. "Crash in my pad" may be colorful and in the other person's language, depending upon who the other person is, but you'll communicate better with, "Why not stay over at my place?"

When veterans were discharged after World War II they were given a small lapel pin to wear. GIs (already a dated word) called the pin a "ruptured duck." Use that slang expression today and few people under forty will know what you're talking about.

Some slang expressions linger on in our language longer than others. It's not wise to even list them here; they may have disappeared by the time you've come to this chapter.

The idea is to use slang expressions and, while we're at it, foreign phrases sparingly. When you do, they can sometimes work to your advantage. They help you to sell yourself.

A common expression in the neighborhood where I grew up, a phrase of the street people, is "Give me five, Brother." No one would think of saying, "Let me shake your hand." One time, in an effort to speak the other person's language, I said "Give me five, Brother!" to a new-car prospect. He did. No sooner did my hand reach his than I thought to myself, Joe, you blew it! The man had lost a couple of fingers along the way. He sensed my sudden embarrassment and saved me from losing the sale of myself and the car. He grinned and shot right back with "I'll give you three and owe you two." Now, that guy had class.

Sometimes, when I knew a prospect was Italian like myself I'd greet him with "Hey, *compare!*" I've said goodbye in German and good health in Polish. Foreign expressions can work for you in speaking the other person's language but only when you are sure of that person's background. When in doubt, don't.

Sixth, *say what you mean*. There is no room for double-talk when it comes to selling yourself. Don't use weasel words or loophole words or words that sound like one thing but that really mean something else. The only place for those squirm-out words is in disclaimers.

Say, "Let's have lunch Tuesday if it's convenient," but not, "Why don't we get together for lunch sometime?" The first says exactly what you mean, lunch on Tuesday. The second almost says I really don't care if we eat together or not.

Think of the times you've been startled by somebody who has missed an appointment or stood you up or ruined the recipe and then said, "But I thought you meant . . ."

Don't do it again. Next time *say what you mean*.

Seventh, *mean what you say*. One way to really mess up the sale of yourself is to have no intention of doing what you say you'll do or going where you say you'll go. Perhaps not consciously, but way in the back of your mind you have your fingers crossed.

I call it using words without backbone. They're the favorite words again of the ATANA people—all talk and no action. Don't use them. You may be tempted to use them because you know they are words that won't let people pin you down. Words like *perhaps, we'll see, sometime, let me think about it, I'll try to get around to it*. There are hundreds more.

The point is, if you want to sell yourself you also want to be pinned down. You want people to know that your word stands for something, that you can be counted on. If you don't mean what you say, don't say it at all. It's the safest course—but whoever said that selling yourself successfully was achieved by taking the safest course? Not me.

Eighth, *forget the profanity*. Some time ago I was in New York City and I was enjoying lunch with a very successful wholesale salesman of digital clocks and watches. No wonder he met me right on time. However, he shocked me by saying that he had had some negative feedback about me and some recent lectures I had given before sales groups. He had heard I had used some profanity—mild, but still profanity. He told me frankly that I didn't need it. He made me promise that I wouldn't use the words again in speech or writing. He cautioned that if I lost one person through the use of profanity, that was one person too many. It would be evidence that I had failed to sell myself.

He pointed out, too, that oddly enough the person who notices your profanity and resents it or is offended by it is often a person who uses it to excess and doesn't realize the image he or she is projecting. Don't be tempted to be like that person. Stand out by being different, was my friend's advice.

Later, another salesman, a retailer of plumbing supplies in Los Angeles, startled me by telling me that he would never go to see or hear the late stand-up comic, Lenny Bruce, nor will he go to see Buddy Hackett. Now, Bruce was very popular, but that did not influence my friend. To him, Lenny Bruce had the filthiest mouth in show business. As if to prove the truth of the New York wholesaler's remark, I noticed that the Los Angeles retailer had an even filthier mouth than that which I was told belonged to Bruce. This salesman had a stock of toilet humor jokes that were in very poor taste, yet here he was telling me now that Buddy Hackett, also a very funny man, should clean up his act.

At Las vegas, I've often watched Don Rickles, who makes an enviable living by insulting people, and he never insults them with a four-letter word. Dozens of other fine comedians have a clean act.

You and I both know that there are people in all walks of life who, they say, have the vocabulary of a marine corps drill sergeant or a waterfront longshoreman. But, you will be surprised and so will they at how well you can sell yourself to them without resorting to profanity. You can search through this book for the blue words, you won't find any, yet I'm selling myself to you in every chapter.

In his book *Yak! Yak! Yak!* Ira Hayes, an executive at National Cash Register and an outstanding public speaker, has this to say about profanity or just plain dirty words: "Don't do it . . . you cheapen yourself . . . when you use profanity. It isn't needed. It can't help you, so why do it?"

When it comes to speaking the other person's language, use their *best* words, not their worst. Again, to quote Hayes:

". . . say nothing that will offend or embarrass them. Profanity will offend half of them and embarrass the other half."

Those eight tips will work wonders for you in helping you to become bilingual in this job of selling yourself. When you remember to speak the other person's language, doors begin to open for you everywhere—at your job, with your family, with next-door neighbors. Speaking the other person's language has started more people on their way to the top and kept them there, has helped people sell themselves more successfully in all their personal and business dealings.

So, get started speaking it now—get bilingual—whether you're a salesperson, a bank teller, a student, a teacher, a homemaker, a toolmaker or just retired. Don't feel for a moment that speaking the other person's language is a one-way street, with all the effort on your part. Not true. People will respond by speaking *your* language sooner than you expect. When that happens you will rarely misunderstand one another. That's when the sale of *you* is easy.

Things to Do NOW!

- Decide that you're going to learn another language—the other person's.
- Decide to become fluent in it—to speak it, read it and write it well.
- Copy the eight tips on a file card and scotch-tape it or thumb-tack it up where you can see it each day.
- Starting now, the first week, see how many "move forward" words you can use with every person you come in contact with. Keep count. Keep it up for an entire week so that it becomes a habit.
- Starting the second week, make an effort to get rid of all the "hold back" words you can.
- The third week, bear down on the simple words. If you're

tempted to use a six-bit word, don't. Use a two-bit word instead.

- Continue with the rules for the eight weeks. By that time they will be a natural part of you.
- This is the way one learns new words in French or Spanish or German, and how one learns the grammar. It works.

CHAPTER EIGHT

Managing Your Memory

Two of the saddest words a person can ever say are "I forgot."

More than that, they are "hold back" words that can wreck your chances of selling yourself and your ideas and opinions. How? What kind of wreckage?

Well, think of the consequences when you forget an important appointment.

Think of the heartache that sometimes results when you forget a wedding anniversary, a birthday or some other special occasion.

Think of the setbacks that can occur if a student's mind goes blank just before a critical examination.

Think of the embarrassment an actor or actress suffers when on stage he or she suddenly forgets the lines.

Think how a sale can be lost because the salesperson has overlooked an important customer benefit during the product presentation.

There are dozens of other times when the simple act of forgetting can cost you the sale of you, but when the ability to *manage your memory* can save the sale.

Consider the Elephant

They say an elephant never forgets, that he remembers everything. But, then, an elephant isn't selling himself or anything else for that matter. The trouble is, an elephant doesn't know how to be selective, how to *manage his memory*. People have the ability to keep the important and let go of the unimportant. That's the difference between elephants and people. Elephants can't control their ability to remember, but people *need* to remember for many reasons, and they also need to remember the right thing at the right time.

They also say one of the most forgetful members of the animal kingdom is the mule. We usually think that the mule is stubborn, that he refuses to do what we want him to do out of sheer cussedness. Animal trainers say this is not so. The mule doesn't do what you want him to do because he simply cannot remember from one moment to the next what it is you showed him or told him. He's a "180" from the elephant.

Fortunately, we are neither elephants nor mules. We can be selective, we can manage our memory, when we know how.

Why is it so important to manage our memory?

The simple act of remembering a name can open doors for you, put people on your side at once, give you an important edge. At the same time, forgetting that name can close doors and shut you out.

Again, failure to be *where* you say you'll be, *when* you say you'll be there (without a valid reason, of course) makes you a loser. Forgetting an appointment might even cost you a job. It certainly can cost you money. Many doctors and dentists now charge for the office appointment that a person failed to keep.

Forgetting your wife's birthday can—well, I don't have to tell you about the buzz saw that can be created in the bedroom.

On the other hand, a good memory can work miracles. Consider, for a moment, just the ability to remember names.

I know several people with remarkable memories, and they have used this ability to achieve great personal success—especially in the area of remembering names, both first and last.

One time I observed Robert Lund, general manager of the Chevrolet Division of General Motors. This was at a convention of the National Automobile Dealers Association in San Francisco. At that particular NADA meeting, Bob stood at the door and personally greeted every dealer by name. He remembers them all. That's remarkable because there are over 6,000 Chevrolet dealers in the United States. This ability of Bob's is only one of the many reasons he is so great a success in the automotive world.

I shook my head in amazement at his feat. "How does he do it?" I asked my companion at the time.

"Darned if I know."

This was surprising, too, as well as amusing, because my companion was my friend William Rohns, dean of the College of Continuing Education at Northwood Institute in Michigan, with satellite schools in Indiana and Texas. Bill has an outstanding memory, too, and he makes people feel important simply by an unfailing ability to recall their names.

I asked Bill how he does it. He mentioned a number of things, and I was pleased to see that most of them fitted into my own set of memory rules.

These rules aren't for everybody, of course. For some people memory comes easily—for others the act of remembering is tougher. Count yourself lucky if you have little trouble. Maybe you can skip this chapter. However, most people have memory problems, and if you share those problems (as I do) then read on and discover some secrets.

String Around the Finger?

My mother always relied on tying a string around her finger when she wished to remember something. Many people do. I mean they really do. But, it's not the best way to remember something, no matter what you've been told. In my mother's case she often forgot why she had tied the string around her finger in the first place. Besides, a string can cut off circulation and you can wind up with a numb finger.

If you must "tie a string" there are many ways to do so without once ever using a piece of string itself. You won't cut off your circulation and you won't wonder what the heck the string was for. The memory secrets I want to pass on to you have no strings attached.

Okay, here they are, and take my word for it, they work:

Ten Memory-Management Rules

1. Open an account in your memory bank.
2. Don't bank trivia.
3. Clean the slate daily.
4. Use word association.
5. Don't trust your memory.
6. Don't muddle your memory.
7. Avoid memory traps.
8. Put repetition to work.
9. Keep your mind busy.
10. Remember to forget.

Let's consider these do's and don'ts carefully.

First, *open an account in your memory bank.* That means you want to manage your memory just as carefully and wisely as you want to manage your finances.

We all have a memory bank. In that respect we are the

world's finest computers. Like any monetary bank it functions as a place where one can regularly make deposits and withdrawals. (The healthy interest comes in the way you find you're doing in selling yourself.)

We make deposits in our memory bank every waking moment of the day, consciously and subconsciously. Often we are unaware that we are doing so. The bank is constantly receiving deposits—names, faces, dates, events, impressions, ideas, facts, figures and other information. Psychologists tell us that even while we are asleep our minds are busy receiving deposits.

The deposits happen whether we tell the bank or whether we don't. Where trouble often sets in is when we want to make a withdrawal. Just as with monetary banks where you've noticed it's never as easy to withdraw money as it is to put it in, our memory banks act the same way.

They're reluctant—they want identification—they demand signatures—they put up roadblocks. Still we *must* make withdrawals and we must do it properly, especially at the time we need to do so the most.

Unlike monetary banks, our memory bank doesn't keep banker's hours. It is open all the time. What a pity, then, that we don't avail ourselves of such a customer convenience.

How do you open an account in your memory bank? Simply by saying to yourself that from now on you will manage your memory the same way you do your finances. You will make a greater effort to control the deposits, a greater effort to decide what is put in. And you will make a conscious effort to withdraw "memory" at the right time. You are telling yourself that you know the memory is on deposit—all you have to do is "step up to the window" and take out what you need.

Picture your mind as a bank. See the tellers' windows. See the drive-in window. See the night-depository slot. See the twenty-four-hour banking convenience area with its push-button operation and its ability to function immediately when you feed your plastic code card into its automated insides.

Picture yourself as stepping up and saying, "I want to deposit *this*" or "I want to take out *that*." And picture yourself getting in return a smiling "yes, sir" or "yes, ma'am."

Know that your memory bank is not going to fail. It is, as they say, insured by a federal agency. That agency is *you*.

Second, *don't bank trivia*. Trivia is clutter. Remember, if you were lucky, the attic at your grandmother's house? You loved to explore it. Fun for you maybe, but something your grandmother was always saying she "had to get around to cleaning." It was usually cluttered with everything the family didn't want to discard. You couldn't find your way around in the mass of things that filled up the cramped space. And, usually, all the things stored there were fairly useless items. (Yes, I know that rare finds have turned up in attics—genuine antiques worth thousands—but these are the exception to the rule. There have also been rare finds of Confederate money.)

Often our minds, like old attics, get just as cluttered with trivia, with useless things, so cluttered that it is hard to find your way around in them. Searching your memory becomes a real scavenger hunt. So, to manage your memory better, keep trivia out of your memory bank.

I don't want to insult the television industry, but TV is one of the biggest contributors of trivia that you could hope to find. I don't need to tell you that it has been called a "wasteland." You've read that for yourself. I rarely watch TV except for worthwhile news events and specials. I think it's important to watch a presidential news conference, but there are plenty of people who will tell me that that is first-class trivia. You must make a decision. There are motion pictures on TV that are classics; there are also films that are junk. There is more junk than classics. I call TV junk food for the mind. Even in color, most TV programming is junk. (Naturally, my own television appearances are an exception.) So, I'm not saying you should cut out TV, I'm simply saying be selective. Don't fill your mind with TV trash. It's only trivia, it clutters up your bank.

The same goes, too, for cheap and sensational newspapers (you've seen them cluttering up the supermarket checkout counters), for pornography in books, magazines and films, and for gossip. All trivia. You know what they are? They are like Jesse James and the other outlaws of the Old West—they are memory-bank robbers.

But, do this: Fill your memory bank with good books, informative magazines, fine art, great music. None of these clutter your mind. Make this a travel pattern—remember that on the way to the bank you will usually find a fine library, an art museum, a concert hall, a book store. Pause and refresh yourself.

Third, *clean the slate daily*. It's important to keep the mind a clean slate, ready to receive new and important information, the kind you want to remember. If the slate isn't wiped clean of the things you've already put to use and remembered, you may be hard put to find room on which to write.

When I was a kid in the third grade I remembered that we took turns cleaning the blackboard at the end of the day. I used to love it when the teacher told me my turn had come. First I would erase all the blackboards around the room, unless there was something on them Teach wanted to save. Then, after erasing, I would use the sponge and warm water and wash the blackboards with smooth up-and-down strokes. I was so short then that I could hardly reach the top of the boards. How proud I was of those clean slates, ready to receive the next morning everything the teacher would put down.

To this day when I set out to wipe my mind's slate clean, I still picture those blackboards in my third grade classroom. I can recall the dust of the chalk, the smell of the sponge in warm water and the look of approval in my teacher's eyes. They are happy memories, and they have wiped out the unpleasant ones —the times I had to stay after school, the fears I had when I took home a bad repor card, the strapping I got in the principal's office.

Actually, we all do this subconsciously as the years go by. We tend to remember good things and wipe the slate clean of the bad. A good example can be seen in our many veterans across the country. As time passes, they forget the unpleasant experiences of war, the heat and the dirt, the horrors of combat, the wounded and the dead. What they now recall are the good things, the letters from home, the week-long furlough, the comradeship of those in their squad or company or battalion.

Wiping the slate clean is a blessing. When we don't do it subconsciously, then we do it consciously. Be like a kid again—wash off that blackboard.

The new things you put on it will look so much better there.

Fourth, *use word association*. It's a fact that one thing usually makes us think of another. Say *Christmas* and you'll think of tree or ornaments or gifts. Say *Hanukkah* and you think of candles. Say *Arab* today and you think of oil.

That's why word association is such a great help in managing your memory. It's ideal for remembering names and places and faces. The word association may have to do with colors, seasons, cities, states, movies, even rhymes. It works like this:

A successful real estate salesman told me that whenever a person's name suggests a color he associates it with that color. It works fine with names like Brown or Browning, White or Black or Blackstone or Whitney, Gray or Grayson, Green or Greenburg, Snow or Snowden. If a person's first name is Rose or Rosemary, Violet or Lily, he uses the same association.

Colors, flowers, combinations of colors are all helpful in remembering names and places.

What if the name doesn't even remotely connect itself with a color? Then, he uses something else. He remembered a Mr. Tim Schyler, a rather short man, by associating his name with two things—Tiny Tim and the sky. He remembered Mrs. Tudor by associating her with automobiles, Henry Johnson by associating him with the late president LBJ.

A builder I knew in the construction business remembered names in connection with the materials he worked with. One of his suppliers was a Chet Brickly who was never aware that in the builder's mind he was always a brick.

A very successful car salesman told me he'd never forget the face of a buyer named Ed Daskiewitcz, who had a mustache and who wore glasses. He might have difficulty with the name but he'd have no trouble with the face. Why? Because to him, his customer Ed's face looked exactly like that of Teddy Roosevelt on Mount Rushmore. In this car salesman's mind, Ed's face was carved in rock.

A daughter of an optometrist I know is a very bright student at the University of Detroit. Here's how she remembers dates in her history class. She associates them with music because she is also an excellent musician. To remember the war between England and America over England's pressing our seamen into their navy, she thinks of the 1812 Overture and, presto, she has it. The war of 1812. She told me that she remembered that Lady Jane Grey was Queen of England for only nine days and then was beheaded at the Tower of London by associating the fact with Beethoven's Ninth Symphony which was his last.

Her way wouldn't work for me because I'm no musician, I'm not a student and I know little of history. But, it might work for you. You get the idea. Relate the name, the date, to something else, whatever serves you best. You can work out your own code. You'll be glad you did.

Fifth, *don't trust your memory*. Memory loves to play tricks. If you let it, it can become a practical joker, but the joke is always on you, and you run the risk of losing the sale when you're trying to sell yourself the hardest.

None of these rules, and this one especially, is designed to turn you into a memory wizard—a Whiz Kid like the ones who used to be on radio when I was a kid. We're talking about *managing* your memory, not *trusting* it, and one of the best ways to do this is to fool your memory instead of letting your memory fool you. The trick you're going to play on it is to *write things down*.

I keep a three-by-five file card in front of me when I'm talking to a person—a holdover from my car-selling days. I jot down stray bits of information—anniversaries, hobbies, sports, new kids, birthdays. I don't make a production of this, I do it as casually as I can. If I'm in a spot where I can't jot things down, I do it as soon as I get back to my office or home.

The next time I'm with that person, especially when I know in advance that I'm going to meet him or her, I refresh my memory from the card and bring up something from it. I'll say, "John, how's your bowling game going? Still playing in your company's league?" Or, "Let's see, Ralph, that little girl of yours is two years old now—right? I'll bet she's a regular little lady." The person is amazed and delighted that I "remembered." He's more than ready to buy me.

I passed on the technique to my dentist, Dr. Gilbert Dilorito, and he's put it to regular use. During visits by his patients, he jots that kind of information down on his regular dental records, along with data on fillings, cleanings, extractions, bridge work and root canal jobs. When the patient returns, often months later, he surprises them with his "good memory" by saying casually, "How was your vacation last summer at Yellowstone Park?" Or, "It's about time to put your sailboat up for the winter, isn't it, Pete?" He tells me it works wonders for the doctor-patient relationship and goes a long way towards putting the patient at ease in the dentist's chair.

The technique is excellent, too, for remembering appointments, upcoming events, scheduling, anniversaries. I have a small pocket calendar with a page for each month of the year, marked off with squares for the days of the month. I carry it with me at all times. On it I jot down such things as (under Wednesday the tenth) *Dinner at Armando's*, or (under Tuesday the sixteenth) *Leave for Phoenix 10 a.m.* It's another way to keep from trusting to memory alone.

Still another technique I use is to mark down *today* appointments I have for tomorrow, or the various things I know I must do. I mark it down on slips of paper which I keep in my pocket. Then at night when I empty my pockets of change I place the slips in order on the dresser or next to my alarm clock. Upon awakening the next day I have right at hand the things I know I have to do that day. *Meet Sam at 9:00* or *Pick up suit from cleaners.*

Sixth, *don't muddle your memory*. That simply means don't get it mixed up. Don't confuse it. The easiest way to do that is to try to make deposits in your memory bank under the wrong account number. The easiest way to avoid this is to make sure *why* you must remember something. The *why* is your account number.

Suppose you wish to remember that on Friday, December first, you want to sell Robert Redford, motion picture superstar and well-known environmentalist, who lives in Utah, your terrific idea for harnessing solar power for home heating during the growing energy crunch. So, what do you deposit in the memory bank and under what account?

Friday, December first? Easy—last working day of the week —last month of the year—first day of the month.

Robert Redford? Word association—a red car—in the Ford model lineup.

Actor? Word association again—motion picture theaters.

Environmentalist? The popcorn litter which people leave in movie theaters.

Utah? Easy—the Beehive state. There's only one.

Idea for solar energy—power from the sun? Word association—sunflower to sun power. Maybe even suntan or sunburn.

To deposit all that would simply muddle the memory. The trick is to be selective. *What is the most important thing to remember?* I think we'd agree it's the terrific idea for solar energy—maybe a new system for mirror reflection. Okay, that's the main thing you want to deposit in the bank. Everything about that idea—what it is, how it works, why it's good. The rest will fall in place. The day and date can be jotted down on your calendar. Robert Redford, the superstar, is not hard to remember. He's on the tip of every movie fan's tongue. If you have to, jot his name down, too.

What you've done is *managed* your memory, not muddled it.

Seventh, *avoid memory traps*. The worst trap you can fall into is forgetting what you said last time. This frequently happens if you don't always tell the truth. I'm not talking about whoppers, I'm talking about the little white lies that we all tell at one time or another. The truth is, it's easier to remember the truth than to remember a lie. That's because we usually find that the first lie demands a second and still another as cover-ups. Truth we remember; our own conscience, I suppose, tries to help us forget untruths.

It's embarrassing, isn't it, when someone says, "How is your headache?" and you blankly reply "What headache?" Then the person says, puzzled, "Why, the headache you had yesterday when I wanted to drop by."

The results can be far more than embarrassing, however, when the untruth relates to appointments or schedules or business arrangements or even important social occasions.

As always, the rule to follow is *tell the truth* and make sure your secretary (if you have one) does the same. Believe me, most callers can tell at once if a secretary is lying or covering up for her boss. Telling the truth keeps you clear of memory traps. You never have to think, "Now what was it I told him last time?" The worst thing about memory traps is that you dig them yourself. Throw the shovel away.

Eighth, *put repetition to work*. This is an excellent technique and, believe me, people will not think that you are hard of hearing or that you are a parrot. It will help you remember names, dates, times, lots of things. It's as simple as this:

When someone tells you something, say quite frankly and with a smile: "What was your name again? I want to be sure to remember it." And, then when you're told, repeat it aloud. I guarantee, the other person will love to hear it played back.

Putting repetition to work is managing your memory by playback. It fixes things in your memory the same way an instant replay does on the boob tube.

Use the technique with other important things.

"What time did you say we are meeting? Nine-thirty?"

"So I'll be sure to remember, when is Phil's birthday? Saturday?"

"Let's see now, where did you say the bookstore was? The Fairlane Mall?"

I'll never forget the way one salesman made memory repetition work for him in selling himself to success. A very fine appliance salesman, he had business cards printed in a series of progressive rhymes. During the course of a sale on the floor he passed the cards to me from time to time, about a half-dozen of them. How could I forget that man and his product—I bought a window air conditioner from him—when he kept handing me cards with his name on them along with rhymes like these:

When you want cool air
I'll treat you fair.
      —Daniel T. Henderson

You'll like the price,
The deal is nice.
      —Daniel Henderson

Our window coolers take the prize,
I've got every model, every size.
      —Dan Henderson

Air conditioning just for you,
On top of that we service, too.
      —Danny Henderson

There were others. They not only sold a fine brand of air conditioners, more important they sold that salesman. Henderson made sure I'd never forget him. And, I won't.

Later on he told me that he got the idea from attending a traveling consumer-awareness presentation by a large appliance corporation. The presentation, a tuneful show with songs and dances, traveled from coast to coast. My salesman friend borrowed that memory device to help his customers remember him.

Ninth, *keep your mind busy*. An unused mind, an idle mind, will not go to work quickly for you when you want it to. Saying the wrong thing at the wrong time not only indicates you forgot the right thing and the right time, it also indicates your mind is lazy.

The best way to put a lazy mind to work is to keep it occupied, keep it busy. Contrary to what you might think, a busy mind hasn't got time to forget things. The busier you keep it, the better a worker it becomes. Again, like a muscle that only grows and develops by regular exercise, a memory only develops strongly through use.

Harry Lorayne, who has been called the man with the world's most phenomenal memory, has this to say in his book *How to Develop a Super-Power Memory*: "I believe that the more you remember, the more you *can* remember. The memory, in many ways, is like a muscle. A muscle must be exercised and developed in order to give proper service and use; so must the memory. The difference is that a muscle can be overtrained or become muscle-bound while the memory cannot. You can be taught to have a trained memory just as you can be taught anything else . . . *there is no such thing as a bad memory*. There are only trained or untrained memories."

Keep it busy, keep it exercised. And watch how, through that training, your memory will grow and develop.

Tenth, *remember to forget*. I've saved this rule for last because it may seem that I am contradicting myself. Not so. It's one of the most important rules there is in managing your memory.

I recall a compliment a neighbor once paid my late mother, one of the nicest I think she ever received. "Grace," the neighbor said, "you're the most forgetful person I know."

Compliment? You bet. My mother was simply remembering to forget, and it was one of the most important lessons she ever taught me.

That neighbor wasn't talking about such ordinary things as leaving the car lights on, or forgetting a friend's birthday or letting an appointment slip her mind. She meant a different kind of forgetfulness, a kind that "brooms" from your mind (as my mother would say) all the petty little things that get in your way when you want to be the best person you can.

It's important to learn that rule for forgetting if you want to sell yourself more successfully. It doesn't matter if you're out to change jobs or to get a date for Saturday night or to sell your husband on the fact that you'd like a microwave oven. My mother knew that a secret in selling herself was to be forgetful. Forgetful of what?

She knew that a person who stores up every hurt, every unpleasant memory, every anger is a person who will soon reflect bitterness. Who wants to buy such a personality? Not you. Not me.

She knew that cruel words from others, or thoughtless acts, would leave their mark. She would have none of that. She "broomed" them.

In the words of the poet, she knew it was "good to forgive but best to forget." In time I learned that others knew her secret, too. I remember a fruit peddler from my boyhood who often suffered taunts and abuse from young neighborhood toughs because of his accent. One day Guido said to me, "Joseph, if I remember their words I will hate them. If I hate them it will show. If it shows who will like me? If no one likes me who will buy my strawberries and oranges? No, it is better to forget."

He was following that wise advice, "Man should forget before he lies down to sleep."

Nickie McWhirter, columnist, writes in the Detroit *Free Press*, that for years she harbored hatred of three schoolmates. She states, "My hatred did them not one whit of harm or good. The only person it affected was me . . . hating drained a lot of energy and wasted it. Hating accomplished nothing of value to anybody, especially me."

It's easy to return insult for insult, to nurse hurt feelings and to hold grudges. But that only makes you a smaller person. Believe me, it is far better to "broom" them. When you do you become a bigger person and it will be much easier for you to sell yourself. Now, do this: Write down those three magic words. Put them in your wallet or purse or pocket. But, take them out often and look at them and think about them. And, *remember to forget*.

There you have them. Ten rules for memory management. I guarantee that if you follow them you won't be disappointed.

We often say "I wish I had a memory like so and so." Wishful thinking won't make it so. You have to work at it but good memory can be achieved.

Certainly memory must be important—look at all the songs it has inspired through the years. "Memories," "Down Memory Lane," "Did I Remember?" "Will You Remember?" "Memories Are Made of This," "Remember Pearl Harbor?" "Always Remember," Do You Remember?" "Give Me Something to Remember You By" and "Just the Memory of You." There are dozens more. But, probably the most popular, most famous of them all, is the one Bob Hope made his signature song—and he never forgets it: "Thanks for the Memory."

The things I do to remember things are not new. I've learned them from others, refined them, made them fit my needs. I pass them on to you. Adapt them to fit your requirements. They'll do the same for you as they have for Elmer Wheeler. The author of many famous "Wheeler-points" puts it this way in his book

How to Sell Yourself to Others: "These are just a few short-order tricks to help jog your memory . . . And if you use them you need never face a friend, a customer, or a client with a red face and have to say, I'm sorry—I just forgot."

Things to Do NOW!

- Throw away all strings, especially the kind people tie around their fingers. They really don't work.
- Decide to open an account in your memory bank now. Picture your mind as a spacious bank. See yourself walking up, making deposits and withdrawals.
- Commit the ten memory management rules to memory.
- Rid your mind of trivia.
- Practice word association.
- Stop trusting your memory. Write things down.
- You can't lie your way out of a memory trap; don't dig one in the first place.
- Keep your mind *very* busy and filled with worthwhile things.
- Carry a card in your wallet or purse that says *remember to forget*. Read it often. Broom out the petty things from your mind.
- And if you're really forgetful, read this chapter twice.

CHAPTER NINE
Telling the Truth

THERE ARE two good reasons for telling the truth—for sticking to the truth as well as you can—in any situation:

First, it makes you feel good.

Second, it's the only way to earn trust and respect from others.

To say it is the *only* way may invite argument, but I'll stick to the statement. You may gain respect for your good manners, your position in life, your acts of kindness, your knowledge and your experience—but to be caught in an outright lie will at once wipe out all the other sterling qualities you might possess.

We need only to look back a few years as a stunned nation watched its president brought down from the heights to disgrace. Richard Nixon lied to his country, and his administration crumbled around him. We saw a vice-president, Spiro T. Agnew, disgraced and forced to resign from office. We were shocked at the sight of high officials in every quarter, from cabinet members to White House aides, lie about their activities and eventually wind up in prison.

There is no doubt about it, failure to tell the truth can have far-reaching consequences. President Eisenhower was one of the most popular presidents this country has ever had. "Ike" was admired as the man who led America to victory in World War II and who came home to lead America in peace.

Yet a day came when he evaded the truth when it came to an issue of a downed U-2 spy plane over Soviet territory. The result? A summit conference involving the United States and the Soviet Union was destroyed. We may never be able to determine what might have been lost in world peace through that act; we do know, however, that America suffered in the court of world opinion.

Senator Joseph McCarthy of Wisconsin had a bright and promising career on Capitol Hill. Then the day came when he stood up and waved a list which he said contained the names of a startling number of Communists in the State Department. It proved to be false, but the damage was done. It set off one of the biggest witch-hunts in the history of our country, wrecking the lives and careers of many innocent people in government, in the arts and in many other walks of life. In his search for "disloyalty," most particularly in government offices, he added a new word to our speech, "McCarthyism," just as "Watergate" was to become a catchword with Americans a quarter of a century later. In his investigative techniques he made public accusations with the most doubtful of evidence. He was censured by his peers; his playing around with the truth eventually destroyed him.

Even before the day when Christ stood before Pontius Pilate and Pilate asked, *"What is truth?"* mankind has asked itself that same question. From the beginning of civilization men have toyed with the truth and they have continued to do so to this day. Just as there have been great speakers of truth in the history of the world, so there have been great liars. Unfortunately it seems the speakers of lies have often outnumbered the speakers of truth. Adolph Hitler made the "great lie" famous. He told the world that if you make the lie big enough and tell it often enough the world will come to believe it. And with the technique of the great lie he almost brought the world to the brink of destruction.

Truth and lies have been thought about, spoken about and written about, most often with seriousness of purpose, but sometimes in comic terms. Too bad, but it is true, that we sometimes enjoy catching one another in a fib. Would that we were more generous with our praise when we catch one another in a truth.

Some years ago someone wrote a book which also became a play and later on, a couple of hit movies. It was called *Nothing But the Truth*. It was about a man who made a large bet that he could tell the absolute truth for a specific period of time. And he did. The mess he found himself in, however, was enough to make you swear off the truth forever.

But, don't do it.

Not if you want to sell yourself to others as a person who can be relied upon, who is honorable and honest in all his or her dealings, who can be believed without the so-called shadow of a doubt. That truth applies no matter who you are or what you do or where you do it. The truth applies to adult and child alike, to male and female, to rich and poor, and to the celebrity as well as the unknown. I can speak as a salesperson.

Certainly the last thing a salesperson—and I have been a successful one for most of my adult life—can afford to do is to play around with the truth, to color it or to stretch it. A salesperson who lies, who comes out with half-truths, will soon find himself without prospects, without customers and without a job. There isn't any room either for false flattery, phony excuses and cop-outs. People can usually see through these like a picture window.

When I was a car salesman I did my level best to give a good deal to my customers. I probably had to work harder at telling the truth than some others in different professions because of the unfortunate image some people hold of car salesmen. They expect to be had, to be lied to. (It is no accident that Richard Nixon came to be known as Tricky Dick; people simply mistrusted him. We all remember the question that swept the country, "Would you buy a used car from this man?" Believe me, it certainly didn't give selling cars a better name.)

Knowing of this image of car salesmen, I worked doubly hard at being truthful. This shouldn't be a matter of pride, and with me it wasn't; it was a matter of survival. *Truth* is what led me to become the world's greatest salesman. I always told every customer, belly to belly, "I not only stand behind every car I sell, I stand in front of it, too." I would never say anything I couldn't back up. It's a standard that I've never regretted.

Many a customer has told me that he or she "shopped around" and could get a better deal elsewhere than the one I offered. Dollar-wise, it might beat mine by $75 or as much as $100. But they would always stick with me. They were afraid of what they *weren't* getting for that $75 or $100. They knew they weren't getting me, and they knew that that counted for something because they could always trust me.

But a good salesperson isn't the only one whose reputation depends on telling the truth. It's true of all of us, whether one's a schoolboy, a member of the armed forces, a lawyer, a politician, a homemaker, a real estate man, a home seller, a teacher. You name it.

The world is full of successes, of people who owe their success to sticking strictly to the truth. The best advertising anywhere, the kind we trust the most, is that which sticks to the simple truth and nothing but . . .

Dutch Cleanser: It chases dirt!
Campbell Soups: Mm-mm good!
Coca-Cola: The pause that refreshes!
Maxwell House Coffee: Good to the last drop!
Kentucky Fried Chicken: Finger-lickin' good!
Morton's Salt: When it rains it pours!
Given time and if you cared to make a game of it you could

sit down and make a list that would surprise you. You wonder why there needs to be such an emphasis on truth in advertising, you wonder why an advertiser feels the need to lie. And when the truth is stretched? Remember Old Gold cigarettes and the "there's not a cough in a carload" slogan? A strange thing to be saying about cigarettes. And, where is Old Gold now?

So much has been written about truth that the truth of what I've said should be obvious.

That great senator from Massachusetts and secretary of state, Daniel Webster, said, "There is nothing so powerful as truth."

The Bible teaches, "Ye shall know the truth and the truth shall make you free."

Mark Twain, who wrote *Huckleberry Finn*, a kid noted for his fibbing, said, "When in doubt tell the truth. Truth is the most valuable thing we have."

Robert Browning, the poet, added, "So absolutely good is truth, truth never hurts the teller."

George Washington, as a lad, may or may not have said, "Papa, I cannot tell a lie," when he chopped down that cherry tree, but we like to believe he spoke the truth.

And one of the things I remember from my own school days is a teacher who told us about some Greek guy, a philosopher who lived in a tub. That alone was enough to make me remember him except for one other thing. One day he climbed out of his tub and, with a lantern, set out to look for an honest man. Even then, honesty was something to look for.

The Story of a Saint

And there is another thing I remember about truth from my boyhood, my teenage years. I have never forgotten this lesson about truth and the importance of sticking to it.

The lesson came from one of the kindest, wisest men I've ever known. I knew him because he was one of a kind, an original. He probably didn't know me other than as "that boy

Joe" because I was one of many young boys who were wild and full of mischief, a kid of the streets.

The man was Father Solanus Casey, a Capuchin monk. Father Solanus served as a simple priest for years at my boyhood parish, St. Bonaventure Monastery on Detroit's east side. From 1924 until 1945, then coming back again to Detroit in 1956 for medical treatment and remaining there until his death, Father Solanus left a mark on the monastery and on the people that will never be forgotten. From my First Communion until I was seventeen I knew him and loved him, as we all did, and, I'm glad to say, I listened to him.

But, first let me tell you the kind of man he was and why we young boys could relate to him so well. In my book he was a saint then and is a saint now. Some day it will be official, God willing.

He was born Bernard Casey in Wisconsin and he had nine brothers and six sisters. He was named after his dad, an Irish immigrant. With that many brothers there was always a great baseball team in the family, a unique team that played many a game with other organized school teams, a team that had enthusiastic sisters to cheer their brothers on. If you know Detroit, you'll know why we kids could relate to a guy like Father Solanus. Detroit is a great baseball town, the Tigers a great baseball team. We had heroes—early heroes like Ty Cobb and later heroes like Hank Greenberg and Mickey Cochrane and Schoolboy Rowe. In Detroit, you grow up with baseball and a guy like Father Solanus belonged.

Not only was Bernard Casey a good athlete in his youth, he also had a lot of guts. Once, the story goes, when he was a young lad in the country, he tackled a wildcat and saved his dog from being torn to pieces. And, he also knew the meaning of hard work. He labored as a farm boy, a logger, a brickmaker, a prison guard (which taught him compassion), and as a motorman on the brand-new electric streetcars in his city.

As a young man of twenty-one he felt a strong call to the priesthood and he entered St. Francis De Sales Seminary in

Milwaukee. He first came to my parish, St. Bonaventure's, at the age of twenty-six, and there became a Capuchin novice, remaining there for two years. At twenty-eight he returned to St. Francis Monastery in Milwaukee, where he was finally ordained a priest at the age of thirty-three. His marks in seminary were not the highest (I could relate to that, too, since my marks in school were the despair of my dad), and, as a simple priest he had permission only to say Mass and he could only absolve a person who might be in immediate danger of death. He was not allowed to hear confessions and he never gave a formal sermon. Instead, his whole life was a sermon, one built upon truth.

It was not until he was fifty-four years of age that he came again to Detroit, this time on an assignment to St. Bonaventure's that would last for twenty-one years. It was during this period that I knew him and came under his saintly influence. He was of the humblest of servants at the monastery, a doorkeeper.

Over and over again I can recall him telling us young boys to always tell the truth. We might fool others but we couldn't fool God. I have never forgotten that. I can see him now in memory, tall and with a big beard, the picture of a saint if there ever was one. And saint he is sure to become. A few years ago, in 1966, the "cause for Beatification and Canonization of the Servant of God, Father Solanus Casey," got under way, with the necessary steps now being taken by the church. His miraculous healings are well documented, people by the hundreds attest to his healings of both body and spirit, yet he always gave the credit to God and took none for himself. Books have been written, magazine articles and television documentaries have told his story. Some of the writers never knew him; they only knew about him.

But, I knew him and each Christmas Eve I return to my boyhood parish to refresh my memory of him at Midnight Mass. Although there are now new faces there among the Capuchin monks, it is always Father Solanus whom I see and Father Solanus's words that I hear. "Tell the truth, you boys, and you will always be able to hold your heads high."

Now, I'm not saying that telling the truth will make *you* a saint, or me a saint, but I will tell you that you will never have cause to regret it.

The Price of Falsehood

Telling the truth is not only a matter of conscience, it is a matter of law. In court, one takes an oath or makes an affirmation to tell the truth, the whole truth and nothing but the truth. The price of perjury comes high. Failure to tell the truth under oath has led to many a person paying heavy fines, and many others finding themselves in the slammer.

Often it seems that many persons in law and government get themselves in that predicament. Those occasions we remember most have seemed to center on congressional and other hearings, hearings which have led to "contempt of court" citations to many. Or, perhaps they stand out more in our memories because of the attention by the media, especially television. And television has become, for many a politician, a mortal enemy.

Sydney Harris, the popular syndicated columnist, is quoted as saying, "Even the above-average politician will double-talk, evade, emit half-truths, make dubious alliances, and do almost anything short of treason to persuade the electorate that he is for them. He is not for them, of course, he is for himself, and he rationalizes by saying to himself what the head of General Motors said openly: 'what is good for General Motors is good for the country.' "

Now, the politician may have gotten away with that in the past, but today the price of falsehood is high. In a recent radio broadcast on Detroit's station WJR, which has one of the widest listening ranges for radio in the Midwest, an interview was held between station producer Hal Youngblood and Nicholas Pennell, a member of the famed acting company of the Stratford

Festival in Ontario, Canada. In it, Pennell made the point that you cannot lie on television and get away with it. The TV camera's searching eye shows up every flickering emotion that betrays the truth, which is one of the reasons politicians have found it so hard to cope with the medium. As John Mitchell, our attorney general in the Nixon Administration, found out, you may think you're fooling someone when you lie, but you are not. The lie always catches up with you.

Today, truthfulness is very important when it comes to a sale, especially, for example, in the sale of your home or property. Under today's laws if one withholds the truth or tells a deliberate lie about the property he or she puts up for sale, the buyer can later sue the seller. The old days of "let the buyer beware" are gone—and nobody misses them.

A lie can cost you business, can cost you friends, can cost you trust, can cause you trouble and can cost you money. Let us all hope that the cost of lying would drive home the value of telling the truth, and that we would all want to stick to the truth because of the trust others have in us, because of our friends and our reputations. We're also human. Usually where we hurt most is in our pocketbooks. Perhaps for some, there lies a motive for sticking to the truth.

Yet, in all honesty, I must tell you that telling the truth may also cost you friends and can also cost you money. You must decide which is most important to you—truth or a friend who ran for cover when the truth was told.

The General Who Told the Truth

A classic example is the famed United States General Billy Mitchell who, in his younger days, was inspired by the idea of flying and studied aeronautics. Even before World War I he warned the nation that someday war would be carried on in the air. He fought for aircraft in the army, he urged a separate air force. In the war to "save the world for democracy," he was the first Yank to fly over the trenches when France was occupied by the Germans.

Always he spoke out the truth, warning, urging, pleading, telling the country and the brass that unless we had air power we could be defeated. After the war, in the early 1920s, he demonstrated the truth of what he was saying by air bombing and sending to the bottom a ship of the battleship class in just a few seconds over twenty minutes. But people sometimes don't like to hear the truth, especially when it hurts, and the military brass hats of that time reacted in the typical manner. Billy Mitchell, despite his dramatic demonstration of the superiority of air power, was court-martialed, relieved of his command and suspended from the service. Was Billy Mitchell telling the truth or were his words lies? Well, one of the truths he forecast was an air attack by Japan which he said would take place on a Sunday morning while the nation, or some of it, was asleep. Remember Pearl Harbor? Yes, the truth can be costly. Billy Mitchell's friends deserted him, thought he was a wild man, failed to stand by him. Brokenhearted, he resigned from the service. But, truth will triumph sooner or later. Events proved that Billy Mitchell told the truth. Time was on his side. From being disgraced for telling the truth rather than lying, he ultimately gained the rank of major general and then was awarded the Congressional Medal of Honor. But recognition came in 1945 and Billy Mitchell had died in 1936—never knowing of the honors which came to him nine years after his death.

And, telling the truth can also cost you money. Again, you must decide which is most important—truth or cash.

My Aching Back

I was drafted into the army on January 3, 1947, at the age of eighteen. I had been in the service for only about three weeks when my unit was sent out on a bivouac. In this instance we were loaded in 2½-ton trucks and transported out to a bivouac area some twenty miles distant, from which we were to walk back.

On the way out I clowned around in the truck, sitting on the tailgate edge and otherwise acting up. We were going down a very rough road when suddenly the truck hit a chuck hole. The vehicle bounced up and I bounced out. I sailed through the air and landed partly on my back and partly on my rear end.

I really felt severe pain as I lay on the road, my breath knocked out of me, hardly able to move. A Jeep picked me up and rushed me back to the army hospital. That marked the end of my army career. I was hurt, yes, but my injuries were slight. I could be fixed up, but not good enough to stay in the army.

The doctors taped me from just below my armpits to just below my belly button. I kept checking in and out of the hospital for a series of X rays, massages and other therapy. I drew light barracks duty. I was not supposed to do much walking and I was not supposed to lift anything.

Shortly afterwards I was interviewed by the army doctors about the accident. I was asked if I had ever hurt my back before. That was the moment of truth. I could have told them no, and probably would have drawn a disability pension from the government from then on. But, I remembered the words of Father Solanus a few years before, about telling the truth, so I told the doctors the truth.

Yes, I had hurt my back when I was about fifteen years old. I had tried a half-gainer from the diving board at my school, Barbour Intermediate. I didn't get out far enough and I hit the board on my way into the pool. I had experienced some pain for a while and then it went away. I had forgotten about it. But, even if I had lied, the X rays hadn't.

Had I clammed up about it in front of the army doctors, however, it is quite possible that I might have gotten away with it. Sympathy and the benefit of the doubt usually go to the serviceman. I might have gained a pension, but I also would have had to live with myself for the rest of my life. That monthly check would have come regularly, and each time it did, through the years, it would have called me a liar—every thirty days—loud and clear.

Yes, it isn't always easy to tell the truth. Sometimes telling the truth can make life tough. The late Martha Mitchell has told how, when she tried to tell the truth of what was happening in Washington high places, she was bound and gagged to keep her mouth shut, that shots were given to her to assure she remained quiet. Her story was shocking. Events later proved that most of what she had to say was true.

But, if you stick to the truth no matter what the cost, you can only come out a winner, not a loser. People who have lied have redeemed themselves by turning to the truth. Peter, the foremost of the disciples, told the soldiers who came to arrest Christ that he never knew the man—a lie which he told not once but three times that night to save his own skin. Yet he reversed his course and went on to become the head of the Church of Rome and to be known through the ages as St. Peter.

Here are some tips—some *do's* and *don'ts*—that I have found helpful in telling the truth. All of them, the *do's* if practiced the *don'ts* if avoided, will go a long way in helping you sell yourself more successfully:

Four Things to Do

1.   Be true to yourself.
2.   Think twice before speaking.
3.   Think of another way to say it.
4.   Temper truth with kindness.

Four Things Not to Do

1.   Don't exaggerate.
2.   Don't cover up for others.
3.   Don't ask others to cover up for you.
4.   Don't tell "little white lies."

Let's consider each one in greater detail.

First, *be true to yourself.* You have learned that in order to like other people you must first genuinely like yourself, that in order to sell yourself to others you must first be sold on yourself. It is just as important that you understand this truth as well. Before you can really be true to others you must first be true to yourself. Let's dig up old Will Shakespeare again. You've heard this bit of advice from him many times, but it never hurts to repeat it one more time, because it is such good advice. Here's what he said, and I'm putting it in Joe Girard language:

"Most important of all, be true to yourself, and just as sure as night follows day you can't be false to anyone else."

So, don't kid yourself, don't try to hand yourself a bill of goods, don't lie to yourself. Down deep in your heart you know you really can't fool yourself. It doesn't work. And when you try it with others, sooner or later you'll get caught in your own trap, your own web of lies.

But, if you tell the truth to yourself, if you face up to the truth, if you're absolutely honest with yourself about your goals, your attitudes, your abilities, your work, your family status, you'll find it a great deal easier to be truthful and to be absolutely honest with others.

Like everything else—charity, respect for others, liking for others, concern for others—truth begins at home.

Second, *think twice before speaking.* It takes a little practice but it can be done. One of the worst drawbacks a salesman could ever have, I had. I stuttered. Can you imagine the effect on a sale of a stammering sales presentation? I went to my friendly neighborhood shrink and he gave me this advice. "Joe, there have been a lot of ways that people have cured themselves of stuttering. Some have tried hypnotism. Some have tried repeating words and sentences over and over again into tape recorders and repeating them once more against the playback.

Still others have put pebbles in their mouths and practiced talking with a mouthful of stones. But let me give you the easiest way of all. Just wait, think for a moment about what you want to say, *and then speak*." I can tell you the system worked for me. I started doing just that, thinking first, and after several months of practice my stutter disappeared.

The same system works for truth telling, too. Think carefully before you speak. Ask yourself, "Is what I'm about to say the truth?" If you can honestly answer yes to yourself, then open your mouth and let the words come out. Believe me, it works. You'll find that fewer and fewer falsehoods, especially the ones you really didn't intend to utter, are coming from your lips, and the ones you may have deliberately decided to say will not be said. You see, many times the fibs we tell just sort of slip out. We regret them later, but there they were. You'll be glad for this tip on things to do because the truth is, we are what we say.

As Jack La Lanne once told me, we are what we eat, and to really nourish our bodies with the right food we must examine very carefully in terms of nutrition what we put *into* our mouths. I say that this is just as true of words, in reverse. We are what we say. We must examine just as carefully what comes *out* of our mouths, in the form of words, because those words are the food for someone else's mind and thoughts. So, think first in terms of honesty and then speak honestly.

Third, *think of another way to say it*. You'll be better liked for it, you'll sell yourself better, you may even become famous for your tact. Both of these facts are true, because I know of the situation: Peggy had a great deal of experience behind her in selling cosmetics over a department store counter. Now she is selling cosmetics door to door and is doing pretty badly. The familiar two-tone chime that could be saying "Peggy Calling" isn't working for her. As a sales manager, you want to keep her but you need to tell her the truth in order to make her more effective. Don't be tempted to say, "Peggy, unless you improve

I'll have to let you go," which might well be true. Think first—think of another way to say it. "Peggy, your experience is truly impressive. Let's see how we can put it to work so that you'll be with us a long, long time." You've told the truth; you've bolstered Peggy.

If you're a car salesman, as I was, you're sure not going to tell a prospect that his ten-year-old trade looks like it came through the Vietnam war, but just, and looks like it may not make it back to the guy's garage. Remember, to the owner it's still his baby and he loves it. He not only came in to buy a car but he came to sell one, too, and it's going to break his heart a little. You've got to think of another way to tell the truth and let him down gently. You don't need to lie and tell him his car is worth more than it really is and then have to jack up the deal on the other end. Say it another way. Try this: "Mr. Smith, it sure looks like your car has given you years and years of service. You couldn't blame it at all if it were tired. Let's see what kind of allowance we can give on such a faithful set of wheels." Years of service is the truth, and with that kind of statement to Mr. Smith, you've told the truth. He's prepared to part with his baby for less, perhaps, than he expected.

With a little practice, you can usually find another way of putting it so that you avoid a lie and stick to the truth. Then, of course, this also holds true. If you can't say something good, say nothing at all.

Fourth, *temper truth with kindness*. Often the truth is harsh but still must be told. Tell the truth—*but*. That *but* doesn't mean it's all right to lie, it simply means qualifying the truth so that it will not hurt a person's feelings or even break his or her heart. Tell the truth, but not if it may embarrass someone else. This fourth tip is closely related to the third, but it means that in addition to finding another way of saying it, also add a touch of kindness. If you do, you'll be adding to yourself a touch of class.

I have watched a lot of people fail to sell themselves in many situations because they put down the other person by telling the strict truth without adding a little consideration. But tempering the truth with kindness may make the other person feel warm all day and especially have warm feelings about you.

Now, let's consider some of the things *not* to do.

First, *don't exaggerate*. The border line between an exaggeration and a lie is very fine. Some people blow things so out of proportion that truth is lost. Worse, soon these people begin to believe their own exaggerations.

Once it begins to be said of a person, "You can't believe a thing he or she says," that person might as well pack his or her bags and leave town.

Don't play around with the truth, or skirt around its edges, or stretch it or color it. Playing around with the truth can have disastrous results.

Remember the story of the shepherd boy who, as a prank one day, yelled "wolf!" Soon other shepherds came running to his rescue. They were relieved to find that the wolf wasn't there. Again, a short time later, the boy cried "wolf!" even more urgently. He was having a high time fooling the other shepherds and he laughed as he saw them coming to his rescue. The wolf had gone away he told them. He tried this a third time and a fourth and each time the shepherds came. By now, however, they began to suspect that they were being had.

You know what happened. One day a wolf actually did show up at the edge of the meadow. Terrified, the boy cried "wolf!" again and again. But nobody believed him, nobody came to his rescue. The wolf enjoyed a good meal.

Second, *don't cover up for others*. You may be asked, and often, to tell a lie for someone else, to cover up for them. Don't. You may have this problem especially if you're a secretary or a receptionist. The boss has told you to tell so-and-so "I'm in conference" if he calls or shows up—or "I'm out of town" or a similar lie. One of the worst things a supervisor can do is to force his employees to cover up for him or make false excuses for him. And, this is one of the most difficult decisions an employee may have to make. Should I lie for my boss, should I cover up for my friend?

Try refusing to do so first. You'll be surprised at your boldness and honesty. Your boss may be even more surprised. He may have brand-new respect for you and never ask you to cover up for him again. But if he doesn't?

My advice, blunt but honest—quit!

Parents, don't lie for your children. Kids, tell your parents you don't want to fib.

And I've got news for you. When you're covering up you never really fool anybody. When a secretary says her boss "is in a meeting" when he isn't, the guy calling can tell if it's true or not in pretty short order. He knows it's a lie and she knows that he knows. So who wins? Nobody.

Third, *don't ask others to cover up for you.* Just as I've said don't lie for anybody, it's just as fair to say don't ask anybody to lie for you. Don't put people on the spot. If you're a boss and you have a secretary, it's just as easy, besides being truthful, to have her tell callers that you've asked not to be disturbed. Why ask her to lie and say you're in a meeting if you're not? Listen, it's a lot easier to tell a single truth than to build a house of lies.

Fourth, *don't tell "little white lies."* This is the big cop-out in the truth game. Take it from Joe Girard, there is no such thing as a little white lie. It's like that old joke, there's no such thing as being a little bit pregnant. A lie is a lie and pregnant is pregnant.

You can't excuse a white lie as a fib, you can't laugh it away, you can't sell yourself with it.

And worst of all, little white lies have a way of developing into big lies before you know it. Before you know it, you're using one to cover up another, or you've forgotten it and suddenly you're caught with egg on your face.

There you have it—some do's and don'ts.

I've never known anyone to really suffer from telling the

truth. But I know many who have gained respect and honor and love by telling the truth.

A tough course to follow? You bet. And, isn't there any time, Joe, you can get away with a lie?

Sure. Join a liar's club. They're fun and you can get it out of your system. You know the kind of club I'm talking about, where the members try to see who can tell the biggest whopper. It's a contest, not a way of life. It's where the great fish stories are born, about "the one that got away," and the source of the shaggy dog stories. It's the only place I know where you can get a prize for fibbing, maybe even be honored with a banquet and get pleasant coverage in the press. So, lie away—but do it somewhere where it will be appreciated.

Outside of that, give truth a chance from now on. You'll be amazed at the sales aid you've got going for you.

Things to Do NOW!

- Pledge to yourself that you will make every effort to stick to the truth.
- Carry a dollar bill with you for one month without spending it. Each morning for thirty or thirty-one days take the bill out and look at the picture of George Washington. Tell George that, like him, you cannot tell a lie.
- Resolve to think first before speaking. Are you sure it's the truth?
- Tell the truth—but, be kind.
- Don't stretch the truth, don't exaggerate.
- Remember, a little white lie is no different from being a little bit pregnant—and you can't fool anybody with that one.

CHAPTER TEN

The Power of a Promise

"PEOPLE WHO are in the public eye soon learn that their good reputation depends largely on how well they keep their promises."

That's Judge Myron H. Wahls, Wayne County, Michigan, circuit court, speaking. Wayne County is in southeastern Michigan and embraces all of Detroit. It has a very large population as counties go, so large in fact that many people feel it ought to be the fifty-first state. Naturally, it has a great many voters, and a judge of the circuit court is elected to that office. The term is for six years.

Judge Wahls, a good friend of mine, does not need to "campaign" for the job in the same way a candidate would get out and campaign for governor or state senator. The office of judge is nonpartisan. A person seeking the office stands only on a platform of truth and justice. There is no opportunity for rough give-and-take speeches or name calling. A judge doesn't make promises such as "I'll cut taxes" or "I promise better roads, or

155

schools, or drains, or mental-health facilities." Judge Wahls can only promise *all* the people that he will uphold the law and deal out justice fair and square. Believe me, that's some promise.

However, Judge Wahls has done his share of campaigning in the past. He once ran for the office of state attorney general, and he may well be Michigan's attorney general some day if he decides to run again. He has high qualifications, including a law degree from Northwestern University.

Meanwhile, he sits on the circuit court bench and, in the words of Robert Frost, he has "promises to keep" to the people and to himself.

Judge Wahls's chambers are behind the impressive court-room on the nineteenth floor of the City-County Building over-looking the Detroit River, which has got to be the world's busiest waterway, and the towering new Renaissance Center which has given a new skyline to the motor capital. It is a fitting setting for the power of a promise. A simple promise.

He puts it this way: "If you don't think you can keep a promise or stick to a commitment, don't make that promise in the first place." That's about as blunt and honest as one can say it. "Promises are meant to be kept," Judge Wahls believes. "I can think of a half-dozen people I know who have made a strong impression on me. All of them are people who follow through. That is, they make promises, but more important, they keep them."

He has a lot of opportunities to meet promise-keeping peo-ple. Because he is known for his service to his community, he is often asked to sit on any number of important boards and committees. He does this on a volunteer basis, however. That is, although he is asked, he considers the request very carefully. He asks himself just how he can serve best. He considers what promises he might have to make and keep. Only when he is satisfied that he can do what he promises does he agree to serve. He knows that reputations are made and broken by promises that are kept or broken. He is convinced that the ability to keep a promise becomes a very strong part of a person's personality and reputation.

He has a keen ability to spot those people who can move programs along, who get things done. They are the ones, he has found, who stand by their commitments and who make good on their promises. And, he's discovered something else. Usually those same promise-keeping people are most always successful in other areas of their lives.

Judge Wahls is right. Keeping one's promises is just as important when you serve on your local PTA or volunteer firemen's group as it is when, as in Myron Wahls's case, you serve on a committee handling larger civic affairs. Keeping one's promises to family and neighbors and friends is just as important as it is to the city or the county or the state. The people or the reasons may be different, but the ability to keep your promises should never change.

"I think that men and women, boys and girls, have a responsibility to others, and that responsibility usually means making promises and keeping them. The responsibility may be to raise a family, educate your kids, find and keep a job, make a successful marriage, get good marks in school or to take care of the sick and the aged. Whatever." It boils down to this: In Judge Wahls's opinion you don't just make a promise, you *owe* it. He has always felt he owed something to the community in which he lives. That philosophy started with his mother who taught him to give and to share. He feels that his education, his experience, his time, should be shared with others. *Sharing* has become a kept promise he made to himself and to others—a promise to "plow back in," as he puts it, what he's been given.

He feels that the many things people have done for him—assistance from others, help with tuition for school, advice and counsel from family and friends—are not debts that he can repay except by doing something for someone else, by passing along what he can do for others.

As he says, "I've collected on promises made to me by others, and I try to pay this back by making promises and commitments to someone else."

Probably the best example of this is the way this outstanding judge has made promises to uphold the law and see that justice is served fairly and honestly. Not an easy job. Whenever you judge something, someone is going to like it and someone is not. There is more to being a judge than just sitting on the bench and deciding cases that come before you. But the job itself has given Judge Wahls a chance to really wrap up all his experience and share it.

A good example is the way he "instructs" a jury. He could use big, legal-sounding words that would be a mystery to most people, including myself, but he doesn't. Law is often hard to understand, but he follows that old rule of KIS—Keep it Simple —and juries as well as everyone in the courtroom appreciate it. To hear Judge Wahls tell a jury what it's supposed to do, what it must consider and what it must not, is a great experience. When he does it at the end of a trial, it is simple and easy to understand. He performs his job of sharing his experience and know-how in a way that shows how he is keeping his promise to see that the law applies to all and is understood by all.

"I have a strong belief in the law as a way of settling problems," he says, "and how I act as a judge is going to reflect the promises I've made to myself and to the people of my county."

Judge Myron H. Wahls is one of the finest examples of a promise keeper that I know. He's a man who sells himself to everyone in many ways, but always as a man whose word can be relied on. He's proof of the success to be found in the power of a promise.

Promises—the Measure of Sincerity

There is a book which I've been told about—I have not read it—called *The Hucksters*. I understand that it is about an advertising man who wanted to make a good impression. He was out to sell himself just as you and I are. He chose his clothes carefully. He shined his shoes mirror bright. And, he put on what he called his "sincere" tie.

Bunk! There is no such thing as a sincere tie or suit or shoes or hat. The only thing that can be sincere is you.

And one of the chief qualities of a sincere person is the ability to keep a promise.

If you want to sell yourself successfully you must never go back on a promise. Never. A promise keeper is a person who means what he or she says. Promise keepers are people you can trust without question.

I know a young man who works in the service department of a nearby automobile dealership. He is a write-up man whose job is to fill in the repair order when someone brings a car in for service. Now, a repair order is also a promise. That RO promises to do the needed service and, in some states, it promises a "not to exceed" price and "not to do additional work unless authorized." Write-up men make promises: "Your car can be picked up at four o'clock, Mrs. Jarvis," or "I'll call you if it's not ready or if we hit a problem, Mr. Mason."

Simple promises. Yet, this young friend of mine sometimes failed to keep his. The car would not be ready when he promised. Or, the telephone call was forgotten. Before long his sincerity rating hit the cellar. People heard his words but they found them to be empty. Customers lost confidence in him and, in time, the service department where he worked. He failed to sell himself, and important service business—even future new car sales—went down the drain.

He had lunch with me one day and poured out his troubles. "Joe, I'm in hot water. I'm pretty sure I'm going to be let out."

"What's the problem, Alex?" I was pretty sure I knew, but I asked him anyway.

"My mouth gets me in trouble. I promise something and then wind up with egg on my face." He gave me the details.

So, over a ham and Swiss on rye, I showed him how he could gain a reputation for sincerity that would change his course and save his job. "Alex," I said, "there are *two* things I'm going to ask you to do, and I want you to do them faithfully for *thirty* days." These are the two rules I gave him:

1.   Force yourself at no matter what the cost to keep the promises you've made to date. No one can force you to do this but yourself.
2.   Think *first* before you make any future promises. Ask yourself, "Can I really do what I'm promising?"

He thought about these rules quietly and then wrote them down on the paper napkin beside him. When he finished, I added: "At the end of thirty days I want you to tell me what happened." I also cautioned that the first rule would be the hardest, but to stick with it because, after all, he was stuck with the promises he had made that day and the day before and the week before. But, that the second rule would keep him from ever being "stuck" again. "Think *first*, Alex, and then only make promises you *know* you can keep."

When we had finished eating I told Alex that if he followed my suggestions faithfully *four* things would result:

1.   Thinking beforehand saves you embarrassment later.
2.   You're saved from having to make apologies or excuses.
3.   People will know that you mean what you say.
4.   Your sincere image will shine through.

A month later he reported back to me. He looked happy and unworried. "I followed your advice, Joe, those two rules, and you're right. Customers are telling me that I've kept my word and they appreciate it. One called me a real sincere guy. People thank me for calling them if we've struck a snag. We're getting more service sales, too. But, you were wrong about four things happening." He was grinning.

"Oh?" To tell the truth, I was surprised.

"There were really five. The fifth is that the service manager said he's happy with me. My job is no longer on the line. How about that!"

Think Before You Promise

It was sound advice I gave Alex. Try it for yourself. Whether they're big promises or little promises such as agreeing to meet someone at a certain time, or a call to your wife to tell her you'll be home at six, the rule applies. Think *first*. Be sure you can do what you say.

Too often we make promises without thinking, yet promises are something we make so many times that they just seem to slip out automatically. Perhaps it is because they are things we say so often that we find it such an easy, unthinking thing to do. Think of the times, the opportunities, when we make promises:

- I promise to be in, Mother, before midnight.
- I'll fill the tank up with unleaded regular, Dad.
- I'll pay you back Saturday, sure.
- I'll write that letter I owe Tim today.
- Your suit will be cleaned and pressed before 5:00, sir.
- I'll fly down Thursday and take care of your problem.
- For every A you get on your report card, Son, I'll give you a dollar.
- Keep up the good work, Tom, and you'll find your paycheck bumped next month.

Try this. Take a piece of paper right now and jot down all the promises you remember making so far this week. Be honest. Then check off those you haven't kept and those which, deep in your heart, you really didn't intend to keep. If you've got only a few checkmarks give yourself a gold star and go to the head of the class. But, if you're like most people, you'll be embarrassed. Tack that sheet of paper up somewhere so that you'll see it every day. Let it be a firm reminder to yourself to do better.

And you want to do better, don't you? Because if you really intend to sell yourself to others—your boss, your coworkers, your girlfriend, your boyfriend, your teacher, your pupils, your parents, your kids, your neighbors—then work at the job of promise keeping. The sale of *you* will be a lot easier.

Why? Because "I promise" are two of the most powerful words in the world.

A Promise Is a Contract

To use an overworked expression, your word is your bond. You're putting your name on the dotted line. And I really mean that a promise is a contract. It should never be thought of simply as an IOU. We all know that IOU's are often not worth the paper they're written on. All contracts are obligations. People who make legal contracts can often get out of them or buy them back, but it isn't easy. And, it isn't easy to buy back a promise. That's why it's so important to think twice.

Perhaps the most dramatic example of this—even in this day of the so-called new morality—is the marriage contract.

Marriage vows are a promise. If you're married, you'll remember when you stood before your minister, your rabbi, your priest, even a justice of the peace perhaps, and when you were asked if you took the person beside you to be your lawful wedded wife or husband, for richer, for poorer, for better, for worse, in sickness and in health, you solemnly promised, "I do."

At moments like that one, the most popular music next to the Wedding March has always been "O Promise Me."

I've often wondered why some people take promises lightly

both in making them and in having them made to them. I think it may be because of the example that has so often been set. We learn by example from childhood on. Parents and teachers and older brothers and sisters must set a good example because children follow what they see and hear. If parents and teachers are promise keepers, children will be, too.

A promise I remember strongly from my childhood—and I still enjoy its pleasures today—began with my mother. She was the finest cook in the world (except my wife), and when I was a boy she always made at Christmas a batch of little Sicilian cookies called *Biscotti*. They are the most delicious cookies you could ever hope to taste. Each holiday season my mother promised to make them and she never failed to keep that promise.

When I grew to manhood, at the holiday season, I'd think back to those days. I'd tell my wife how Christmas brought back those memories of *Biscotti*. And my late wife, who was not Sicilian, would smile and say, "Joe, I'll make them for you." Chances are I would forget about it the next day but then, a week later, I'd walk in the house and all of a sudden I was eight years old again. My nose cancelled more than forty years from my mind. June had made *Biscotti*. She never went back on her promise either.

How wonderful it is when a promise is kept!

But, as adults, when so many things seem involved in politics of one sort or another, we tend to grow cynical about promises. It is unfortunate that the most publicized promises are those that politicians make. The example is justified, however, because politics, like sex and marriage and work and play and study and physical and mental health, are as much a part of this book as anything else.

Sydney Harris, the nationally known syndicated columnist, writes: "For every officeholder who is corrupted by money, a dozen are corrupted by the desire for reelection, which compels them to say anything they think will ingratiate themselves with the voters." Oh, the promises that are made to get votes.

And Judd Arnett, another popular columnist in the Midwest, says: "This is what is making such a dreadful mishmash out of American politics. You knock yourself out working for some character, then a short while after the election he turns 180 degrees from what he promised."

The truth is, in the long run, if a politician doesn't keep his promises he won't get reelected. He or she should never make promises idly, promises that aren't possible to keep. Yet, so often, that is the example set for our young people. No wonder they are cynical, no wonder they find it easy to make and break promises lightly. But there is a lesson in political promise-keeping for all of us. When a mayor or a governor, for example, promises a tax cut and then finds he can't meet the payroll, he must go back to the people and say "I'm sorry." To change the words a bit of the famous line in the movie *Love Story*, keeping promises means you never have to say you're sorry.

The guy in the song got out of saying "I'm sorry," and he got out of delivering roses, because he actually said, "I never promised you a rose garden."

Don't promise roses if you can't deliver roses. And if you follow the rule, *think first*, you won't promise roses.

You can keep from breaking promises, even if you have *thought first*, if you follow another simple rule:

Let the person know—by phone, by letter, in person—that you may have to replace one promise with another. If, for example a delivery is promised by a certain time and then something unforeseen pops up—a breakdown in equipment or parts or supplies—it's the simple thing, the right thing, to do—the making of a phone call to explain.

How much better it is to call up and say—"I know I promised to see you tomorrow morning at nine, but I've got to put out a fire in one of our branches. Can we set a new appointment?"—than it is to break your promise completely. Explaining the situation creates warm feelings. Breaking promises puts your sincerity in question.

You only get one shot at it. Break a promise and I've got news for you. You won't be able to promise much again to that person. You've lost the sale of yourself, as well as anything else you represent. A fellow car salesman found that out to his regret a year or so ago. One of his customers had a vacation coming up and his new car was going to be the vacation transportation. The customer had booked a condominium in Florida some seven weeks from the day he bought his car. No sweat, the car salesman assured him. You'll have delivery with all your options in seven weeks for sure. As it turned out the customer didn't get delivery until eleven weeks later. He was robbed, in effect, of four weeks' vacation at his condo. That was bad enough, but he checked up and found out that the salesman knew all along that the car would not be ready in seven weeks.

How much repeat business do you think that salesman got from that customer? You're right.

Promises kept are so important that even the Bible speaks of a homeland for the children of Israel as the Promised Land. Can you imagine how Moses would have felt if God had failed to keep His promise to the people that Moses led out of Egypt?

If you can, you'll have no trouble imagining how people to whom you make promises must feel if you break them.

Have you ever promised to bring your kid something when you come back from a business trip and then forgot it? And can you remember the terrible, hurt look on his little face when you told him you forgot? Or, if you're not a parent, can you remember when you were a kid and your old man told you he was sorry, but that he'd forgotten?

And, here's a final word. We often will find it easier to keep our promises to others if we first learn to keep the promises made to ourselves. You know the kind I mean. That promise that you'll give yourself a week's holiday trip if you break your quota. That promise that you'll make three extra prospecting calls each day. That promise you'll cut your calories to 1,200 a day and lose twenty pounds. That promise you'll hold your temper. That promise you won't nag.

Sometimes the most important promises we make and then break are the ones we promise ourselves. So, do this: Make a firm promise to yourself right now. Now, wait a minute—*think first*—are you sure it's a promise you can keep? Okay. Now that you've made that promise to yourself write it down on a piece of paper. Fold the paper and put it in your pocket. Keep it with you for ten days. When you change your suit, make sure you transfer that paper to the new suit. Women, keep that paper in your purse. Kids, keep that paper in your jeans.

Ten days, remember. And, each day take a good long look at it. But, ten days is a minimum. If it's a long-range promise such as losing ten pounds you may carry that paper for some time. On the other hand, if it's a short-range promise such as baking a lemon pie for your neighbor, you may carry the paper for only a day. The point is, you can't toss the paper aside until you've kept your promise to yourself.

Do this with two or three promises you make to *you* and you'll soon find it a challenge to keep your promises to *you*. Before you know it, you'll find you're doing a much better job, too, of keeping promises to others.

The power of a promise is a tremendous force in helping you to sell yourself successfully. Business success, marriage success, family success, more congenial relationships with others, more downright enjoyment in life can come about through keeping the promises you make.

A kept promise builds faith and confidence in you by others. A broken promise can not only shatter that confidence, it might also break a heart.

A promise kept is a shining thing.

Things to Do NOW!

> Promise yourself that you will keep your promises to others to the best of your ability.

- Write that promise down on a piece of paper and carry it with you.
- It's a contract with yourself because a promise is a contract.
- Think first before making promises. Ask yourself, can I really keep this promise?
- If you sense that a promise made may be difficult to keep because of unforeseen circumstances, let the person(s) know, and renew your promise according to the circumstances.

CHAPTER ELEVEN

The Sensation of a Smile

THERE IS something sensational about a smile. It can light up the sky. It can lift the spirit. It can change those around you. It can change you. It's easier to sell yourself with a smile; it's a rough job without one.

One of the first lessons I learned when it came to selling yourself was this: Your face isn't only for eating, or for washing, or for shaving if you're a man, or for makeup if you're a woman. Rather, it was actually made to order for the greatest gift God ever gave a human being—a smile. Made to order? You bet. It takes a lot more muscles to make a frown than it does to make a smile.

The more muscle you use to put on a frown, the more "muscle" you'll get back from others. But, if you give a smile the odds are ten to one you'll get one back.

I have a little sign in my office right where I can look at it all day long. It reads: *I saw a man who didn't have a smile, so I gave him one*. I don't know who first said that, but I don't apologize for using it and I wish I could give him or her credit for the way it brings a smile to the lips of everyone who sees it.

Maybe that's why songwriters have written so many tunes about smiles. They tell us that when you smile the whole world smiles with you . . . that you should pack up your troubles in your old kit bag and smile, smile, smile . . . that there are smiles that make you happy . . . that you should let a smile be your umbrella . . . that you should smile, darn you, smile . . . and that when Irish eyes are smiling, they'll steal your heart away.

I've got news for that last songwriter. When Italian eyes are smiling, or German, or Spanish, or English, or Russian or Greek, or *anyone's* eyes are smiling, they'll do the same thing. A heart just isn't safe from theft.

That's giving a lot of credit to a smile, isn't it? But, why not? As I said, a smile can smooth out many a bumpy road when it comes to selling yourself. A grouch is going to get stuck in the ruts.

Let me tell you about some positive examples of smile power.

The Blind Date Who Opened My Eyes

Quite a number of years ago, when I was seventeen, I double-dated with a buddy. The arrangement was the standard one. His girlfriend was going to line up her girlfriend for me. A grab bag. Anyone—man or woman, boy or girl—who's been fixed up with a blind date at some time in his or her life will understand at once the nervousness connected with it. What will the blind date be like? Will we hit it off? How did I ever get in a spot like this?

That night, so many years back, we drove in my friend's car to this girl's house. A honk of the horn and out comes my blind date. At first glance I thought she had to be the ugliest girl in the history of the world. A real dog. My heart sank down around my socks.

But, when this girl got into the car and her girlfriend introduced me to her, she suddenly lit up that car with a smile that was simply terrific. Easily one hundred watts. Inside that first sixty seconds of meeting, that girl became the most beautiful girl I had ever seen. She kept up that smile all evening. It was in her eyes, in her voice, in her personality. I never had so much fun before as I did that night on that blind date.

Although I was blinded by her smile, she opened my eyes to just how sensational a smile can be. She sold herself by the sensation of a smile. To this day, I still remember it.

A Real Problem-Solver

Claudio Carlo Buttafava, an Italian like myself, is the general manager of the famous Savoy Hotel in London, which is now almost one hundred years old. Buttafava is very efficient in his handling of the dozens of problems that crop up each day in a four-hundred-room hotel—problems regarding reservations, sleeping arrangements, linens, food service and often the temperament of the guests.

That's easy to understand when you realize that over the years the Savoy has put up (and still does) everyone from practically every walk of life: kings and queens, movie stars and opera singers, golfers and prize-fighters, generals and prime ministers and presidents.

As you can imagine, the dozens of details daily usually mean as many problems. As general manager, Buttafava not only has to supervise a large staff, from bellhops to bakers, from maids to musicians, he must also be a problem solver. Here's what he has to say about it, as quoted by Israel Shenker in the *New York Times*, and his method is simple, his advice good for everyone:

"I smile a lot," Claudio says. "It comes from my character. You can always—or 90 percent of the time—avoid problems with a smile."

Now, you are probably saying, "Wait a minute, that's too easy, you can't solve problems with a smile." I say that you can because, as Claudio Buttafava learned, you solve problems best by avoiding them in the first place. The idea is to head off the problem before it happens. And a genuine smile, seen or simply *heard* in the voice, is a great head-offer. Selling yourself *first* can often keep a problem from popping up later on.

Why Are Those Skies So Friendly?

Selling yourself first with a smile is a policy with the number-one commercial passenger carrier, United Airlines.

United Airlines is listed in the 1979 *Guinness Book of World Records* (page 339) as the commercial airline carrying the greatest number of passengers in 1977—35,566,782—in a fleet of 352 jet planes owned by a company with 49,866 employees. (I can't help being impressed; after all I'm in the same book of world records.)

As you know, United Airlines claims that its sky is a friendly sky. But, that friendliness starts right down on solid earth. Don't be misled, this isn't a plug for United—I fly all the airlines. It's really the story of Grace, my daughter's, experience.

Recently, Grace was interviewed for a job at United Airlines. Since she is known by our actual and legal name, Girardi, there was no way of anyone at United connecting her with me. No pull. No strings. She was on her own. Incidentally, she got the job.

When interviewed, she learned that her work would largely be done over the telephone, particularly in the area of reservations, cancellations, changing and confirming flights.

To her surprise, during the interview the interviewer deliberately turned his back to her while talking. But it was not because of rudeness, he told her later—far from it. It was done so that he could listen for a "smile in her voice." A smile was all-important. He wanted to feel her smiling, to sense her smile, which he told her must become one of the greatest assets in her job. He told her at the time that one of the main reasons she was hired was her smile. It fit the policy of United like a glove.

Not many people would see it, would know the pleasure of its warmth face to face, but they would know it was there all the same, over the telephone.

A Smile Never Disappoints

Another example—an outstanding one—of a "smile in the voice" is that of Jimmy Launce. Jimmy is one of the most popular deejays in the metropolitan Detroit area. In fact, his popularity extends far beyond the limits of Detroit, because WJR, the radio station on which he has been heard for over twenty years, is one of the most powerful in the midwest. Jimmy's morning show is heard not only throughout both peninsulas of Michigan, but in Pennsylvania, Ohio, Kentucky, Indiana and Illinois. There have even been times when listeners in the Deep South have written to Jimmy, the man with the smile in his voice, to say that they have heard him and his genial program and to tell him they can see his smile over the airwaves.

It's true. Listening to his lighthearted, carefree commentary, one can literally see the smile that lights up Jimmy's features. Many others have a chance to see it in person, myself included, because Launce is also the actor-manager of one of the Midwest's finest professional dinner theaters, located in metro Detroit's most elegant mall, Somerset, and operated in connection with the excellent gourmet restaurant Alfred's.

Jimmy is not only a producer known for his good taste, but he is a fine actor as well. Leading roles in such hits as *Private*

Lives, The Prisoner of Second Avenue, The Owl and the Pussycat, Don Juan in Hell, Don't Drink the Water, A Man for All Seasons, Our Town and *The Man Who Came to Dinner* have earned him a loyal and enthusiastic following.

When he is not appearing on stage, he likes to step before the audience and, in broadcast language, "warm the folks up." Because many of his audiences are made up largely of radio fans, he smiles and starts off by saying, "And *you* don't look like I thought you would either." But, that's not quite true. Jimmy tells me that one of the most frequent comments audience members make to him during the "afterglow" in the cocktail lounge, following each performance, is, "Jimmy, your smile is exactly like I imagine it when I listen to you on radio. I was afraid I'd be disappointed. I'm not."

A smile never disappoints. People ask Jimmy why he is always so cheerful. His secret is that he never tells others his troubles. Instead he always shows a genuine interest in people. "My job is to entertain," he says, "and to make life enjoyable for others. It starts with a smile, but that smile must come from inside." It is no accident that Jimmy, successful in a highly competitive field, long had for his program theme song "Put on a Happy Face." He has put a smile in his voice to match his God-given talent and years of dues-paying experience. "Others will like you more when you smile," he says, smiling, "and besides, it makes you feel better. It doesn't cost anything and it earns dividends that no blue-chip stock could ever pay."

Jimmy Launce—proof of the sensation of a smile.

A Smile That Melts Steel

Not too long ago, Dolly Cole, wife of the then president of General Motors, said to me, "Joe, I'm the chairperson this year of the March of Dimes campaign and we're having a number of celebrities in to help us on our drive. I'd like you to join us."

Although I didn't count myself a celebrity, I told her I would be honored to help out. Then, I added a condition. "I'll do it, Dolly, if you'll introduce me to your husband, Ed." I figured this was a reasonable request; after all, I'd been selling his cars for the better part of my career. Dolly smiled and agreed.

I'll never forget that occasion. When Dolly did introduce me he was in the company of Phil Donahue, the talk-show host. Dolly must have told him about me, because he turned to Donahue and said, "Phil, this is Joe Girard, the world's number-one retail car salesman. He's the guy who makes my assembly lines move!"

Who could top that for openers? But Ed, himself, did, because then he turned on a sensational smile as he shook my hand. It was a smile so big, so warm, so full, it could melt a piece of steel.

Now, he didn't have to sell himself to me. In a very real sense he was my "boss" at the time. But he sold himself with a smile, the same smile that moved him to success after success in the world's greatest automotive company. We became friends and remained so until his too-soon tragic death in an air crash.

A Smile That Made the Sale

A couple of seasons back there was a gigantic boat show held at Detroit's Cobo Hall, the convention center which usually hosts the automobile show. Crowds came to look over, compare and buy every kind of marine craft you could think of—small sailboats to luxury cabin cruisers.

One day during the run of the boat show a fantastic sale was lost—and made. Here's what happened, as one salesman at my training school told me, and as it was reported on the business pages of the Detroit press.

An extremely rich man from one of the Middle East oil-rich countries was at the show. He stopped at one of the large boat displays, approached the salesman there and calmly said, "I want to buy twenty million dollars worth of boats." Now, that's something to make anyone put out the welcome mat—or so you'd think. Instead, the salesman is said to have looked at the prospect as if he was crazy, as if he was simply somebody who was taking up his valuable time. And the one thing his look didn't have was a smile.

The oil sheikh looked at the salesman, read his unsmiling face and walked away.

He went on to the next boat display and this time was greeted by an enthusiastic young salesman with a welcome-mat smile on his face. It was a smile as radiant as the sun in Saudi Arabia. That sheikh was being made to feel at ease and at home by that greatest gift God ever gave us—a smile. So, again he said, "I want to buy twenty million dollars worth of boats."

"Sure," said the second salesman, still smiling. "I'll show you our line." He did just that, but he had sold himself first; he had sold the world's greatest product before anything else.

This time the oil sheikh stayed put. He put down a five-hundred-dollar bill on deposit and said to the salesman, "I like people who show they like me. You have sold yourself to me with your smile. You're the only one here who has made me feel welcome. Tomorrow I'll be back with a certified check for the full twenty million."

The sheikh was true to his word. The next day he returned with his certified check, added it to his five-hundred-buck deposit and the sale was closed.

The salesman who sold himself first with a smile, and then his marine product, is said to have made 20 percent on that sale. He is probably set for life but I'll bet he won't stay idle. He'll go right on selling himself and smiling his way to success.

It is not known what the unsmiling first salesman is doing now.

Now, you and I know that it takes more than a smile to make a sale like that. It takes a good product, it takes product knowledge on the part of the salesman, it takes training and it takes a willingness to be of help. What really happened was that the lack of a smile on one salesman's face moved a ready-to-buy prospect over to competition.

How many sales of products, of services, of people have been lost—and made—that way? Think about it.

That happening at the boat show proves the words of a short poem I keep framed in my office. I don't know who wrote it but I'd like to share it. It's called *Good Business*, and one of its verses says:

> The reason people pass one door
> To patronize another store,
> Is not because the busier place
> Has better silks or gloves or lace,
> Or better prices, but it lies
> In pleasant words and smiling eyes.

Given at the right time, at the right place, a simple smile can work miracles.

Here are seven simple rules to follow if you want to get extra "smileage" out of life. Each of them will make it easier to sell yourself in any situation.

How to Get Extra "Smileage"

1. Smile when you don't feel like it.
2. Share only your positive thoughts.
3. Smile with your whole face.
4. Turn the frown upside down.
5. Exercise your sense of humor.
6. Smile out loud.
7. Don't say "cheese," say "I like you."

Although the seven rules are simple ones, they still take practice if you really wish to master them. Let's consider each one briefly.

First, *smile when you don't feel like it.* I put this rule first because it's probably the toughest one to follow. So, you ought to get a head start on it. Say to yourself that no matter how you may feel deep inside at a particular moment, that is, moody or blue, you're not going to let others know it. Keep your troubles to yourself. Make people believe you are having a wonderful time. It is better to have others ask "What has he or she got to smile about?" than to say "He or she has every right to wear a long face." In selling yourself, it is always better to keep them guessing.

One of the most famous paintings in the world, the Mona Lisa by Leonardo da Vinci (a fellow Italian, by the way), which hangs in the Louvre in Paris, is known for the mysterious smile that plays about the woman's lips. For centuries, people have asked, "Why is she smiling?" No one knows the answer and no one ever will. But why do people flock by the thousands each year to see this work of art? Not because of the artist. Not because it has been stolen several times, cut from its frame, but luckily found again. Not because of the coloring or the brush strokes. Not because of the model who posed for it. No, it is because people are fascinated by the smile.

It's a good rule to follow. Keep them guessing—and the best way to do that is to keep smiling even when you don't feel like it. Whenever you feel the least like smiling is the time to smile the most. It has often been said that the Mona Lisa smiles because her heart is breaking. But, if that is really true, she's not letting anybody else know it.

Second, *share only your positive thoughts.* And, spread them around. Like so many other things that are positive, a smile is very contagious. When you smile, people think you feel good and are happy. Soon they're smiling with you. It's practically impossible to smile if you go around putting out negative vibes. There are a number of things to remember about this rule: Spread only good news; stop discussing stories in the papers that deal only with crime and violence; instead, talk about the positive things that are happening in your community; do things that will gladden the hearts of others, not depress them; and if you can't say something good about someone, keep your mouth shut.

The sooner you start sharing only positive thoughts with others, the sooner you'll discover that a smile just goes along with them like eggs with bacon. And, speaking of eggs, as the song says, keep your sunny side up.

Third, *smile with your whole face*. A beautiful smile doesn't belong to the lips alone. A smile also means eyes that twinkle, a nose that wrinkles and cheeks that crinkle. A good smile covers the whole map and is a delight to see. It's almost impossible not to smile right back.

The entire state of Michigan, my state, knows the sensation of the full-face, million-dollar smile that belongs to its governor, William Millikin. His face simply lights up. Sure, it takes more than a smile to win elections (and his latest return to the governor's seat was by the largest vote, a landslide, ever in Michigan), but Bill Millikin knows it certainly helps. Nobody can warm a Michigan winter as he can with his ready, eager, sincere smile. Spread all over his face, his smile inspires people with confidence. It causes people to trust him. It may even carry him someday to the White House.

Another full-face smiler, one who owes a great deal of his success to his smile, is Robert Binsfield. For a long time Bob was an instructor at the Girard School of Salesmanship. Every eight weeks he faced a new group of salesmen/students who were eager to learn how to sell themselves and, at the same time, learn how to do a better job of selling their products.

On their first day, their first hour, those students are not sure of what to expect. This is a new experience for most of them. Some are uneasy, some are slightly skeptical, some are eager to "get on with it," and some are worried about getting up and participating. I have never seen anyone put a group at ease as quickly as Bob could, with his wide, happy-face smile. It's a smile that says, "Trust me, have confidence in me, I am your friend." He warmed the group at once. His smile sold him as an instructor before he ever said one word of instruction. Bob and his smile give my school an extra plus.

There have been and are now a lot of full-face smilers. Besides my governor, Bill Millikin, and my instructor, Bob Binsfield, I have a list of six others who readily come to mind. Here is mine—and, why don't you make your own list, too?

The late first lady, Eleanor Roosevelt; the sportscaster and former Miss America, Phyllis George; and the poster beauty, Farrah Fawcett-Majors. As for the men, Oral Roberts, President Jimmy Carter and my editor, Michael Korda.

Each one of them, I've noticed, smiles with the entire face. How nice to see it!

Fourth, *turn the frown upside down*. When you do, it becomes a smile. But again, it takes practice.

Frank Bettger, author of *How I Raised Myself from Failure to Success*, tells that as a young man he was a sour puss. A first-class, number-one frown. He also knew that if not corrected, that frown would spell sure failure in everything he set out to do. His boyhood had been touched by so much sickness, hunger and misfortune that, in his words, there wasn't much to smile about. In fact, he says, the family was actually afraid to smile and act happy. He grew into a sourpuss.

Then he decided that if he wanted to be a success he'd have to change his attitude and overcome the handicap that worry and hardship had written on his features: a permanent scowl, a frown. He set to work, absolutely determined to wear a big, happy smile, to turn the frown upside down, to make it an honest smile, from deep inside, one which would reflect an inner happiness and an inner goal. He was going to do more than just put on a happy face; he had to take off the unhappy face first.

It wasn't an easy thing to do. As soon as Frank had fears and worries, the smile would disappear. Fears, like frowns, and smiles just don't go together. Still, he kept at it. From a fifteen-minute workout of smiling at the start of each day, he carried the exercise into the day itself. Before entering an office, a room, a situation, he'd think of reasons to smile, of things he was thankful for, and he'd turn the frown upside down into a smile. What happened, of course, was that this became habit forming. Working at happiness created a face of happiness. Working at smiling began to create the feeling of happiness inside. Good results began to show up more and more in his business, socially and at home.

Frank Bettger says: "You can cultivate happiness with a smile. Try it just for thirty days. Give every living soul you meet the *best* smile you ever smiled in your life, and see how much better you feel and look. It's one of the best ways I know to stop worrying and start living."

Turn that frown upside down!

Fifth, *exercise your sense of humor*. You have one even if you don't think you have. Admit it, you enjoy a good joke as well as the next person—and I don't mean off-color jokes or practical jokes at the expense of other people. I mean a good, really funny story.

The more you respond to them the more you exercise your sense of humor and the more you'll be smiling. That doesn't mean you need to be able to tell a good joke—some people just can't; you know the type, they always manage to louse up the punch line. But, it does mean to let yourself go. If you've heard the joke before don't spoil it for the teller, keep your mouth shut and smile all over again. Try to see the humor in situations and respond to it. Don't be a tease, because teasing isn't funny and it usually hurts the other person—no matter what you've heard, people don't enjoy being teased, especially young people. But here are two good tips about exercising your sense of humor: one, smile and roll with it when the joke's on you and, two, smile *with* the other person, never *at* him or her.

Sixth, *smile out loud*. If a smile is sensational, then a good, hearty laugh is super sensational. A laugh is an out-loud smile. Have you noticed how contagious a laugh is? Go to the movies to see a good comedy. Someone in the audience starts laughing. It's picked up by somebody else. Soon the whole theater is rocking with laughter. Later, you may see that same comedy on TV in the privacy of your living room. You may smile now at the same jokes, even chuckle, but laughing in private is harder to do.

Smiling out loud takes practice, too. The next time you smile, turn it lightly into a chuckle. And when you feel like a good belly laugh, don't hold back, let it come out. You'll enjoy it, so will others. Laughter is one of the finest exercises in the world. It does wonders for your body. Laughing until your sides ache is pain that really doesn't hurt. Nobody has ever been harmed by his ability to laugh; instead people have sold themselves to success with a hearty laugh. Two people come to mind at once, Phyllis Diller and Carol Channing. Take a minute to think about it and you'll come up with a lot more.

And, seventh, *don't say "cheese," say "I like you."* Ever since the invention of the camera, photographers have said "say cheese" when they wanted the subject to smile. The word "cheese" just seemed to bring the corners of the mouth up into a smile.

I've learned that the words "I like you" bring a smile that's even bigger.

Sometimes, during a lecture, I try this little experiment. I call two people from the audience to join me on the stage or platform. Before I tell you about this experiment, let me also tell you that when I was actively selling cars I used to begin the sale this way. I knew that most new-car buyers are a little fearful. They know they're making one of the largest investments of their lives, second only to buying a house. They are about to spend a lot of money and they've got a right to be nervous. They want and need to be put at their ease.

So, the first thing I did was to smile and hand the prospect a big, round lapel button that read: *"I Like You!"* The prospect would look at it and in just a second or two he'd start to smile. He was pleased at what I'd done. He'd start to relax and would begin to feel more comfortable.

You know, it's hard to say "I Like You" aloud or even in print without smiling and getting a smile right back.

As I branched out from selling cars into other fields, I found the "I Like You" technique worked just as well. So I started to use it while lecturing. As I said, I'd use a couple of volunteers from the audience. I still do.

I give each one a mask to wear, exactly the same mask, one with absolutely no expression on the face at all. Then, I ask the audience which of the two people on the stage they like the best, which of the two do they warm up to. Almost always, the answer is the same. Neither one. The masks are without expression. There is no choice between them.

Then I ask the volunteers to remove their masks. Now we have two separate personalities on the stage, two different faces. I ask one volunteer to fold his arms, scowl and say nothing. I ask the other to open his arms wide, smile and say "I Like You" to the audience.

Next I ask everyone in the audience, "Now, which of these two people do you respond to the most?" The answer is always the same: They pick the smiling "I Like You" person and he wins hands down.

A stunt? Sure. But, it serves to break the ice for what I do next. I ask the audience members to turn to each other and say "I Like You" once or twice out loud. When they do, the smiles light up the auditorium like a searchlight.

Saying "I Like You" is one of the easiest ways to make a smile. This country of ours has a physical fitness week each year. I think we should have a national "I Like You" week.

Seven simple rules. Try them.

Remember the famous catch line that swept the country? "Smile! You're on Candid Camera!"—Alan Funt's great TV show which had started out as "Candid Microphone."

What a wonderful world it would be—and how much better we'd do at selling ourselves successfully—if we went through life never quite sure if we were on "Candid Camera" or not—but, just in case we were, we'd better smile.

It's a great thing to be caught with your smile showing!

Things to Do NOW!

- Put this little sign up where you can see it: *I saw a man who didn't have a smile, so I gave him one.*
- Be sure to do it every time you see an unsmiling face.
- Try smiling away problems before they happen. At least it will help in keeping small problems from becoming big ones.
- Practice putting a smile in your voice. The easiest way to do this is to smile when you speak. People who can't *see* you will *hear* the smile all the same.
- Stand in front of a mirror and practice smiling with your whole face. Smile with your eyes, spread out that grin. You may feel silly at first and you may laugh out loud. If you do, that's great.
- Decide to make your smile your welcome mat to everyone.
- Put the seven "extra smileage" rules to work. You'll be amazed at how they help you sell yourself.

CHAPTER TWELVE

Being a Second-Miler

*"And if anyone forces you to go
one mile, go with him two miles."*
—Matthew 5:41 (RSV)

THAT'S ONE of my favorite verses in the Bible, not only because it is part of the beautiful sermon Christ preached on the mountain, but because it's such good, practical advice.

Force, as the Scripture verse says it, is a pretty strong word. In this day and age, in America, it's not likely that you are going to be *forced* to do anything. So, I'd like to put it this way: If anyone *asks* you to go one mile, go with him or her two miles. On top of that, do it even if you aren't asked.

That's just another way of saying that you should always do more than you're asked to do if you want to sell yourself successfully. Put forth a little extra effort. Go out of your way to help someone. *Reach* out. The stretch will do you good.

The Seventh-Inning Stretch

Is there a better feeling than that which comes when you give a good stretch? You reach way up, extending your spine, standing on your toes, stretching every grateful muscle in your body, loosening each one, feeling the tensions slip away in neck and shoulders and back, relaxing. You've done yourself a big favor and you're a better person for it.

I don't believe there's anyone in this great country of ours who doesn't know what you mean when you say "seventh-inning stretch." It's as much a part of baseball as peanuts and Cracker Jack, hot dogs and beer, doubleheaders and designated hitters.

Nobody can take a bigger seventh-inning stretch than I can when I'm at a ball game. And, the best reach-out stretch I've ever seen on the diamond is the one Pete Rose makes when he's rounding second for third, or third for home. It's more than a stretch, it's a long, graceful dive for the plate, and Pete Rose has used that *extra effort* to make him one of the highest-paid players in the history of major league baseball.

Part of the secret of selling yourself is learning how to make a seventh-inning stretch—a great big reach-up and reach-out. You must make it a part of your life, your personal life, your job life, your home life, your school life, *your whole life.*

A college student whom I'll call Ralph came up to me the other day and said, "Joe, I'm in a history class, but I don't seem to be a *part* of the class. Like I'm outside looking in."

"You mean you want to do a better job of selling yourself to the class?" I said.

"I guess you could put it that way."

"What better way? You're the world's number-one student, right? Now, just who isn't buying?"

We talked. I soon learned that Ralph's problem wasn't his instructor. His grades were good because the learning process came easily to him. But, he felt like a stranger to his classmates. He'd been with them half a semester. He hardly spoke to them or they to him. Pressing a little, I learned it was pretty much the same in his other classes, too—biology, English and government. I knew Ralph was shy, but he felt there was a wall between himself and the others. How many of us sense walls between ourselves and others?

"Stretch," I said to him.

"What?"

"Take a seventh-inning stretch." He looked puzzled, so I explained. Instead of stretching *up*, which is physical exercise, I told him he should stretch *out*, which is mental exercise because it calls for a different attitude. A second-miler attitude. I wanted him to extend his *outreach*, stretch his viewpoints about others, reach out each day a little further, touching the lives of others he lived with, studied with, worked with, played with and shared his hopes and dreams with.

Ralph felt that he had no contact. I told him, "You cannot touch others unless you reach out. It often takes stretching to make contact, but it is wonderful exercise."

I also told him that it might well mean going the second mile with someone. For example, if a classmate asked him for an hour of his time to help with an assignment or to bone up on an exam, give him two hours instead. Or, when his instructor asked for a class volunteer to give a report, I suggested that Ralph should put out just a little extra effort to overcome his shyness and volunteer. The instructor would be surprised and pleased, the class would be surprised and, more important, Ralph would be surprised at his courage. The class would regard him with new interest. He would be a *part* of the class, not just *in* it.

"Then," I added, "reach out to someone in your class in a way that has nothing to do with history. You'll never feel better."

Ralph wasn't sure. "How can I do that, Joe?"

"Make an effort to ask someone about his hobby," I suggested. "Or, ask another what she likes to read or still another what films he likes. Share your likes—but never your troubles. Look forward to reaching out as though it were a good seventh-inning stretch. And, be a second-miler. If somebody asks you for a lift part of the way home, go out of your way and take him right to his front door. That's the best way to topple the wall you feel is between you and your classmates."

The advice is good for all of us. Are you a loner? Are you a shy person? Do you feel left out of things? Are there walls between you and others? Is life whirling by like a merry-go-round without you getting a chance to grab the brass ring? Are you having trouble selling yourself? You can never grab the brass ring unless you *s-t-r-e-t-c-h* out and reach for it. As one poet said, "Stretch a hand to one unfriended/And your loneliness is ended."

You'll be stretching yourself in a way that's good for you when you walk that extra mile, when you put out that extra effort, when you hang in there just a little longer. *The more you reach out by extending yourself, the more people you'll influence for good.* And that, basically, is what selling yourself successfully is all about: Influencing others; getting rid of walls.

Incidentally, Ralph took my advice. He told me that since he tried being a second-miler, tried the seventh-inning stretch, he doesn't need to knock down walls. He simply scales them with no trouble at all. He sold himself.

Positive Results

Being a second-miler means that you go out of your way to do your job better or faster or both. The rewards are very real. They may show up in your paycheck or as a promotion. Aside from that you'll take new pride in your work, and usually personal satisfaction can mean more than money or recognition from others.

Sometimes the payoff lies in just the way you've exercised every attitude-muscle in your body, how you've actually lubricated them by walking the second mile. Extending yourself is the best exercise for the mind and spirit that can be found.

Sometimes the payoff is just in surprise and delight and gratitude. A neighbor once said to me as she was speaking about still another neighbor, "Mr. Girard, that Mrs. Kelly who lives across the street is simply super! You know, I didn't even have to ask her, yet she insisted on driving me to the store when she knew my car was in for service." I didn't mention it to my neighbor, but I will say it to you. That Mrs. Kelly was really selling herself.

And we've all seen the gratitude on the face of a blind person or an elderly person who has been helped across the street or steered through traffic. You don't have to be a Boy Scout to do a good turn daily. You shouldn't even do a good turn expecting a payoff, but you'll get one anyway. Being a second-miler means that you give of yourself in ways that may not even be asked for.

Sometimes the positive results show themselves in increased happiness through the years. No better example exists than that of marriage. Nothing demands more second-miling than marriage, where each partner must compromise and give just a little *extra* to make it work. A little thoughtful but unexpected gift. A backing down on demands. A little tenderness. A telephone call if you'll be home late, so that a wife or husband won't worry. My wife, June, and I had twenty-eight wonderful years because each of us so often extended ourselves a little more for each other. The divorce courts are full of wrecked marriages where no one ever walked the second mile.

Sometimes the payoff is in greater understanding of another. Often walking the second mile means you travel the same distance, but you do it in the other person's shoes. You know the saying, "Walk awhile in his moccasins if you want to know how he feels and what makes him tick." Eleanor Roosevelt began walking the second mile in the shoes of her husband, Franklin, the moment he was stricken with polio. She knew better than anyone else the personal torment that was to be his the rest of his life.

And as for walking in the other person's shoes, attend an AA open meeting and see what life is all about from another's viewpoint.

And, sometimes the payoff in traveling the second mile comes with a welcome second wind to help you sell yourself. Runners—and running has become one of the most popular sports activities today—know a lot about the importance of second wind. I'm not a runner and I'm not planning on entering a marathon, but here's something that happened to me which proves the point.

Recently I was asked by the Boys Club of Royal Oak, Michigan, a northern suburb of Detroit, to act as an auctioneer during a day-long effort to raise money for the club. It's an annual event, and local businessmen, sports figures and personalities from radio, TV and the newspapers are asked to auction off a wide variety of useful and expensive items that have been donated by local merchants.

I was teamed with Mickey Lolich, former ace pitcher for the Detroit Tigers and now with the San Diego Padres. We had a half hour allotted to us and, taking turns, we were supposed to auction everything from sporting goods to stereo and from T-shirts to trips to Walt Disney World.

It's a fast track in a fast half hour. The hall was jammed with bidders and had been all day long. I stood on the sidelines waiting for my and Mickey's turn to go to work. While waiting and watching I learned that one of the auctioneers, scheduled ahead of me, had been unable to show up. His partner would have had to go it alone, a strenuous job. That's when a small voice seemed to say to me, "Go ahead, Joe, fill in for the missing guy. It won't hurt you and you need the exercise." I didn't bother to label it as being a second-miler; there wasn't time.

My partner for this extra half hour was a newspaper reporter from the Detroit *News*, Fred Girard, who is no relation. Fred took the podium and I worked the floor. Work is right—and I worked up a sweat chanting, "Come on, gimme higher bids . . . let's make money for the kids." My half hour with Fred was very successful but I was exhausted. Now, I had to do it all over again with Mickey Lolich, my assigned partner. The old law of second miling didn't fail me. Without realizing it, my little extra effort had really sold me to the crowd. I was all over the floor, on my knees and in their laps and this is what happened. Going the second mile gave me second wind. I no longer felt tired. My voice was no longer hoarse. The bids came faster and they came higher. If anything, my second half hour was more successful than my first. And, when Mickey and I were finished he looked as if he'd just pitched a shutout, and I felt more refreshed than when I had started.

But the wonderful thing, really, was the way the people had responded, how they had dug deeper into their pockets. You see, each time we reach out to do more than what is expected, we add just a little more positive goodness to the world. That goodness showed up in the way those bidders helped the kids.

Where the Sale Begins

A second-miler's cup is never empty. The more he or she tries to empty it, the more it fills up. No extra effort, no bending over backward to help somebody, no gesture, however small, is ever lost.

That's why being a second-miler is to have the most rewarding philosophy of life that can be found—a philosophy which has paid dividends to me all my selling life.

With many salespeople the sale is finished the moment the

deal is closed. Nothing is further from the truth. That's when the sale really begins. A salesperson-customer relationship should be a long-term marriage. Repeat business is what adds up to success. This is as true of selling furniture or insurance or real estate or appliances as it is of automobiles. It's also true of selling ourselves. It's sad, but many a salesperson has killed all chances of repeat business the moment the sale was closed. He or she did so by forgetting that this is where the SALE begins.

I have always said that I not only stood behind the car I sold, but that I also stood in front of it. That means that the customer buys me first. And, if you are a salesperson of a product or a service the customer should be buying you first. It works like this. When you stand in front of your product, it puts you between your customer and what he's bought. After the sale is made, you become his friend at the dealership—in fact, you must make it a point to do so.

Because the product he's bought may be mechanical, such as an automobile, or may have a defect in manufacture, such as a suit of clothing, the odds are that something may go wrong or may not fit exactly right. It takes time to work the bugs out of mechanical things. A defect may not be noticeable at first. Being human, the odds are that the customer will probably be unhappy about it. He or she may come storming into the dealership or store ready to chew someone out.

Now, I have seen salespeople who, when they see an unhappy or angry customer come back after the close of a sale— "Here comes that creep," they'll say—will actually hide. They will duck into the washroom. They'll go out back. They'll ask others to cover for them. They'll do anything to avoid facing and handling that customer.

Or, sometimes they'll slough the customer off by saying, "Go out through the back door, turn left and take the first door on the right to the service department and ask for Mr. Finnegan. It's his worry, not mine."

Whether you've ducked the customer or passed the buck, that was the moment the long-term SALE was lost. Yet, it really should be where the long-term SALE begins, especially if you remember to be a second-miler.

Because I "stood in front of the product," I couldn't hide. Instead, I would put out that little extra effort to be nice, to take care of something, to go out of my way on the customer's behalf even though there was no immediate commission in it for me. I would smile and say, "Mr. Jennings, you're having a service problem, right? Let me handle it. I'll go back and talk to the service manager. You don't have a thing to worry about." And then I'd do what I promised.

You've already read about the power of a promise, so how could I lose? Ten minutes of my time perhaps, time during which others thought I was making nothing. Wrong. I was saving a sale.

Sometimes, to walk the second mile, I'd put a little of my own money into a deal. You are probably aware that with all the wonderful warranties on a new car, the factory doesn't warrant front-end alignment. So, at the close of a sale I'd remind the customer of that fact and say, "Now, I know, Mr. Bates, that it's possible you might hit a chuck hole and throw your front wheels out of alignment. I value your business so much that I'm going to give you a certificate for a free wheel alignment if you should need it." That certificate cost me only a few bucks. Still, other salespeople would say to me, "Joe, you're nuts. You don't have to do that. You wouldn't catch me doing it." Too bad, but I extended myself anyway and it paid off over and over again in customer goodwill.

That willingness to walk two miles with a customer instead of the one that was required of me is what helped to bring the customer back again and again. No wonder my repeat business was 65 percent. It's what made me number one.

Being a second-miler is what gets and keeps a sale. That's the way it works with a product or a service. Imagine how much more it means when you act that way about the world's number-one product—*you*.

Selling yourself again and again becomes far easier when

others see how willing you are to go out of your way for them —asked or unasked. And, it becomes easier, too, because you become a better product.

Becoming a second-miler calls for making certain resolutions about yourself and your attitudes. If you stick to these rules you'll soon see how much better things will go for you, how much better you'll be at selling yourself. Here they are:

Ten Second-Mile Rules for Success

1. If you're a salesperson, make one extra prospecting call each day. Or two.
2. Work a little longer at the office or the shop than you need to. Or, come in an hour earlier.
3. Do something useful around the office, or house, or apartment without being asked.
4. Give a little gift to someone special even though there's no occasion for it.
5. Give a little gift to someone not-so-special; it may make them feel special for the first time.
6. Go out of your way to help someone; just be there when he or she needs you most.
7. Pay a compliment to someone each day.
8. Take a load *off* someone's back instead of being *on* someone's back.
9. If you're a student, put in a little more time with the books. You might learn something.
10. Do something for someone, or some cause, without expecting any pay for it.

There are a lot of ways in which we can walk the second mile in life. You can become a Big Brother . . . you can volunteer to serve on a committee when it seems as if you're too busy to do so . . . get active with the Boy Scouts or Girl Scouts . . . read textbooks to a blind student . . . give a pint of blood to the Red Cross . . . extend a welcome hand to a new member of the team or the organization . . . visit someone sick or shut-in . . . umpire a Little League game . . . be a Candy Striper in a hospital . . . bake a pie or cake and take it to your neighbor . . . baby-sit for someone who can't afford to pay . . . don't just give your broad shoulder to lean on, give your *shoulders*.

In short, get involved with life. Get off your duff. Remember this: *You can't walk a second mile sitting down.*

Things to Do NOW!

- Copy the Bible verse, *"If anyone forces you to go one mile, go with him two miles"* on a card and carry it in your wallet or purse. Read it daily.
- Take a seventh-inning stretch and reach out each day to others.
- Repeat these words three times every morning upon arising: *"The more I extend myself to others, the more people I'll influence for good."*
- Start walking awhile in the other person's shoes.
- Start following the ten-second-mile rules for success as they apply to you and stick to them. The results will amaze you.

CHAPTER THIRTEEN

Selling Yourself as a Woman

RECENTLY A woman wrote to Dr. Joyce Brothers, psychologist and popular syndicated columnist. The woman, a mother, was concerned about her daughter and wrote primarily for understanding. Dr. Brothers published the letter and her reply.

It seems the daughter was quite happy being a service-station or garage mechanic, she had plotted her life to include eventual marriage and children and had, as a work goal, a desire to own her own service station and still take a hand at servicing automobiles. The mother found this difficult to understand. In her day, she pointed out to Dr. Brothers, girls, if they chose a career at all, chose "women-type" occupations. Furthermore, the mother added, when she was a girl she didn't have things all planned out. Why was her daughter like she was?

Dr. Brothers replied, in effect, that today's world is a different world and that many of today's generation of young women do not see themselves in traditional women's roles: motherhood and homemaking to the exclusion of all else, while the male is the breadwinner. In addition, sexual roles were no longer that clearly defined, that it was quite acceptable for a woman to choose a job that was previously considered only man's work, such as a garage mechanic. To the mother who wrote to Dr. Brothers, these new attitudes are probably hard to accept.

Do all these new roles for women, the national search for equal opportunities, downgrade the traditional paths that women have followed for centuries and found contentment, happiness and a sense of fulfillment? Not at all.

One of the greatest ways a woman can sell herself today, *as a woman*, is through marriage and motherhood. The building of a successful marriage imposes just as many decisions and demands upon a woman as does a career away from the home. Maybe even more. If a woman doesn't like the demands made upon her in business or the professions, if she doesn't like or agree with the demands made upon her as a stenographer, a secretary, a salesclerk, a cashier, a model, a waitress, a reporter, a teacher or even a job which may have been thought of as a man's job, she can, at best, transfer or, at worst, quit. She can move over or out and no one will criticize her or think less of her.

But the same opportunities for adjustment or escape do not exist in marriage. A woman cannot simply walk out because she resents the demands of marriage and child raising. Today's society still does not excuse such actions. Marriage and motherhood require a commitment and a devotion stronger than any made to a career or a job. In fact, most women I've talked to on this subject, despite all one reads of "women's liberation," tell me that marriage and motherhood are still the most satisfying careers for women today, the most rewarding and the most fulfilling. It is even more enriching, today, as husbands and fathers come to see themselves liberated from traditional male roles and feel free to share with their wives the responsibilities of homemaking and child rearing.

Fast disappearing, or at least it should be, is that derogatory phrase about women, "Keep 'em barefoot and pregnant." Such an unenlightened viewpoint is degrading to women; and it casts an even worse reflection on men.

A woman doesn't just become a mother because of the fact that she gave birth to a child. Some of the best mothers have been foster mothers and stepmothers; some of the worst mothers have been natural mothers. The daily press is full of stories of natural mothers who have given their babies away or, worse, have simply abandoned them. At the same time we read of wives and husbands, denied children of their own, who learn that the demand for adoptive babies far exceeds the supply. They live with hope, but often with broken hearts.

No, motherhood is something more than pregnancy and birth. It's a "job title" earned through the years, one that is measured in sacrifice and hard work as well as happiness and love. Motherhood calls for a special kind of salesmanship on the part of a woman. A woman can leave behind a fantastic sales record just by the way she brings up her children and the influence for good that she exerts on them. A mother is selling herself every moment of the day, as a woman, and when she does so successfully there is no more noble calling.

But, what of the woman who wishes to seek fulfillment in other fields, or who wishes to add a career to marriage and motherhood? What is the outlook for selling yourself as a woman in the business or professional world?

Comedy, Songs, Fashion and Food

Here is some good advice from four women who are tremendously successful. They happen to be in several fields, ranging from show business to fashion design to cooking. Still, their advice holds true for all women who set out to sell themselves successfully, regardless of their line of work. All of them are quoted by James A. Randall, writing in *Mainliner* magazine, which I chanced to read on one of my recent cross-country flights. I have added my own comments to each quote.

Carol Channing, superstar of *Hello Dolly* and many other Broadway musicals and motion pictures: "Success is sticking to one job, not changing your mind suddenly, deciding, 'I'll make furniture.' In the theater, talent counts. But it is definitely secondary to experience, and experience comes with time. And something else. I remember my father telling me to make the man above you look like a great guy and you'll succeed."

I agree with Miss Channing 100 percent. I've always said that success comes from sticking to one job. People who moved from job to job really move nowhere. Of course, there are always exceptions, and a woman should feel that she does not have to remain frozen in one job or in one income-category. She must realize that she can make choices. To do so wisely calls for self-confidence and courage, and in another chapter I've already covered ways to build those qualities and how to use them.

Dolly Parton, superstar of country music, who is reaching out to sing other types of music as well: "You make your own luck, so being successful means hard work, determination and a willingness to sacrifice. I've been inspired by many people but influenced by no one. I've done my own thing my own way, but I've had lots of help from good people."

Again, I couldn't agree with Miss Parton more. I carry a card in my wallet that reminds me of this truth every time I open it: *If it's to be, it's up to me*, which is the same thought as Dolly Parton's words, "I've done my own thing my own way." She believes that "hard work, determination and a willingness to sacrifice" are what leads to success. She is right. As I've always said, *the elevator to success is out of order, you have to take the stairs one step at a time*.

Diane Von Furstenberg, internationally known fashion designer: "Success is having an idea that makes sense and then being able to focus on it and carry it all the way through with a lot of drive and nerve, regardless of difficulties."

How right she is. Part of selling yourself successfully is having a goal, realistic and attainable, then sticking to it and putting everything you've got into your efforts. This has always been true for men; it is equally true for women, perhaps even more so. Why? Because, in past years, few women were particularly goal oriented. They were not encouraged to have goals beyond homemaking. Women must be educated to focus on goals if they wish to be successful in careers.

Bert Whitehead, head of the Business Department of Marygrove College in Detroit, had this to say about realism in goals when he spoke recently before the Michigan Federation of Business and Professional Women (as reported in an article in the *Birmingham Eccentric* by Carol Mahoney): "A woman must decide that what she wants is the most important thing in her life. You can't be president of General Motors if you have to be home to make dinner at five o'clock."

Julia Child, renowned chef, author of many best-selling cookbooks and syndicated columns on food preparation and gourmet recipes, and star of her own syndicated TV show on cooking: "A great deal of my success I owe to my husband . . . since our fields are so different, we don't have the sense of rivalry that can sometimes spoil a career."

Mrs. Child knows what she's talking about. It used to be said that behind every successful man stands a woman. Julia Child proves that today it might be said just as truthfully that behind every successful woman there also stands a man. In today's business world women often find themselves in direct competition with men; many even enjoy the rivalry that takes place. But Mrs. Child's career provides this guidance for many women —choose a field different from your husband's so that possible rivalry will not exist. A number of women film and television stars today, as in the past, are married to men who are not actors. They may be in the same profession, such as producers, directors or writers, but they are not in front of the camera. No rivalry—happier careers.

Successful Women Through the Years

Some women have achieved success in the past because they chose fields that were considered at the time to be acceptable for women. Nursing was one such field (no longer, many men now enter the field of nursing). Two outstanding examples of nurses who made names for themselves are England's Florence Nightingale, who reduced the death rate of soldiers in hospitals during the Crimean War from 42 to 2 percent, and Clara Barton, American nurse in the Civil War and founder of the Red Cross.

On the other hand, some women achieved success but found it necessary to hide behind masculine identities. Two such examples were writers. One was the noted French author George Sand, who was really Amandine Lucile Dupin, and who was also the lover of the composer Chopin. The other was George Eliot, who was really Mary Ann Evans and who, through her writings, was to finally earn praise on a professional level equal to men.

Selling oneself as a woman has had, through the years, many built-in difficulties. Rejection, refusal to be taken seriously and outright opposition were faced by women. It is hard to believe today that being an actress at one time was not considered respectable. In Shakespeare's day men and boys played the women's parts. It was tough for a woman to become a doctor in the past; it is still not easy for a woman to be accepted into medical school today. And, since women were not even allowed to vote nationwide until the passage of the Nineteenth Amendment to the Constitution in 1920, you can imagine how difficult it was for a woman to break into politics. Until the right to vote was won, it was often said that the only vote a woman had was in the bedroom. Yet despite the difficulties they have had breaking out of the molds of schoolteaching, nursing, secretarial work or homemaking, despite the tough job of selling themselves successfully in business, the professions and trades, and politics, women have not given up. They continue to break down doors.

The roll call is impressive. It was a woman, Marie Curie, who discovered radium. Frances Perkins, as secretary of labor in the administration of Franklin D. Roosevelt, was the first woman cabinet member. Oveta Culp Hobby, secretary of health, education and welfare under Eisenhower, was the second. As of this writing, President Carter has two women in his cabinet, Juanita M. Kreps, secretary of commerce, and Patricia Roberts Harris, secretary of health, education and welfare. There have been many congresswomen in our recent history. To name just a few, Margaret Chase Smith was senator from Maine, Bella Abzug made Congress lively for a time, and Clare Boothe Luce was not only a member of Congress, she was also America's ambassador to Italy and a successful Broadway playwright. Oddly enough, her biggest hit was called *The Women*. There have been women governors, many women mayors and councilwomen and women judges. I'm proud to say that currently Mary Coleman is my state's new chief justice, the first woman ever to preside over Michigan's supreme court.

Women have made a name for themselves in sports (Mildred "Babe" Zaharias), aviation (Amelia Earhart), racing (Janet Guthrie), government (Golda Meir), economics (Sylvia Porter), broadcasting (Jane Pauley, co-host on the *Today* show, Barbara Walters), and religion (Ruth Carter Stapleton). Women have show themselves to be highly qualified cadets in the military, naval and air force academies of the United States.

All right, none of those glamor careers fit you, you say. You're just an ordinary working girl trying to get along in a man's world. What about women who aren't famous and who don't move around in the rarified air of sports, broadcasting, aviation and politics?

I know of three women who have done a great job of selling themselves as women. They don't trade on their sex but they do use it to good advantage. Two of the women are business successes I've read about because, even though they are not celebrities in any sense of the word, their occupations have made news. The third woman is one whom I've known and admired for years.

A woman named Sondra Iwrey has an X ray recycling business. She buys up old X rays because they contain silver in the negatives. In fact, Sondra states that you can get an ounce of silver when you burn a pound or so of old negatives. Actually, it is a competitive business because there is a demand for silver. It seems that the darker the negative the higher the silver content, so that's the kind she looks for. She collects 700 to 1,000 pounds of negatives on a good day and sells them to companies who burn them and "pan for silver" out of the ashes.

Since she has to deal with women receptionists and assistants in doctors' offices, hospitals and clinics, and, I imagine, dentists and dental assistants as well, Sondra finds there is a definite advantage in being a woman. Determination, persistence and imagination can move a woman along in business just as they do a man.

Setting your sights on a career in engineering is not something that should scare you away. If women can enter other professions, why not engineering? Even automotive engineering. With a background in cheerleading, of all things, Rita Dalton is turning her back on a future such as between-the-half entertainment for the fans of the Dallas Cowboys and has her sights set on a solid business background. She'll make it, too, because she has the same determination and stamina that led her to place second in the All-American Cheerleading Squad competition held in Cypress Gardens. According to press reports, Rita was a champ at aerial somersaults, running leaps and double flips.

The important thing to remember is that you do not need to hesitate, if you're a woman, to take a running leap into what has long been considered the domain of men. Be it engineering or driving an industrial tractor with loader and backhoe, you should not abandon the idea simply because you're a woman. Do it *because* you're a woman. Hang up the pom-poms, if that's been your symbol of womanhood, and pick up the T-square, the surveyor's rod, the keys to the forklift truck or whatever, if that's what you want to do.

Or stay within the feminine context if you prefer.

My friend, Theresa Merlino operates Terry's Place, a resale clothing shop for women in a nearby suburb. She brought to her business considerable experience, having worked with a retail drug chain for fifteen years. When she moved to Florida a while back, she gave up working. But, she didn't forget her retail background. Upon her return to Michigan she decided to use her retailing knowledge and make it in a man's world by being her own boss. But at what?

It was other women who gave her the idea. At card parties and social gatherings she often heard them comment that they wished there was a really good resale shop for clothing that was chic, in style and of known quality.

Well, why not? Theresa thought. Seeing the need in her area, and with nothing fulfilling that need, she opened Terry's Place, and it's thriving. People bring their women's and children's clothing in, cleaned and ready for resale. Theresa sells it and splits the price fifty-fifty with the donors.

"I feel it will serve me well in good times as well as in tough times, if we should have a recession," Theresa says, "and I'm ready to tackle it if it comes."

Retailing—the operation of a retail business—has basically been thought of as a man's profession. Theresa is proving that that's a myth. She operates in a man's world, she uses her feminine instinct in fashion and good taste to succeed. A celebrity?

No way. An everyday gal just like most of you women readers. If Theresa Merlino can do it, so can you.

And speaking of breaking out of molds, the daughter of a salesman friend of mine was a sister in a Roman Catholic convent for nearly a decade. She left the life of a nun, married and entered the world of big business. In addition to being a wife and mother, she is now a highly regarded and well-paid executive with General Motors. She sees no reason why the president of General Motors cannot someday be a woman.

All these women have sold themselves *as women* in what was long held to be a man's world. Add to those the many women across the country who are seeking equality in a man's world through active campaigning for the Equal Rights Amendment. They have able spokeswomen in such leaders as Gloria Steinem, Betty Friedan and Midge Costanza, who served on the senior staff of President Carter and whose outspokenness during her twenty months in the White House is still talked about in Washington.

Yes, opportunities for women to sell themselves as women are ever widening. There have never been such great opportunities for women to say to men, "Move over, buddy!"

Recently I talked to two women who are very much aware of opportunities and who have done a great job of selling themselves as women. One is a relative newcomer to a career in the business world. She is Delvern Bell, a teller at the First Independence National Bank of Detroit. The other has had a great deal of experience. She is Maria Piacentini, a successful real estate salesperson for Real Estate One in Dearborn, Michigan.

I Love Being a Woman

Miss Bell, a native Detroiter, smiles a lot and has a pleasant attitude. She has worked since graduation from Detroit's Central High and a year at Eastern Michigan University and has been with the First Independence National Bank for over a year. She went through the bank's standard training program before she actually was assigned to her first window.

Miss Bell likes her job very much, and she plans on staying in banking. She doesn't feel that anything stands in her way, especially as a woman, but she does realize she can benefit from more education. But, she adds, that's just as true for men. Part of her career plan calls for going back to college and earning a degree while continuing to work for the bank.

Her plans do not rule out marriage and children but, for the moment, that's still down the road. At the same time, she doesn't feel that a successful life necessarily has to include marriage, that a woman can be happy in her life and career and remain single. Women don't have to remain in the sort of roles that men have tended to put them in. Susie Homemaker, as she says with a grin.

She admits to a sense of security in that the other tellers are also women, and feels no frustration about the fact that the single male teller was the one promoted "upstairs" to the accounting department. She views her work as neither female nor male in nature and would like to see more male tellers. She does not feel that being a woman holds her back, but she is aware that more men than women seem to "get the breaks" even if they are equally qualified. Her attitude is that she must simply sell herself as a woman twice as hard, study, work hard, show enthusiasm *and be prepared to step up*.

"I would set out to be just as skillful at performing a job or being prepared for a promotion as a man would be," Miss Bell said. "My sex should have nothing to do with it. A man can't trade on his sex, nor should I."

In other than job life—social, school, home—she has never felt she was handicapped by being a girl. "I love being a woman. I wouldn't trade it for anything."

Those words of hers are probably the major reason Delvern Bell has managed to sell herself in her business career—and elsewhere. *I love being a woman*. What finer attitude could there be? She not only likes herself, something which I've pointed out as being absolutely necessary, but she loves *who* she is and *what* she is. She is proud to be a woman. She is proud of her job. She refuses to be pigeonholed because of her sex. Good for her!

Don't Trade on Your Sex

Don't trade on your sex—that's the advice of Mrs. Maria Piacentini. She is a career woman with a family. She has been a real estate salesperson—actually an independent contractor—for fifteen years.

She deals with the buying and selling public both in residential and commercial properties. However, she admits that more commercial property sales and purchases—large tracts of land, office buildings, stores, etc.—are handled by men.

She works with a home seller, mainly, and prefers to work in the area of listings. In her particular office two-thirds of the sales force are women, while the office supervisor is a male. Even fifteen years ago she found real estate a field that was open to women. There was little resistance to female salespeople. But, there is still some resistance she feels to women entering the commercial real estate field. At the same time she is sure that women can sell themselves successfully in that area if they wish, and they can function on equal terms with men without entering into male/female competition. In the long run, competence, knowledge of the business and experience are what count, not sex, and the commercial area is one that is widening for women.

Although the office supervisor is male, there is nothing that would stand in Mrs. Piacentini's way of becoming a supervisor —least of all the fact that she's a woman, because there have been two women supervisors in her office in the past. But, Maria Piacentini isn't interested in such an administrative position. She desires to keep career and home life in balance. She wants to make sure she sells herself as a woman equally as well in business as she does in terms of marriage and family. To her they are separate worlds. She enjoys cooking, homemaking and dressmaking. She is a private person and keeps her home life private. She is ready, however, to talk of her business life fully and openly.

"I work both in an office and in the field on about a fifty-fifty basis, and I enjoy it. I enjoy getting out-of-doors and being with people." Working both in and out means that Mrs. Piacentini has to have, in part, a double wardrobe: clothing suitable for both office wear and outdoor wear. In the latter case boots are often necessary because she may find herself ankle deep in mud or on nonlandscaped property. "The main thing," she says, speaking of suitable clothing in her work, "is to always dress professionally. I want to look attractive, but I don't think it is wise or even necessary to advertise the fact that I am very feminine by nature by wearing something frilly."

That is probably a major reason why Mrs. Piacentini has managed to sell herself successfully as a woman in the business community. She hasn't *made an issue* out of being a woman, of being feminine, and she hasn't traded on her sex. A man cannot sell an item of real estate better simply *because he is a man*, she believes, nor can a woman *because she is a woman*.

But, she is quick to point out, selling yourself as a woman does play a part in the selling techniques that she uses. For example, in showing a property to a husband and wife she often finds herself focusing more on the wife—woman to woman—noting that women are more concerned with kitchen area, bathrooms and visualizing where their furniture will fit, while men tend to respond to family room, basement, wet bar, fireplace and garage. Those features usually sell themselves to a man.

Although when selling a property in the past she had found that the bulk of the women clients were homemakers, she has now noticed that more and more women feel freer to come "out of the kitchen" and into the business world, neither using nor ignoring their sex, but preparing themselves *as women* just as men have prepared themselves for success. She feels women are ready for success everywhere on an equal basis with men.

Ten Rules for Selling Yourself as a Woman

Regardless of your job (waitress, clerk, stenographer, secretary) or your trade (there are some good, well-paid female plumbers and electricians and assemblers) or your profession (teaching, nursing, law, medicine, nutrition), regardless of your position in the business, academic or work world, these ten solid rules will help you sell yourself more successfully. All of the women I've talked to made contributions to these rules. They work for them and they'll work for you.

1. Stay upright. You'll get to the top quicker on your feet than on your back.
2. Dress to suit the job. Unless a uniform is a requirement, your clothes should show good taste and good judgment. Simplicity and good grooming are always in good taste.
3. Go easy on the makeup.
4. Save the jewelry and the glamor until after five, unless your job requires glamor after five.
5. Keep your private life separate from your work life.
6. Don't flaunt your sex appeal and don't tease. The office flirt never rises higher than the water level in the water cooler.
7. Watch your language. Don't tell off-color stories. They won't get you accepted by men. Experience and job know-how will.
8. Keep away from office (work, shop, school) cliques. The only time to concern yourself with politics is if you're actually *in* politics.
9. Watch the social drinking or the "three-martini lunch". What is acceptable in drinking by men isn't for women.

10. Remember, aim high *as a woman* not because you are a woman. Your sex is not what makes you special. You are special because you are a human being.

Self-Management

Obviously, following these ten solid rules for selling yourself successfully as a woman calls for a certain amount of discipline. Granted there is a lot of "give and take" just as there is in anything else, and granted a certain amount of "luck" is helpful. These principles, among others, of giving and taking and of appreciating "luck" are discussed in *Super Self*: *A Woman's Guide to Self-Management*, by Dorothy Tennov, a professor of psychology at the University of Bridgeport, Connecticut. Dr. Tennov's book is one of the finest step-by-step guides for women who are seeking fulfillment in every field including homemaking.

I say that following the rules I've set down calls for discipline. Dr. Tennov likens this to self-management. Her summary-explanation of self-management is to the point and one of the easiest to understand and follow. She states: "A French book teaches French. A math book teaches math. Self-management gets you to study. A diet book gives instructions on how to lose weight. Self-management gets you to stick to the diet." Following Dr. Tennov's principle of self-management will help you stick to the ten rules I've given you. Do so, and you'll soon be seeing results. I guarantee it.

In the long run, selling yourself as a woman is simply selling yourself successfully as a person—a person who is number one.

Things to Do NOW!

Decide today that you will not be forced into roles determined by men.

- Be the woman you want to be for no other reason than that you want it.
- Be the woman you've decided to be and *stick to it*. Set goals important to you.
- Write on a card, *If it's to be, it's up to me* and carry it in your handbag. Read it every day for building self-confidence.
- Say to yourself each morning upon rising *I love being a woman*. Repeat it three times. Smile and enjoy what you are.
- Don't trade on your sex. Instead, resolve now to work hard, study hard and be prepared to step up.
- Put the ten rules for selling yourself as a woman to work now. Follow them faithfully. You'll soon see results.

CHAPTER FOURTEEN

Selling Yourself as a Young Person

THIS ENTIRE book is for everybody regardless of age, but this chapter is especially for young people.

Who are young people? I'm talking about youth of high school and college age and those who have stepped into the work world.

A lot of young people still seem to think that anyone over the age of thirty is over the hill. They soon learn that that's not true, but I'll go along with that age limit for now and say this chapter is talking to all those under thirty—male and female, single or married.

It often seems that young people have twice as hard a job selling themselves as others do because they sense that older people—

1. Don't listen to them.
2. Don't take them seriously.
3. Consider them too idealistic.
4. Consider them too radical.
5. Think most of them are into drugs.
6. Figure they're still wet behind the ears.

Many older people have as mistaken an idea of youth (they forget all too quickly that they were once young) as youth has of oldsters. Young people, just as much as people in other broad categories, have an image problem. It takes a lot of self-selling to show the world the true image of youth. What is the true image? It's this:

1. Young people have plenty of ambition and the energy and drive to back it up.
2. Young people want to make a secure place for themselves in the world.
3. Young people are full of new ideas, new ways, new hopes and new dreams.
4. Young people still want to "set the world on fire"—and there's nothing wrong with that.

Selling yourself as a young person presents a lot of opportunities.

The student has a job of selling to do with his teacher. How well he does it will be reflected in his grades, even perhaps his entire future.

The athlete still has to sell himself to the coach and to his teammates, as well as to the fans in the stands.

The son or daughter still sells himself or herself to parents or in-laws.

The young member of the armed forces must sell himself to fellow servicemen and to his leaders.

The young husband and young wife are still selling themselves to each other. It is said that when either one stops selling, the honeymoon is over.

But, probably the most challenging sale of all is when the young person is faced with selling himself for the first time, or first few times, in the job market. You know the feeling well. Suddenly, during that first interview, that first sizing up of each other, job applicant and hiring agent, you know that super salesmanship is called for—or else. The tough part is that few young people, yourself included, no doubt, know how to go about the job.

Young people just out of high school or college, for example, do not have experience beyond, perhaps, part time jobs or summer jobs, which can include such work as delivering papers over a good-sized paper route, "bagging" in a supermarket, parking or washing cars, baby-sitting, being a lifeguard or a camp counselor. Those are just a few. The list of every young person's efforts to "make a few bucks" would stretch from here to Wednesday.

Jobs, yes—experience in a particular field in the labor market, no. So, what you are probably selling chiefly is the ability to learn and the eagerness for a chance.

A number of young people have discovered ways to take that first step out into the job market and succeed. Others simply have muffed the chance to learn from their mistakes. I'm going to let all of them speak for themselves. They all point up the fact that there are about eight sound rules for young people to follow in selling themselves.

Eight "Young People" Rules

1.   Be glad you're young.
2.   Set high goals.
3.   Be a young whirlwind.
4.   Offset your lack of experience.
5.   Hide your feelings.
6.   Watch your language.
7.   Keep your eyes open.
8.   Be persistent.

Let's consider them one at a time.

1. *Be glad you're young.* First of all stop thinking you can't get anywhere because you're young, that older people "put you down" as having been out to lunch when the brains were passed out. I'll tell you this. You have one thing that everyone envies. Youth. And, businesses today know that they must hire young people and build them up to take over management responsibilities and leadership tomorrow.

You're wanted, believe me. Being young is no handicap, so it's nothing that you have to overcome. Time will overcome it all too quickly as it is. Instead, your youth is something to merchandise and sell. Pitch in and show everyone you're glad you're young by proving you can get along with people of every age—children, other young people, the middle-aged and the elderly. Your youth and energy will be contagious. The very young will look up to you, the oldsters will feel young again in your presence.

Since a person is usually hired to work with others and not by himself, it's important to know how to get along with others. Be glad you're young enough to be wide open—to like others and to learn from and listen to them.

To acknowledge your youth and to be glad about it is one of the best ways to sell yourself as a young person. I know a little girl down the street who sells more Girl Scout cookies than anyone else in her troop. She is not allowed, of course, to go from door to door alone; she is too young. So, her older sister, all of seventeen, goes with her. The little girl's standard pitch goes like this: "I'm selling cookies and I'm eleven years old. My daddy thinks I'm too young to sell cookies but I'm glad I'm young. If I was older I couldn't sell them. I'd have to do like my sister and go along with me, because she's older. That's dumb."

It sells cookies. Don't ask me why, but it does.

Be glad you're young.

2. *Set high goals*. Set high goals for yourself. Many a young person during his or her school years gets overloaded with athletics or baton twirling or baby-sitting to earn money. Sometimes this results in lower grades—C's, instead of B's and A's. If that has happened to you, don't be satisfied with just slipping by. Bring those grades up without sacrificing important after-school activities. Doing so shows you have the ability to set high goals, that you want to be tops in all you do. Don't be fooled. Future employers notice your grades and are influenced by them.

Ann Crowe, a young student at Michigan State University, makes sure she keeps her grades up by studying hard, yet at the same time, she works in the kitchen of her sorority house and does tasks ranging from meal planning to food ordering. While working for her degree she serves on a dozen committees at college. Upcoming, too, the week she came to my attention, was a job interview with a major corporation. She's a fireball on the campus, and she sells herself positively every day.

She has high goals. According to Tom Easthope, vice-president of student services at University of Michigan—another of our fine state universities—(and as reported by Susan Forrest writing in the Detroit *Free Press*), big people on campus are found in every class . . . they are highly social beings . . . (and) research finds them more successful later in business than most.

Miss Forrest knows what she's talking about.

Setting high goals, working hard, keeping up grades, selling oneself in a dozen ways to others can lead to business success later on—and, I've found, to success in marriage and family relationships as well.

3. *Be a young whirlwind*. Lowell Thomas has called me a human whirlwind. At my age that's a terrific compliment. But, don't wait until you are as old as I am to practice and get in shape. Be a *young* whirlwind starting now.

One of the busiest examples of a young human whirlwind

that I have heard of is Steve Spivey, in his early twenties, who is a graduate student in animal husbandry at Michigan State. A quick rundown of Steve's activities would leave most people breathless. Look at this whirlwind schedule (again as reported by Susan Forrest in the Detroit *Free Press*).

"Steve Spivey's outlook is displayed on the walls of the tiny office he occupies as a $500-a-month graduate assistant who counsels students.

"There are an Olivia Newton-John poster, a 'Go State!' sticker, a poster of an Aberdeen angus cow and calf and a slogan 'Men, like racing machines, are at their best only when performing at maximum output.'

"Spivey puts himself through his paces, indeed, like a machine: 20 hours a week on a committee to select a university president . . . every afternoon in the office counseling, hours on academic council steering committee, council of graduate students and student council.

"Late this month (November) he'll take delivery of 75 bulls which he'll feed, slaughter and test for the next nine months on a master's degree study of weight gain.

"A friend recently criticized Spivey for not being introspective enough, and he agreed. His manner is all-business, and, says an acquaintance, 'that's Steve.'

" 'There are times when the schedule gets so hot and heavy that I kind of wonder if I'll come out the other side. I actually have turned down some committees because I didn't think I had time.' "

It's a funny thing, but I've observed that human whirlwinds seem to find more time to sell themselves than any others. Considering the corner that young people have on energy, *young* human whirlwinds should do even better. Start being one now. How? Schedule your activities and stick to the schedule. Get up a half hour earlier each morning and go to bed a half hour later each night. Put idle moments to work. You can study in the bathroom. I know a guy who carries a bookbag. It goes with him wherever he goes—on buses, trains, planes, subways. He told me, "It was the only way I could get around to reading all the books I meant to read but couldn't seem to find the time. Yes, I miss a bus or a subway stop sometimes and I've had to walk back several blocks. So what? My mind is getting a work-out, so are my legs. The exercise walking back is good for them."

Take the example of Steve Spivey and others to heart. Be a young whirlwind starting now.

4. *Offset your lack of experience.* Here's a question that's put to me over and over by young people:

"How can I get a job with no experience and no track record?"

Obviously you have to offset the lack with something else. Let's be honest. We all know the expression, "It's not what you know but *who* you know." Sometimes that is the best avenue for a young person who must break the "lack of experience" barrier, and no one ought to be ashamed to use it.

A personnel officer who deals with young people and with high school and college guidance counselors on a regular basis was frank in his advice. "It pays to know someone," he told me. "One of the best ways for a young person to get a job in a particular plant or office is to know someone—a friend or relative—who works at the same place.

"Although this may sound a little like the old saying, 'the best way to get ahead is to marry the boss's daughter,' there is still a germ of truth to it. Many long-time and respected employees will come to their supervisors and ask if they'll interview and consider their son or daughter, nephew or niece. Supervisors are usually happy to find people this way, they feel that someone in the company who knows and recommends the applicant is not going to give them a bum steer."

So, don't hesitate to use this route to offset your lack of experience. Some time ago there was a large furniture outlet in metropolitan Detroit that used as an advertising slogan to the public, "You've got an uncle in the furniture business." You had a friend, in other words, at the store, one who would look out for you.

The same thing may work for you in getting your first job. Let me tell you about Linda. She is not yet twenty-five, and she has been selling a nationally advertised brand of cosmetics door to door for six years. And, doing so very successfully. But, at first it was tough going when just out of high school she went job hunting. Her chief qualifications were two years as captain of the cheerleading team and an attractive, unaffected personality. She heard there was an opening, a new territory, in which to sell cosmetics. Unfortunately, so had some thirty others. But, Linda "had an aunt in the cosmetics business" who worked for the same firm. A little pull, yes. A good word for her niece and Linda was given a chance. She was also given a short training course and then sent out to beat the bushes. Beat them she did.

"I put the 'who you know' bit to work after several weeks of ringing doorbells," Linda told me. "From using it to get a job, I went on to use it in selling. I would sit down in a prospect's living room and say, honestly, 'I've never really done much housework, but Mrs. Giddons down the street bought this hand lotion from me, and *she* says it's super. Do you know her? Why don't you check with her?' "

Linda was letting Mrs. Giddons, *who she knew*, do her selling for her. She is very successful at it.

But, you say, "I don't have a relative or a friend who can help me out. I don't have any inside drag. Any suggestions?"

Sure. This is what another young woman told me. Ruth recently went to work as a keypunch operator in the office of a large trucking firm with headquarters in Ohio.

"I didn't wait till the last day of the twelfth grade," she said. "I started to get my job during the first month of my last school year. I picked out the company I wanted to work for and sent them my application—just a letter, really. I didn't know anyone there, I sent it to the office manager. The manager was a woman and she sent me an application form. I filled it out and mailed it back.

"Then, about four or five times during my senior year I'd write or phone the company to tell them that I was getting nearer to graduation and that I was preparing to work for the company and that I wanted them to know it. I kept them aware of me all the time. What was really happening I guess was that I was making a friend of the office manager during that year. She had to be thinking about me for my whole senior term. When I graduated and said I was ready to go to work I was no longer a stranger. The company said 'come ahead.' "

Ruth proves that the sale of yourself doesn't start the day you go to work for a firm; it may start a year ahead of that. The sale of *yourself* is often the only way to make up for lack of experience and no track record. Do this with several personnel officers and you'll soon find that they are out selling for you.

5. *Hide your feelings.* Learn to hide your feelings, unless they are feelings of enthusiasm and confidence. One young man told me how he lost a chance at a job as a circulation manager for a newspaper substation.

"I blew it," Roger told me, "because I lost my cool. I'm a big guy, six feet two, and I weigh two hundred pounds. The man who I went to see about the job was short and he seemed to be very conscious about his small size. He kept saying negative things about people who were big. I didn't like it, and pretty soon I didn't like him. I was totally turned off by him and it showed all over my face, I guess. I didn't get the job. I'm pretty sure it wasn't because I'm a big guy, but because I couldn't keep a poker face about his mouthing off. I guess he read me like a book."

Remember, you're after a job and that's what you've got to keep your eye on. You may not like the interviewer's hairstyle, his clothes, his politics or his unfunny jokes. Forget it. Don't show it or you'll blow it.

6. *Watch your language.* I don't mean profanity. I do mean that you should make sure you and the person you hope will hire you are on the same wavelength. (You already know the importance of that from my earlier chapter Speaking Another Language.)

One young man, Lance, lost his chance because he was talking to an older interviewer who didn't understand certain words of the street. "I really wrote off that one," Lance told me. "I was applying for a job as a clerk in a lumber company. The older man asked me how I knew there was an opening and I said, 'this cat told me.'

" 'Cat? What cat?'

" 'This guy,' I said. But I had no business saying that to him. He was older, from a different period of time. He put me in a certain category because of the way I talked. Too bad for me. The category he had me in was one where he didn't want to trust me, as a clerk, with his money. He wouldn't even take an application from me."

In our wonderful and sometimes confusing language, *cat* doesn't always mean a furry, four-legged animal and *dog* doesn't always mean man's best friend and *gay* doesn't always mean happy and *cool* doesn't always mean temperature. So, when you're seeing a person about a job make sure he or she and you speak the same language.

7. *Keep your eyes open.* Be alert when you set out to get a job. Most individuals who have offices will have things around them which they like or which have special meaning for them. Pictures, trophies, models, flowers. A picture on the desk or wall of a family group lets you know the person you're seeing is probably a family man. Cups and trophies let you know the person is interested in sports and is probably very competitive. Models of ships or automobiles or planes tell you things about

the person's hobby or interests. Flowers and plants can also tell you quite a lot if you keep your eyes open.

A young man I know noticed that a person who was about to interview him had several pictures of Little League baseball teams on the wall, and that a wall shelf held Little League trophies.

"After I was asked to sit down and the interviewer opened the conversation casually by asking me what my interests were, I made sure *his* interests were mine also. I told him that I had noticed his trophies and mentioned that I had umpired a few Little League games for my kid brother. He showed new interest in me right away. The interview got off to a good start. When we got down to talking about the job—I was after a spot as a book salesman—I said that I wanted to get out of the on-deck circle and step up to the plate. He came right back with that he'd give me a job in the outfield, which meant sending me out of town. That was all right with me. I got the job. I was on solid ground the minute I zeroed in on where he lived—baseball."

So, keep your eyes open. There may be clues about the interviewer's likes and hobbies all around you.

8. *Be persistent*. Recently a young man, now twenty years old, told me how he sold himself to a sheet-metal company which makes heating ducts, heat-transfer units, cold-air returns and other made-to-order metalwork for new home and commercial construction. He's the nephew of a guy I used to work with in the building trade.

Roy was just out of high school, and college was something he wasn't too interested in. He liked to work with his hands. In high school he felt he had learned marketable skills in his shop classes.

He called on the sheet-metal company and was told there were no openings. Roy was willing to try anything—shipping department, truck driving, anything that would let him get his foot in the door. Still, there was nothing, they said, and, on top of that, turnover was slow.

Roy asked for an application anyway and was given one. He filled it out carefully and attached a letter of recommendation from his high school shop teacher. He dropped back at the sheet metal company the following Monday at 8:00 A.M., left his application and asked for an interview. The personnel director spoke to him briefly, but again told him that there were no openings. Besides, he told Roy, when they did put someone on they wanted a worker with experience.

The same old story. The company wanted experience, but how could a young man get experience if no one would give him a chance?

Lacking a track record, Roy knew that all he had to sell was himself—his enthusiasm, his high energy, his willingness to work and learn, his promise to be a reliable and loyal employee.

So, he thanked the personnel director for taking the time to interview him, left the plant and began his strategy. One week from the day of his interview he came back at 8:00 A.M. and asked to speak to the personnel director again.

"I know you're busy and I won't stay but a minute. But, I was passing by and I thought I'd stop in and see if there was any action."

"Sorry, nothing."

One week later Roy dropped by again at 8:00 A.M. He was just passing by, he said, and wondered if—.

"Sorry, young man."

Roy kept up these tactics for six weeks. Every week at the same time, on the same day, he would stop in. He was, by now, on a first-name basis with the switchboard operator. The guard at the plant gates would shake his head; the kid didn't know he didn't have a chance. The personnel director joked that he could set his clock by Roy every Monday morning. He started telling various department heads about "my young friend." It became something of a guessing game—would Roy show up or wouldn't he?

Roy figured that the one way to get himself really noticed—and wanted—would be to break the pattern. Do the unexpected. So, on Monday morning of the seventh week, a few minutes before 8:00 A.M., the personnel director called several of the department heads and told them to synchronize their watches. Roy was due any minute. "You gotta say this for the fellow," said the head of machining, as Roy later told me, "that guy really hangs in there."

But, 8:00 came and went. No Roy. The personnel director was so upset about that that he drank more coffee than he should have. The unexpected had happened. At 9:00 A.M. the phone rang. It was Roy.

"I'm sorry, sir," he told the director, "but I was on my way in and I had a flat. I changed the tire myself. I'll be by in just a few minutes." Then he hung up before the personnel director could say a word.

Roy showed up as promised. The head of the machining department was beaming. The personnel director offered him a cup of coffee—and a job. That was two years ago. Roy is now one of the company's most valuable employees. His persistence in selling himself paid off.

Another success story of a couple of young men selling themselves through persistence began over fifteen years ago. I know one of the young men personally—Lee Skelton—and the other by reputation—Chuck Leslie.

My friend Lee had just come out of the service. He and his buddy Chuck set out to get jobs at the Rouge Plant, Ford Motor Company, in Dearborn, Michigan. They went out every morning for over two weeks, very early, about 6:00 A.M., in order to be first in line.

"Each morning," Lee told me, "when the guard opened the gates at 8:30, he'd say, 'no jobs today.' But, he couldn't help notice me and my buddy standing there. He would look at us like he was thinking we ought to quit wasting our time. Then, the third week, when he gave us the standard bad news and the men began to scatter, he pointed to us and said, 'you two kids, come here! You fellows must really want a job. I notice you here every day, early enough to be first to knock the gates down.' We said, 'yes, sir.' He said, 'come on, let's see what we can do for you.' Maybe he just got tired of seeing us, but I don't think so. He knew we wanted to work. Ford gave us jobs in the frame shop, welding. Today, my buddy who was out there first in line with me, Chuck Leslie, is a Detroit attorney. And I'm a personnel director."

True. Lee Skelton has been with Faygo Beverages, Inc., as personnel director, for over eight years. Faygo markets a wide line of soft drinks which is extra popular in my area. You probably recall how Harold Peary, the original Great Gildersleeve made Faygo Red Pop a best seller via TV and radio commercials.

Faygo has its offices, manufacturing facilities, bottling plant and distribution center in Detroit, and it sells its products in thirteen states. As of this writing, it has over 560 employees. That represents a 100 percent increase over the previous year. To reach that employee level, Lee interviewed over 1,500 people, most of them young. For many who were hired this was their first job. Certainly few can speak more to the point about the important subject of the interview than Lee Skelton.

Interviews and Applications

Lee points out that most interviews begin with an application for the job. An application form is a screening tool. It helps a company, plant, firm, store or office decide just who it wishes to see in person. The application form is usually filled out some days, even weeks, ahead of the interview.

Consider the form itself. On it you are asked to indicate specifically the job you're interested in. Be definite about it and everything else you put down. Remember, the application form is a piece of yourself. It's what gets you called in. It speaks for you, as your résumé, in advance. It will probably set the tone for your entire interview.

Later, when an interview appointment is arranged, you must be prepared to talk about that job. Nine times out of ten the interviewer will have your application form in front of him. When you appear in person, everything from your attitude to your posture, your personal appearance to your clothing should reflect what your application indicates. The combination of advance application form and face-to-face contact should point to your interest in and readiness for work at that particular company, plant or place of business.

Lee Skelton goes on to emphasize that, most likely, other young people will be interviewed for the same job that you're interested in. "Odds are," he says, "a half dozen are probably being considered. You have competition right off the bat. You are competing the moment you turn in your application. You are still competing even though you managed to get your foot in the door. You are competing when the telephone call is made to you, or the letter sent, asking you to come in for an interview. You are competing with those who finally get past the personnel director to be interviewed further by department heads, superintendents, sales managers, foremen and so forth. You must sell yourself all along the line.

"Knowing that, you must be very careful and thorough about filling out the application that you hope will get things rolling. What you say or don't say tells a lot about yourself. If you have a Social Security number and the application calls for it and you neglect to give it, you've just said something about yourself. Something negative.

"Avoid being flip or clever or saying things you might think are 'original' and will call attention to yourself. You've all read where one young man who, in filling out an application, put under the heading *Sex* the statement *now and then*. Or the one who wrote after *Marital Status* the word *swinger*. This kind of nonsense, if true, might cause a chuckle in *Reader's Digest*, but it will get you absolutely nowhere in an interview."

Lee Skelton and other personnel directors I've talked to tell me there are a number of things you should know about in filling out an application for an interview or in answering a letter that asks for more information about yourself. These come under the heading of "knowing your rights of privacy under law." Take heart. Employers cannot ask for and you are not required to give the following information.

- Your sex
- Age (although later your date of birth may be required for insurance purposes if hired)
- Marital status
- Race
- Religion
- Color
- Anything relating to personal background
- Any information that you feel may be embarrassing or damaging

Further, this has happened in my state and may be happening in others—let's hope so. Governor William Millikin of Michigan recently signed into law a bill forbidding employers from giving lie detector tests as a condition of employment. Sooner or later one's individual rights win out.

How to Handle the Interview

Many young people ask me, "How should I act during the interview? What should I wear? What do I say?"

Those are good questions. Young people are understandably nervous about their first interview—or their first few interviews.

In fact, even old hands at it are still uncertain at times as to what to do, say and wear.

Here's the advice I've gathered from a number of personnel directors who spend hours interviewing and screening young applicants.

The rules add up to a baker's dozen.

Thirteen Interview Guidelines

1. *Relax and be comfortable.* The first time out is never easy, but if you're uptight you'll have a tougher time of selling yourself. Quiet the butterflies in your stomach. How? First, remember that the interviewer once went through the same thing that you're doing in order to get his job. Second, take three deep breaths before you go into the office to help you relax.

2. *Dress for the job.* Wear clothes related to the type of work that you're being interviewed for. *Young men*: An hourly rated job in a plant or shop does not call for a suit and a white shirt. Wear a clean shirt, trousers and a neat jacket. For an office or salaried job, a tie is called for during the interview. *Young women*: Dress neatly. For a job other than office work, a pantsuit is okay. Otherwise wear a simple, neat dress. No one wishes you to lose your femininity.

3. *Be well-groomed.* By law you won't be discriminated against because you have long hair (but you may have to wear a hairnet on the job). All things being equal, if the job narrows down to two people, the person with the haircut, or the clean fingernails or the shined shoes is going to get the job. Your image speaks for you before you open your mouth.

4. *Put your best face forward.* It isn't necessary today for a guy to be clean-shaven, but if you do wear a mustache or beard keep it trimmed neatly. If you don't sport a beard, then shave—a five-o'clock shadow will get you nowhere. Girls, go easy on the makeup. The less rouge, lipstick and eyeliner the better.

5. *Don't jingle-jangle.* Girls, cut down on the jewelry, the

necklaces, the dangling earrings, the rattling charm bracelets. Men, leave the chains and beads at home. And, since
you are, you can button your shirt back up again above the
navel.

6. *When you walk in, remain standing* until offered a seat by
   the interviewer. Never sit down of your own accord. Remember, this is the interviewer's office, not yours.

7. *Regard the interviewer as a friend.* Think of the interview in
   terms of a visit to a friend. This creates a warm feeling on
   your part. The more warmth, the easier the job of selling
   yourself.

8. *Put the interviewer at ease.* Do everything possible to make
   him feel comfortable, too. How? Look interested by not
   slouching. Don't yawn or you've had it. Smile a lot. Make
   your smile a big, warm expression of pleasure. Don't frown
   or look stern. Stern is a turn-off.

9. *Listen and question.* Listen a lot to show the interviewer
   that he has your attention. Ask questions designed to show
   that you have digested what the interviewer has said. Example: If the interviewer has just told you the office hours
   are nine to five, Monday through Saturday, it's smart to
   ask if overtime might ever be required.

10. *Don't be too easy to get.* Even if it's your first job, don't
    sell yourself cheap. This rule is a toughie, but important,
    and the best thing to do is play it by ear. Ask about fringe
    benefits, sick leave, overtime, working conditions and other
    aspects of the job. It may turn out the place isn't the heaven
    you thought it was and you'd be better off someplace else.
    Remember, the interviewer is also trying to sell you on
    joining his or her firm. So, be an interested *buyer* as well as
    a seller.

11. *Don't smoke.* And, don't ask if you can. The interviewer
    may look upon your pack as a portable death warrant. On
    the other hand, if the interviewer lights up and invites you
    to do the same if you care to, then it's okay. If he invites
    you to smoke and he doesn't, then skip it.

12. *Never chew gum.* The Doublemint twins may never forgive
    me, and I know spearmint is what probably built Wrigley
    Field in Chicago, but in my opinion gum chewing is one of

the most revolting habits a person can have. It's murder in an interview.

13. *Know when to leave.* Watch for signals that the interview is over. You don't end it, the interviewer does. If he pushes back his chair, if he leans forward at his desk, if he rises, or if his secretary seems to come in for no reason at all, the interview is finished. Thank him—and keep your hopes up.

Keep On Selling

Your job of selling yourself doesn't stop once you've nailed the job. You are usually on a trial basis. You may be hired for a probationary period during which the company has a chance to evaluate you. For a salaried position this might be from sixty days to six months. For an hourly rated employee it might be from thirty to ninety days. So, you don't stop selling once the interview is over and you're accepted. Stick to the job, keep your nose clean, work hard, learn, ask questions, give a little more of yourself than is asked for and remember you have something wonderful going for you in selling yourself—*youth.* The truth is, most people envy you.

The Importance of Preparation

Here's my final advice to young people. Above all else, the ability to listen is, in my opinion, the most important aspect of preparation for your future. (Go back and reread the chapter Learning to Listen.) And, be concerned about what you're hearing. Listen carefully. Don't sell something short because it came from an older person, and don't be too quick to buy a viewpoint or opinion simply because it came from someone older.

Most people are crying out for someone to listen to them—

young and old alike. The more you listen without making value judgments the better person you'll be. But if you listen without making critical judgments then you'll go whichever way the wind blows. You can't prepare yourself for the future without an open mind. If you listen carefully you'll find that older people have more respect for you than you may have thought; you may also learn, wisely, that maybe you weren't as smart as you thought you were.

By listening you show that you are concerned about the other person, you show that you care. Do everything you can to make people feel good, to let them know that they have touched you in some way. They, in turn, will want to be with you regardless of your young age. This comes from being a good listener and a giver, not a taker. If you don't have the capacity to give of yourself, you will never really feel good about yourself.

Give older people respect. Don't be afraid to use words such as *sir* or *ma'am*. You'd be surprised at what door-openers they are. Like *please* and *thank you*, they are vital aspects of preparation.

And, get all the education you can. Technology is going to make education doubly important. No longer will you be able to say "anything" when someone asks you what you can do. The "anything" day is disappearing. The world is changing.

Preparing yourself for tomorrow's world today and selling yourself today go hand in hand.

Things to Do NOW!

- If you're just beginning your last year in high school or college, start lining up the job you're after *now*. Write, phone, call in person and tell the company to be ready for you upon graduation.
- If you have friends or relatives working in a company that you'd like to work for, ask them to see if they can use their pull to get you an interview.

- Pick up several application blanks and study them. See what is called for. Even if you don't intend to use them now, get familiar with them.
- Copy the eight "young people" rules on a card and carry it in your wallet or purse. If you're a student, use it as a bookmark. Read the rules often.
- Each morning, on arising, say to yourself three times, *I'm glad I'm young.*
- If you've got an interview coming up, study the baker's dozen guidelines before going in. They'll help you make the interview a success.

CHAPTER FIFTEEN

Selling Yourself in Maturity

*"Aging . . . brings wisdom only as long
as we continue to remember our youth. (But
not in sense of comparison, such as 'when
I was a boy . . .')."*
—*Sydney Harris*

As I said in Chapter Fourteen, this book is for everybody, no matter what his or her age. But, this chapter is especially for those folks who have reached a number of years that mark them as mature, well-seasoned individuals.

Just as young people, in selling themselves, have to overcome a wrong image held by many as "wise guys," disrespectful kids and rude, so must mature people overcome false images expressed in words such as "over the hill," or "put out to pasture," or "the graying of America."

Older person after older person has proved such images to be lies, proved them by the lives they've led and the accomplishments they've chalked up.

Maturity is something to wear with pride. It is a state of being, not a label. I hate labels that get tagged on to older people such as Senior Citizen or Elder Statesman or Golden Years or, worse, Sunset Years. Most older people I've talked to hate them even more than I do.

"Cut that stuff out, Joe," they say. And I say right back, "You can count on it, pal!"

A citizen is a citizen. He or she does not become a better one simply by the fact of reaching sixty-five or some other magic age.

A statesman is a statesman. He could be a lousy politician or statesman at thirty-five. Once he reaches sixty-five or so he most likely becomes just an older lousy politician.

I'm not going to put an age on maturity. There are a lot of mature people of thirty; there are also "kids" of fifty-five. I'm told there is a line in a play called *Family Portrait* that someone, talking to the brother of Jesus, speaks: "James, you were born middle-aged."

But, if I'm not willing to put an age on maturity, business and government are. Certain rules concerning mandatory retirement in business or in public school systems, for example, define maturity to suit their policies. (A new federal law forbids forced retirement because of age before seventy.)

The government's Social Security legislation, although it is ever changing, makes sixty-five the magic number, with an allowance for "early retirement" at sixty-two. Look for that to change one of these days. Many unions have negotiated contracts with retirement clauses such as "thirty and out." That means that a young person who started in a plant at age nineteen, for example, could retire with a pension at forty-nine. That's hardly old by anybody's timetable.

As far as I'm concerned, maturity is an open-ended age,

starting maybe at fifty (that's where I am right now) and running all the way up to whatever number of years the good Lord gives one to be active, useful, healthy and alert.

Take my grandmother, Vita Stabile. The number of years she's been given so far is ninety-seven. She has every intention of outdistancing everyone, and knowing her as I do I believe she'll make it.

You would think a person of ninety-seven would no longer feel it necessary to keep selling. But, not Grandma Stabile. She is still busy selling herself to everyone she knows or meets and she is still earning respect, acceptance and love from all who know her.

Vita Stabile—And Patience

Vita Stabile is my mother's mother and she's simply dynamite. She can hardly see—she has cataracts in both eyes and can just make out images dimly. She can barely hear—she has about 10 percent hearing in her right ear. Yet she laughs away her lack of sight and hearing. These are no handicap to her at all in getting around. You should see her walk. She can walk as fast as I can. There isn't a person who can keep up with her. Actually, she's five feet of enthusiasm, with a disposition as sunny as Sicily, and she is always smiling.

Last Christmas I bought her a big basket of fruit as her gift—oranges, apples, tangerines, a pineapple—and I said, "*Nonna*, look what I brought you."

She could just make it out. "Why did you do that for me?" (She said this in Sicilian. She only knows two words in English, *hello* and *goodbye*.)

"Because you're my baby," I said, grabbing her by the cheek.

"Look, I only got three teeth, but I'll manage it."

No sad song for her, no "poor me, I've only got three teeth." Instead, she sold herself a million times over again to me with her "I'll manage, with *pazienza*." Patience. That has been her philosophy of life.

She has lived by that word all the way up to her ninety-seventh year. She lives each day at a time, turning her back on yesterday and looking forward to tomorrow. But, she doesn't rush tomorrow. *Pazienza.* It impresses everybody who meets her. Whether it's a patient bite at an apple, or a patient expectation of all that life still offers her, Grandmother Stabile refuses to do anything but look ahead. "That way," she tells me in Sicilian, "I always know where I'm going."

She has sold more people on herself by her attitude and by her own patience with life as she heads toward a century of making others feel happy and loved.

Look at What You've Got Going for You

I once asked an older person of eighty what he had going for him at that age. He laughed and said, "Time." Winston Churchill is reported to have growled, when asked what it was like to be old, that it had its drawbacks, but that it was greatly to be desired when you considered the alternative.

Take it from me, you've got *time* going for you. You've got it on your side, no matter how old you are. Fifty, sixty, seventy, eighty—time is still working for you. *It's not how much time you've got left that counts, it's how you use what you've got left.* The biggest drawback to a mature person's successful selling of himself is to have a negative attitude about time—to carry the feeling that time is running out. The famous song "September Song," though nice to listen to, is sad and negative because it has such words as "one hasn't got time for the waiting game."

Bull. Mature people really have time as their friend. It's a shame that our American society seems to worship only youth and often pushes the elderly aside. Oriental peoples, on the other hand, have great respect for age. In Asian countries older people have a friend in time. They are looked up to, their advice is sought, they are treated almost with reverence. This is also true in many European countries. But, things are changing for the better in America, too. The voices of mature people are being heard. People are living longer, thanks to better medical attention, better eating habits and more exercise. And, business and industry are beginning to realize that mature people have something special to offer: *experience*. Experience comes only with time.

Time is your friend no matter how much over fifty you are. For many people, time means a positive change. Napoleon Hill, in his book *You Can Work Your Own Miracles*, states that "Time trades . . . youth for maturity . . . and wisdom . . . (and) time is our most precious possession, because we can be sure of no more than a single second of it on any given date or place."

If what Mr. Hill says is true, and I believe it is, then we should sell ourselves in maturity using all the "smarts" that we have, and we should never stop (just as my grandmother has never stopped) because time is the greatest possession that we have.

Let's look at how some mature people used that great gift of time in the past and how some are using it today.

Were These People Over the Hill?

Anna May Robertson "Grandma" Moses began to paint after she passed her seventy-fifth birthday. She was the wife of a farmer, had had no training, yet her works which portrayed the farm scenes of her childhood brought skyrocket prices from art collectors everywhere.

Bernard Baruch, financier and statesman, continued to advise presidents until he was in his late eighties. This millionaire's favorite "office" was a park bench.

My countryman, the composer Giuseppe Verdi, worked right up to his death at the age of eighty-eight, after giving the world such great operas as *Rigoletto* and *Aïda*.

George Bernard Shaw, who lived to be ninety-four, continued to write plays and startle the world with his wit, wisdom and critical comments well past his ninetieth birthday.

Henry Ford lived to be eighty-four. After giving up the presidency of the Ford Motor Company to his son, Edsel, he took on the job again upon Edsel's death. He ran a tight ship well past his eightieth birthday.

My late wife, June, who dressed in very good taste (and did so even when we were on a very limited budget), told me that Coco Chanel, who made her No. 5 perfume world famous and who designed the "basic black" dress that was considered correct to wear anytime, was still a queen in the world of fashion when well into her seventies.

General Douglas MacArthur's long, brilliant and often controversial career took place in a lifetime of eighty-four years. The country remembers the late general for many things—from leadership in its wars to military service in peace—but it will always remember him for his farewell speech before Congress in 1951, in which he said, "Old soldiers never die."

The late general's words have special meaning to all people who are still bent upon selling themselves in maturity. William Manchester, in his biography of MacArthur, *American Caesar*, reports that the general once wrote, "People grow old only by deserting their ideals. Years may wrinkle the skin, but to give up interest wrinkles the soul . . . You are as young as your faith, as old as your doubt; as young as your self-confidence, as old as your fear; as young as your hope, as old as your despair . . . when . . . your heart is covered with the snows of pessimism . . . then and then only are you grown old . . ."

I like MacArthur's words. I believe in them. *You are as young as your faith . . . as young as your self-confidence.*

Are These People Ready for Pasture?

As young as your faith. Remember I told you earlier that my friend Norman Vincent Peale told me that the most powerful word in the world is *faith*? Look at Dr. Peale today. He is in his eighties and is as active as a man half his age, traveling worldwide and preaching regularly at The Marble Collegiate Church in New York.

Lowell Thomas, in his late eighties, is still roaming the world and reporting what he sees with all the enthusiasm of a man in his twenties.

Lillian Gish, famous star of silent films and equally renowned on the stage, who is still active in motion pictures, TV and the theater, has now added writing and lecturing to her accomplishments. She admits, with a lady's privilege, to being "nearly eighty-five."

Richard Rodgers, who wrote the music for *Oklahoma!*, *The King and I*, *South Pacific*, *The Sound of Music* and many other hits, is still going strong in his seventy-seventh year.

Colonel Sanders, who started an entire new career late in life with his Kentucky Fried Chicken franchises, is still an active consultant with the company about the quality of the chicken and the service.

Eugene Ormandy, well up there, too, and conductor of the Philadelphia Symphony, says, "I'll never stop conducting until I drop."

Artur Rubinstein, the Polish-born pianist, in his nineties, still gives concerts before an adoring public.

George Cukor, the film director, directed Katharine Hepburn in the made-for-TV movie *The Corn is Green*, telecast in 1979. He is right in there, working steadily, at the ripe old age of seventy-nine. Miss Hepburn is seventy-one. Cukor has been quoted as saying, "If there is such a thing as a Cukor style, I guess it arises out of two principal factors: My own person-alized perception of the world and my ability to deal profes-sionally with actors." As cited in *Modern Maturity* magazine, Cukor, noted for his wit and style in films, has had many years to personalize his perception of the world and to learn how best to get along with people, especially performers. He also has the class to recognize those on the way up. He pinpoints the great-est change in the motion picture industry as "the great influx of imaginative young people."

The daily papers and magazines are full of accounts of film superstars active as young colts although they are well up in the mature years. The *National Enquirer* recently highlighted a few. I found the comments they make about age to be real food for thought.

Joan Fontaine, star of *Rebecca* and dozens of other film hits: "Oh, how marvelous it is to have the past all behind you—not to have to apologize for anything."

Kirk Douglas, star of *The Champion* and a score of films that have been box-office champs: "Aging is just a part of changing. I've accepted change. I feel better at this age. I feel more confi-dent in dealing with life."

Gloria Swanson, star of the silent screen, critically acclaimed in *Sunset Boulevard* and still going strong: "I have no sense of being old, young or anything. I'm just here. Recently somebody said to me, 'Why do you always tell people what your next birth-day is going to be?' I said, 'Because it's kind of fun.' "

And, William Holden, who was in *Golden Boy* many years ago and was star of *Network* more recently: "God gives us compensations for growing older. I wouldn't trade a minute of today for an hour of yesterday."

But, you say, those are famous people. They're well-heeled. Money cushions the fact of growing old. They can have any-thing they want. What about the ordinary man or woman? The person nobody ever hears about? What has somebody like that done?

Plenty.

I checked recently with James Stone, president of the Small Business Management School in Michigan. The school's courses, geared to the operation of small businesses, are offered on university campuses around the country in conjunction with continuing education programs. Many retired people, "second chancers," avail themselves of the courses as they plunge into new and often different ventures in their mature years. There have been some eye-openers in all-new careers that I now know about and admire. Here are some examples:

A retired man and his wife grew tired simply of taking care of the garden, doing things that needed doing around the house and waiting for life to run out. They decided to do something with their time and augment their retirement income as well. The guy remembered an essay he once read called "Acres of Diamonds" and figured that maybe his opportunity was right in his own backyard. It was. He and his wife looked around their neighborhood, did a survey to determine the need, found that there was a need and, as a result, started a catering service for the extremely elderly and shut-ins. For a small, affordable fee, they bring prepared food, warm, to people who wish to stay home and be independent instead of going to nursing homes, but who find it difficult to shop for food and then prepare it.

The couple work as a team. The wife prepares the meals, three a day, and the husband delivers them ready to be oven warmed or popped in a microwave oven. He delivers dinner and at the same time leaves behind the prepared packages for the following day's breakfast and lunch. The wife is a good cook, the meals are nutritionally planned and every aspect of their operation is scrupulously clean.

Retirement didn't stop this couple. They are performing a useful service and augmenting their income at the same time.

A mechanical engineer was forced to retire at sixty-five. As with so many people, he was immediately confronted with the problem of what to do with himself. He did what he knew best: engineering. He offered his services as a consultant and found that he was in demand. In fact, his former company used his services gladly. His skill was engineering, but whatever your skill, you'll find that if it was marketable before retirement, it will be marketable after. But the good part of it is that, like this engineer, you can pick and choose projects after retirement to suit your need or mood. The important thing is that, in maturity, you're still in control of your life.

A fellow who had been an office worker most of his life began to plan for his retirement—which is a very sensible and necessary thing to do. He started planning five years ahead of the retirement banquet, the speeches and the gold watch. He looked around the field and picked a venture. Most of his colleagues thought he was slipping a cog. But the more he read and studied about the venture he was planning, the more excited he got—which is a great way to approach retirement. Beats gloom any day.

The new venture? Raising earthworms. Friends asked him, "How many worms can you sell to fishermen and make a buck?" But this guy had boned up on his new venture. He startled his skeptical friends. "I'm not concerned about the bait business," he said. "I guess you don't know much about earthworms. Worms are extremely high in protein and they provide protein as a food supplement, not only in pet food, but, believe it or not, as necessary protein needed in many underdeveloped countries. Raising earthworms is an industry that runs to several billion dollars a year."

I'll stick to worms for fishing. I hope I'll never need 'em as a protein supplement. But, that's beside the point. That guy saw a new opportunity, got ready for it, entered into it with both feet in maturity and has a brand-new and profitable career.

And this story involves another couple who did something new, yet familiar, in retirement. The guy had been a music teacher all his life. He, too, planned ahead. When retirement time came he was ready for it. Using a portion of their savings, he opened a music store, a small one, with several soundproof booths in the rear. He continues to give lessons, and his wife sells all kinds of musical instruments, new and used. They have a new career in later life, are making a comfortable living and have refused to step aside for youth. Good for them.

An important thing to remember, and one I learned from the Small Business Management School, is that all those examples I just cited indicate that the people developed their ideas, basically, before they settled down too deeply into retirement, and that they took some courses to gain some basic fundamentals in operating a small business. After all, they were entering fresh fields and they needed new savvy.

The list could go on and on: people who sold themselves, and are selling themselves, successfully to the public when well into their seventies, eighties and nineties.

Because of the shame of mandatory retirement in many areas of business life, it is hard to single out individuals today who are still selling a product or service in their later years. But, they are out there. I know of several:

"Debbie" Drummond, of Boston, is still selling a product for rodent control, is doing well at it and he's into his eighties. If he has days when he isn't feeling as up to par as on other days, he shrugs it off. He gets out and sells.

Jamison Handy, head of the Jam Handy Organization, is still selling hard-hitting audio-visual communication programs. He is in his mid-nineties. He still swims daily to keep his body trim and lean. An Olympic swimmer, Handy represented the United States in 1904 and again in 1932—twenty-eight years apart, an almost unheard-of feat. What is his secret about selling yourself in maturity? A couple of years ago he gave a talk before the Detroit Producers Association. "I never bother with birthdays," he said. That's good advice. Women have known the secret of "forgetting birthdays" for years.

So, go ahead, forget birthdays, but don't forget who you are. Part of selling yourself in your later years has to do with those concerns that apply particularly to mature people. People like yourself are demanding and getting better legislation in many areas, from raising the limits of Social Security earnings to gaining better housing and better health insurance programs. Organizations such as the American Association of Retired Persons, which work in your behalf, are steadily building greater clout.

There are a number of broadcast programs which cater to the mature person. One of the best is *Over Easy* starring Hugh Downs. It's a daily Public Broadcasting series for older Americans and one of PBS's most popular programs.

Downs, who for almost a decade came into our living rooms as host of the "Today" show, is still very active in television—most recently as anchorman of "20/20." He also appears often on the lecture circuit, pilots a plane, skin-dives and writes articles and books. As of this writing, Downs is fifty-eight, but he is making plans to celebrate his one-hundredth birthday. Now, that's really selling yourself on yourself. He writes in *Modern Maturity* (Dec.–Jan., 1978–79): "Reaching a full century is not an unreasonable hope . . . If I don't make it, it will be because I got too sick or had too bad an accident. It will not be because I got too old. (Indeed, it will be because I didn't get old enough.) Old age never killed anyone. When anyone cashes in, at any age, it is not because he is old, but because he *wasn't old enough.*"

Mr. Downs's article appears in a magazine devoted to forward-looking, mature people. *Modern Maturity* is a bimonthly publication of the American Association of Retired Persons. The association itself is concerned with pharmacy service, travel service, insurance for the mature person and retirement research. The association also publishes a monthly (except August) news bulletin with up-to-date information for older people. Although it is an association for retired persons, it is concerned with people having a long and productive work life. You do not have to be "retired" in the fullest sense of the word to belong—you only need to be fifty-five. On top of all the fine things it does on behalf of the older person, the association and its publications are chiefly concerned with showing you how to sell yourself better as a person day by day. As a *mature* person. For example, you would be selling yourself if you still actively offered your experience in some capacity, but you would be failing to do so if, in maturity, you offered yourself only to a rocking chair. Others feel the same as I do.

Senator Frank Church (Idaho), who is chairman of the Senate Special Committee on Aging, believes people need a longer work life and shorter retirement. As reported by Elliot Carlson in *Modern Maturity* (Dec.–Jan. 1978–79), Senator Church "believes that times have changed, and as a result he proposes that working Americans reexamine their retirement ideas. And he thinks the Federal Government should modify some of its rules, counterbalancing old policies that encourage retirement with new ones that promote a longer work life . . . To make a real impact, [Senator] Church believes Congress will have to bolster the incentive to work. The problem now, he says, is that incentives work in the other direction, tempting people to retire early rather than at age sixty-five or some later age."

That's as it should be. If you want to sell yourself successfully, my advice is to resist temptation like the devil when it comes to retiring to the front porch and the rocking chair. Unless a guy or a gal has back problems, all a rocking chair does is reveal his or her age. (The exception is President Jack Kennedy who made his rocking chair famous—but, remember, he did have back problems.)

Wear your age proudly—but you don't have to reveal it if you don't want to. However, sometimes you may reveal it when you don't want to. If you want to sell yourself successfully in maturity you must maintain a youthful outlook on life. Not a face-lift, lady—that's on the outside only. A youthful outlook comes from the inside. You may look fit, may *feel* young, but then you let your tongue, your clothing, your associations, your habits, your outlook trip you up. How to avoid this? First, I've listed ten things that I think you ought *not* to do in your *mature* life. They are freely "borrowed" from a list of twenty-one in the book *For Men Only,* by my friend, Jack La Lanne, written with Jim Allen. I don't think Jack will mind my spreading his gospel. I'll go Jack one better, however, and point out that this counsel is equally good for women.

How to Blow It as a Mature Person

1. You wear fuddy-duddy clothing and never discard a suit until it's worn out.
2. You tell kids how easy they have it compared with the way things were when you were young.
3. You keep telling the same stories you've told so many times before.
4. You don't read any new books or go to the movies.
5. You discuss your ailments with anyone who'll listen.
6. You haven't made a new acquaintance in over a month.
7. You're bothered by the noise and slang of youth.
8. You haven't learned any new activity or taken up any new interest in several years.
9. You can't decide where to spend your vacation because you'd just as soon stay home.
10. You'd never attend a party if you were going to be the only person there over thirty.

On the other hand, here are ten positive rules to help you look age in the face and say "scram!" They'll also help you to sell yourself as successfully now as you did in the past.

Ten Positive Rules for the Mature Person

1. Make your slogan that of the popular cigarette, *you've come a long way, baby!* Then add to it, *you've still got a long way to go!*
2. Think twice about retiring. If you're not forced to retire, stay on the job. Experience counts.
3. Get regular medical checkups. Make sure you're as healthy as can be.

4. Eat sensibly. A little goes a long way.
5. Get plenty of rest. Take a short nap each afternoon. You're entitled.
6. Read a newspaper every day. Don't lose touch with the community and the world.
7. Make some young friends. They'll keep you young.
8. Find a hobby—woodworking, painting, flower arranging, anything creative.
9. Challenge yourself and others. Play bridge, chess, checkers, backgammon—anything to keep you on your toes and competitive.
10. Keep in shape. Watch your weight. Do something to exercise your muscles every day. Keep the skin tone firm, make your blood tingle.

That last rule is really important. There are a number of exercises that older people can perform each day to keep muscles firm and skin taut. Stretching and bending, done to music, is ideal. Play golf, shuffleboard, jog if you're able. One of the best forms of exercise is walking. Harry Truman, right up to the last months of his long, active life, made walking a daily habit. Again, the same advice I gave elsewhere in this book: *Do not begin an exercise program without first checking with your doctor.*

Live for Others

The other day a successful lumber company executive asked me about ways to continue to be influential in his community, even in his former company, now that he had retired. I said, "Walt, this is straight from the Girard philosophy of life—kick *yourself* in the backside and get lost!"

"What do you mean, Joe?"

"Up to now, Walt, you've been living for yourself, right?

You worked hard, kept plugging away, got some breaks, pretty much kept your eye on number one. You don't need it anymore. You can stop living for yourself and start living for others. Here's what to do. Since you don't have to get down to the office anymore, see what you can do to help somebody else out."

Walt said, "There's a guy a couple blocks over from me who's trying to build his own house. I don't think he knows a two-by-four from drywall—he's working nights and weekends on it—"

I looked at Walt, he looked at me, and he got my point. He walked over, introduced himself and offered to give the young do-it-yourself builder a hand. As far as I'm concerned that's a bigger sale of himself than Walt ever made when he was handling truckload sales of lumber.

Let me again quote from Napoleon Hill who said, "Recognizing that . . . my allotted time on the earth . . . is limited, I shall endeavor . . . to use my portion of it so that those nearest me will benefit by my influence . . . [and] Finally when my . . . time shall have expired, I hope I may leave behind me a monument to my name—not a monument in stone, but in the hearts of my fellowmen—a monument whose marking will testify that the world was made a little better because of my having passed this way."

If the world was made a little better by your having passed this way, then, my friend, you have sold yourself very successfully indeed.

Things to Do NOW!

· Like the song from *Gigi*, say to yourself every morning, *I'm glad I'm not young anymore* and mean it. Your years have given you experience.
· Join the American Association of Retired Persons today. The address is 215 Long Beach Blvd., Long Beach,

Calif., 90801. The phone number is (213) 432-5781. The annual dues are only $3, and this includes a subscription to *Modern Maturity*.

- Regardless of what time it is right now, start planning your next vacation. It will keep you young.
- Start a new book today, go to a movie this evening, begin a garden if it's spring. Any of these will make you a more interesting person and will help you sell yourself.
- Memorize the ten things *not* to do if you don't want to give away your age.
- Memorize the ten positive rules for selling yourself in maturity and put them to work starting now.
- No matter how far away it is, or how close, start planning your one-hundredth birthday party now.

CHAPTER SIXTEEN

Selling Yourself and Your Ethnic Background

WHILE I'M out selling myself and telling others how they can do it, too, I'll often have people come and say to me, "Joe, everything you say sounds good—getting enthusiastic, wearing a big smile, keeping promises and all that, but that's for the other guy. It may work for him okay, but not for me."

"Why not?"

"Because, man, I'm black!" (Or, "You forget I'm Polish." Or, "People get the idea that just because I'm Chinese I either sell egg rolls or do laundry.")

I can get a dozen more answers like that, depending on whom I'm talking to, but all running along the same line.

The black person, or the oriental, worries about his color. It gets in his way. The Polish or the Italian guy thinks about the Polish jokes or the Italian jokes and he gets hopping mad. The Jewish guy worries about a move-over image.

And so it goes, so many people I meet think that what I'm preaching is for the all-American white, came-over-on-the-Mayflower, clean hands and white shirt guy or gal. Forget it. The chapters in this book are for everybody. I don't even know what an all-American person is anyway.

When it comes to ethnic backgrounds my city, Detroit, takes a back seat to no one. If America is a melting pot, Detroit didn't get the word. The people here have as many backgrounds as there are nations—we've got entire communities of them. Detroit is a French name to start with; it means "on the straits." We started French when a guy named Cadillac came canoeing up the Detroit River and set up housekeeping to the amazement of the Indians. To this day we have more streets with French names than New Orleans: names like Lafayette, Duquesne and Beaubien.

Then, the British came and the Indians had a great time playing them off against the French and back again. In the War of 1812 my hometown went American. Under three flags—French, British, Yank—that's Detroit.

Today you could add another forty or so ethnic backgrounds. If their flags don't fly over the city, it doesn't matter. The people have left their mark and are still doing so.

We have Germans and Poles, Hungarians and Italians, Chinese and Mexicans, Puerto Ricans and Jews, Slavs and Scandinavians, Irish and Greeks, Canadians and Arabs. And a score of others too numerous to list. It's wonderful!

We are one city with many communities. Corktown, the home of the Irish, Little Mexico, Little Hungary, any number of Polish, Jewish, German and Italian neighborhoods and a Greek town that is the heartbeat of the inner city and a black population that has spread beyond the inner city to our surrounding suburbs.

So have other cities, you say. True, but not like Detroit. A few statistics: The mayor of our city is black, one of the few black mayors of major American cities. The mayor before him was Polish. Before him Irish. Before him Italian.

We have more Arabs in Detroit than anywhere in the world outside of the Middle East.

Our International Institute, with its fall fair, is larger than the one in New York. Daily it helps the flood of new Detroiters from Europe, the Orient and Latin America get "settled in," find jobs and become productive members of the community, *without losing their ethnic origins*. That's probably the most important thing of all.

Annually on our waterfront we stage the world's largest outdoor international festival, weekend after weekend, all summer long. The air rings with the music of the world, the afternoons and evenings are filled with native dances and the good smells of ethnic foods floating above the crowds of people. In every corner of the city are to be found great restaurants with foods from around the world and Polish halls, Italian halls, Hungarian halls, Spanish halls, Scandinavian halls—all jumping and bouncing with dances, weddings, receptions and music.

And, once a year, Detroit, which is on the border with Canada, connected by tunnel and bridge to Windsor, stages a joint freedom festival with its Canadian neighbors on the Fourth of July.

It's wonderful!

Do we all get along like ham and eggs, waffles and syrup? Of course not. We get along just as members of any large family do. We quarrel, we make up, we haul off at one another, we love one another.

I'm telling you all this to point out that in my city, when it comes to selling yourself you simply have to sell your ethnic background as well. We've got the qualifications. Maybe Detroiters know how by instinct, but I don't think so. We still have to work at it. I've got some tips to pass along to all of you with ethnic backgrounds—all those of you who think, "I can't do it because I'm black/Polish/Chicano/Yugoslavian/Dutch." And I want to tell you about five people I know who have done a great job of selling themselves and their ethnic backgrounds, each in a different way. One is black, one is Jewish, one is Japanese, one is Mexican and one is Sicilian like myself.

Your Competition Is Prejudice

First off, get this straight. I believe people like people who are proud of who they are. It doesn't matter what the nationality is.

One of my black friends likes to kid me about this and still make the point. "Joe," he'll say, "it's too bad that we all can't be black. It's a great color—it's the only one Henry Ford liked —black is beautiful!" Then, I'll grin and come back with, "But white is right." And, he'll come right back at me with, "But white is too hard to keep clean." We keep that up, sparring around, trying a little one-upmanship, kidding and loving each other. We can, because deep down each of us is proud of *who* we are and *what* we are. Each of us knows it about the other, and that's why we like each other so much. *Pride in who you are is important in selling yourself and your ethnic background.*

Not long ago a friend of mine was staying at a motel in Palm Springs, California. He is a car salesman and he told me this story—it's not about cars. The motel had an Olympic-sized swimming pool, and because it was hot the pool was getting a good workout. There were people of all races, including a number of blacks. One guy, standing nearby, who was white like my friend, shook his head and said to my friend, "They let anybody in these days don't they?" My friend said that at that point he lost his cool a bit, turned to the guy and said, "Don't worry about diving in, buddy. The color won't rub off on you. But, maybe you'd better stay poolside, because I'm going in and

I'm Russian. You don't want to swim with a Commie, do you? The red might rub off."

Thinking about it later, my friend said to me, "Joe, I guess I shouldn't have sounded off at the guy. I really wasn't selling myself, was I?" I told him that, yes, he was selling himself, perhaps never so well as then, when he let another person know how he felt and where he stood when it came to racial prejudices.

And, it is racial prejudice, bigotry open and hidden, misunderstanding and sometimes fear that you must sell against when you're selling yourself and your ethnic background.

Keep the Rope Tight

William Bailey is the president of the First Independence National Bank of Detroit. It's a small bank with its principal office in the inner city, where Bill runs the operation, and there are also two bank branches. It's growing. It has sixty-two employees. It has been in existence for over seven years, and my friend Bill Bailey was called in to be president a little over two years ago. He and the bank have made great strides in getting established and being competitive with other banks. Detroit was and is a second city for Bill, who is a native of Buffalo, but he knows it well.

By the way, William Bailey is black.

He has faced his share of racial prejudice because of this. Yet I don't know anyone who has done such a terrific job of selling himself and his ethnic background—his blackness—as Bill.

"You've got to start very early in life to develop confidence," Bill tells me, "confidence that you can achieve your goal —whatever it is." (I have Bill's hearty endorsement of my chapter Building Self-Confidence and Courage.)

"My mother was a very strong and sincere person who tried to instill in her children confidence in themselves. She taught us to believe we could gain success regardless of the obstacles we faced. Of course, in the beginning, the biggest obstacle I guess was being black. But, I didn't know it then.

"With that kind of shove-off, I think I was able to face each obstacle as it came up and lick it. Because of my mother, I guess I've never really lacked the confidence I needed to achieve what I set out to do. I grew up in a poor setting in Buffalo. My brother, my sister and I had to work very early in life. I've been supporting myself since I was eleven years old.

"I worked my way through college, spent four years in the air force and, while going to school and working, raised a couple of kids.

"I tell everybody, you've got to have confidence in yourself in order for your ethnic qualities to sell themselves right along with you. Of course, you don't just whip up confidence overnight.

"I've always kept this one thing in mind. If you're black, or an ethnic in some way, and prejudice is an obstacle, you take one step at a time, build your confidence one step at a time, and you do those things you can do to overcome whatever obstacles there are.

"Sometimes you run into stone fences, but even fences can be gone over or under or around if you do everything you can do.

"There's an old saying I live by—about taking up slack in the rope. If you keep your rope taut, things will work out. I don't buy a lot of today's advice to 'stay loose.' I think sometimes young people misinterpret what this means.

"I believe in keeping things tight because sometimes, when things are too loose, you're not doing everything you can to get over the hurdles. For example, if you're an ethnic person and you're working on a job and people dislike you because you're black or Turkish or Indian, don't let them also dislike you because you don't wash or shave or come to work on time or do a good job. In other words, don't confirm the negative stereotyping.

"If you do all the other things you're supposed to do on the job, if you keep the rope tight, then most likely the other problem, the ethnic problem, will go away, too. If it doesn't go away, at least you're prepared to move on and you're carrying some pretty good traits to accomplish what you'd like to do.

"I don't believe in letting one single thing create slack in the rope. I like to keep it tight, be prepared. In my business I have to sell myself every single day. I have to be patient and have the disposition to confront many different personalities and problems. It's a necessary thing when you're dealing with the public."

Bill Bailey's been doing a good job of keeping a tight rope for quite a while now. Being black started posing problems for Bill first at school then later on in college. He did not go to an all-black school. And, there was only a sprinkling of blacks at the University of Buffalo at that time. I asked Bill:

"Bailey, just what were some of your problems then, just how did you go about selling yourself to your classmates and teachers along with your ethnic background?"

"Joe," he told me, "they were the usual ones blacks face. Cracks about sexual prowess. All that watermelon crap. Amos 'n' Andy stuff. Sometimes the racism was subtle and sometimes it was right out in the open. But, here's what I learned:

"That kind of thing was *their* problem, not mine. I quickly discovered that many of my problems were self-created, psychological problems of confidence, problems I created myself by just making mountains out of molehills, becoming upset at subtle forms of discrimination, not maintaining a kind of toughness and stick-to-it attitude, trying to get ahead in a setting where you're not welcomed by 100 percent of the people.

"Now, that's a very hard thing for a lot of young black kids to overcome. But, here's what I did.

"I always tried very hard to see that I and my blackness fit in. I made sure I was friendly—that's important for an ethnic person. I always tried to pull my weight—on the basketball team or in group lab problems. I always tried to do my share or even more. I always tried to be the very best. And a lot of times I didn't make it. I remember a white classmate of mine saying to me, 'Bill, you're a real friendly guy.' Then he used an expression that I've never forgotten. He said, 'you're a guy who's easy to laugh with.'

"I think it's absolutely essential in selling yourself to become an outgoing person, a man or woman with an outgoing personality. Be easy to laugh with."

Bill did a hitch in the air force. He traveled in a lot of countries. He had a lot of opportunities to talk to Americans abroad. He had a chance to see his country through the eyes of foreigners. He found it looked pretty good. Most of all, associating with others in the service and abroad, Bill woke up to the importance of education and training.

It was while he was a graduate student that he first took the step into banking that has led him to where he is today. He was always interested in economics but had done nothing about it. One day, taking a long look at himself as a fifth-year college student, with a wife and two children, he said to himself, "Hey, it's time I went out to work again."

"My mother at that time," he told me, "was the housekeeper for a very wealthy businessman who was a director of a bank.

" 'Bill,' she casually suggested to me one day, 'why don't you go down and apply for their training program?'

" 'Come on, Ma, they won't talk to me,' I told her.

" 'Adam told me'—she first-named her boss—'you should go down and mention his name and they'll talk to you.'

"She was right," Bill told me. "I went down to see them and they did talk to me. I guess I had some other things going for me, too. It was the mid-sixties, at the height of the civil rights activities, and banks were just beginning to reach out a bit. I just walked in the door at the right time. I was the first black in their training program, but things worked out."

Bill tells me things have changed for blacks. Racism is decreasing. There are still problems. But, people are realizing blacks are here to stay. To be a racist today is just old-fashioned. That opinion from a black shows that guys like Bill Bailey are doing a pretty good job of selling themselves and their ethnic backgrounds.

His wrap-up advice: "Don't dwell on the blackness. Keep your sense of humor by not taking yourself too seriously. Start controlling life by controlling your own head first. Don't come down hard on yourself. Explore your strengths, shrug off your deficiencies.

"And keep your rope tight!"

Find Yourself a Market

Saul Wineman is an assistant professor of humanities in the Wayne State University College of Lifelong Learning. He didn't grow up in a ghetto, but in a nice, middle-class, Jewish neighborhood of Detroit. His father was a food jobber who distributed cheeses, smoked meats and fish, candies and other items to a number of small grocers during the heart of the Depression. His boyhood gave him a box of memories, many of which are tied in with Detroit's bustling Eastern Market.

The Eastern Market, a sprawling, outdoor-indoor feast of sounds and sights, is a link to his youth and his present life. It helps him to keep in mind his own ethnic background as well as that of all the other ethnic groups that make up our urban metropolis.

In using his ethnic background to best advantage, Saul leads a double life. He is not only Saul Wineman, but to millions in the metropolitan area of Detroit he is also Paul Winter, radio broadcaster, star of the former radio show, "The Paul Winter Connection," film reviewer on the airwaves, heard all the time on both AM and FM radio, and is producer of special projects on Channel 56, Detroit's Public Television station. One of his projects was a film called *Only Then Regale My Eyes*, which won a special midwestern award from PBS as the best cultural documentary by a local Public Television station.

He is also an actor of note with such regional and dinner theater credits as *The Fifth Season, Thurber's Carnival, Ulysses in Nighttown, The Marriage-Go-Round* and *The Sunshine Boys*.

And, he writes songs. "An album of mine sold about a thousand copies," he said, grinning, "almost entirely to Yale students. Why? You should only ask!"

I first got to know Saul Wineman/Paul Winter when he did a series of commercials for the large automobile dealership where I worked. I've seen a lot of him since. He's a happy guy, always ready with a joke or a song.

However, Saul/Paul likes to quote an anonymous writer who, he said, sums up what it means, for him at least, to be Jewish: "A Jew's joy is not without fright."

There is delight in being a Jew, and yet to be one in the twentieth century—as for centuries before—means there have been many moments of fear. One only need recall the countless persecutions suffered by Jews throughout the ages.

For some Jews, being a Jew is special—"a peculiar treasure" as it says in the Old Testament. Chosen people. Very religious, and they see themselves that way. Paul is not that kind of Jew. On the other hand, some Jews pretend that they're not Jews, and they sell themselves that way. Paul is not that kind of a Jew either. "I'm not religious in any way. But, I'm Jewish and I'd never pretend that I'm not." He is emphatic about that.

"I've been successful in one profession as Saul Wineman. And, I've been successful in another as Paul Winter. I believe the secret of selling yourself and your ethnic background is to borrow from both your worlds, your past and your present. With me, one of the secrets was in my name.

"At the time I changed it to Paul Winter it seemed necessary to Americanize my name somehow—just like Bernie Schwartz who became Tony Curtis in the films. (I could relate to what

Paul told me. After all, I dropped the *i* from Girardi and became Girard for much the same reason.)

"Today it isn't all that important," Paul said. "But, back then I set out to find a name that would probably be somewhere in between my Jewishness and the WASP world where I worked."

It has been a good Jewish identity for Saul/Paul. The tie that binds the two together is still the Eastern Market. Here, at dawn every Saturday morning, the assistant professor loses himself in Detroit's busy East Side, and the personality of the airwaves also disappears. He is once again a small boy, basket in hand, shopping for the fruits, vegetables and fish as he did with his father years ago. Literally hundreds of people know they can set their watches by Saul/Paul at the Eastern Market Saturday mornings. And, they know why. It is not because of what the market offers in the way of food for the body, but what it offers in food for the soul.

"To forget one's ethnic background, whether it's Jewish or Arab, Yugoslavian or Scandinavian, is to cheat yourself. When people 'buy' Paul Winter," he says, "they also 'buy' Saul Wineman. I am more than *me*. I am the product of six thousand years of Jewishness and that makes me, like good whisky, aged to perfection.

"I've never failed to sell myself or my ideas because I'm Jewish, I do know, however, that I could fail if I denied it.

"Our parents wanted us to become Americans, yet somehow remain Jewish. Most of them were immigrants and they became Americans because they set out for here instead of someplace else. Here was where there was land. Here was a chance to grow. But, we children were Americans by birth. What we needed to get was what our parents had, the *Jewishness*. My father, maybe without knowing it, showed me how.

"He gave me a place to hang on to, the *market*, and that's where I go once a week. And, that's why I go—to remember. Every person of ethnic origin should have such a place. If he does not, he should find one. Once you've found it, make it a part of your life. You'll do a better job of selling yourself from then on, every day to everyone."

Who You Are—by What You Do

My friend, Lawrence K. Shinoda, is president of Shinoda Design Company. A good many of the cars you see on the road—maybe even the one you're now driving—carry the Shinoda design touch somewhere. Or, maybe your recreational vehicle is of Shinoda design. Or, perhaps your piece of farm equipment came in whole or in part from Larry's drawing board.

As a designer, Larry's skill has carried him far. He is in great demand. As a person who, like all of us, is selling himself in many ways every day, he has an ethnic background to sell as well.

Lawrence Shinoda is a Nisei. That is, he is of Japanese-born, immigrant parentage, but he was born in the United States, in California.

As a young boy of twelve, when the Japanese bombed Pearl Harbor, Larry and his family found themselves cruelly uprooted from their home—as did thousands of other Japanese-Americans. His parents operated a wholesale flower market and nursery, but, suddenly, they were parted from it. Larry's family was "relocated" for more than two years at camps which, although they had a different name, were nevertheless concentration camps. Those, along with Indian reservations, make some of the shameful episodes in our country's history.

Young Larry faced a reverse type of discrimination however, once he was in the cold, dusty camp in the Owens Valley of California. From facing the hostility of whites once the war broke out, he now found a different kind of bigotry. Raised American, his family having freely mixed with other Americans, he found himself interned in a totally foreign environment at the relocation camp. You see, he could not speak Japanese.

Larry, who has a keen sense of humor, can still see the humor in his situation. "There I was—a Japanese kid—surrounded for the first time by Japanese and Nisei—and I was shunned because I didn't know the language. Hell, I was too American."

Larry passed the time as kids do, playing ball, working with his family, and making sketches of life around him. He had, as one of his designer friends later told him, "an educated pencil."

When the war was over, his family eventually found its way back to Los Angeles and their nursery (after a sojourn on a relative's farm in Colorado). Larry entered high school, where almost at once he faced a lot of racial hard feelings leftover from the war. He was one of the few orientals in the school. He was faced with selling himself along with his ethnic background to the whites, to his fellow students, his teachers, his teammates and to hoped-for dates. It wasn't easy. A date that he might arrange for on the telephone would suddenly be canceled once the girls saw him and saw that he was oriental.

"I mean a date with a nonoriental," Larry told me. "It wasn't really the white girl's fault. Young kids like myself didn't have racial prejudices. It was usually her parents' doing. They wouldn't let her go out with me."

As a young man then he faced the same false views that many whites still hold today about those who are of a different race or color or national origin. You know, Mexicans or Chicanos are all cherry, strawberry and lettuce pickers, or blacks are porters or roustabouts, or Jews are in the junk business, or Japanese are mainly gardeners.

To sell himself and his ethnic background, with anybody in an impressive position in the design field—or any field—at that time, Larry tried flip answers.

"I'd have a smart crack for everything. Maybe I'd have a comeback for somebody who had made a racial slur—or maybe I'd be a smart mouth just to head off bigotry or rejec-

266   **HOW TO SELL YOURSELF**

tion. It wasn't the way to go, of course, but I had to learn that later."

Larry was not the kind of guy to turn the other cheek. He was a scrapper, a born fighter, and he ended up in quite a few physical brawls, usually over a remark such as, "Why don't you go back and cut grass?"

He began to develop a stock answer which, if it wasn't polite, got results. He'd say to anybody who took a crack at his Japanese background, "Hey, the war's over, so stop bombing me, huh?"

But, Larry realized soon enough that that was not the way to sell himself and his ethnic background. He was just reacting, not acting. He decided to tell people to "stop bombing" him in a different way, without words, but through actions. He would show them he was someone to be reckoned with.

"I did it by drag racing to start out with," Larry says. "And it was a way, in college, to reverse any negative image about myself. I'd always been interested in motor sports, in racing, so I began to race in my little '29 Ford roadster. Letting 'em eat my dust was a better way than my telling them what they could do."

Soon Larry was into other racing vehicles and he was breaking records at such events as the Bonneville Nationals. It was rough, tough, hard work, but it was his way of showing that ethnic people could work as hard if not harder than anyone else at their jobs.

Along with his interest in driving was an even deeper interest in drawing. In school, just as he had in the detention camp, he made sketches and paintings of cars and trucks. "Then," Larry continues his story, "when I was in the service, during the Korean War, I met some guys who were going to what is now the Art Center College of Design in Los Angeles, one of the better schools for learning industrial and transportation design. They got me interested in it and I enrolled in the college.

"So, after driving cars I started to design them." Larry made the changeover as easily as he says it. Along the way he designed such winners as his Shinoda Chopsticks Special, with an Ardun-head Mercury V-8 engine. It was the Dearborn, Michigan, and national record holder in 1955. A year later his John Zink Special, built by A. J. Watson, was winner of the Indianapolis 500. It was also the pole winner in that race.

His first regular job as an automotive designer was with The Ford Motor Company. Larry went to Dearborn, Michigan. Although there are a great number of ethnics, Poles and Arabs largely, in Dearborn, they are clustered in East Dearborn. West Dearborn tends to be "pure" white Anglo-Saxon.

Larry found it very difficult to get housing. It was the same story as in high school and college when he tried to get dates with girls other than orientals. "I'd call in answer to an ad for a house or apartment and everything would be fine. Then, I'd show up and the property was suddenly not available. Of course, this was before there were laws about that sort of thing."

Larry was piling up expenses, living in and commuting from a downtown Detroit hotel. Finally, the Ford Motor Company found him a place to live. He had put it to them bluntly. If he was good enough to work for them they'd have to "buy" his ethnic background as well. It was—and always would be—part of the sale. "Take me as I am, here in Dearborn, or I'll go back." He almost fell back on his old flip answers, but didn't. Instead he made his ethnic price tag so high that he, himself, was amazed when they took it.

After a period with Ford he joined the old Studebaker-Packard Company for several months and then he went to General Motors. He remained there for twelve years, eventually becoming chief designer/coordinator for special vehicles.

Finally he stepped out on his own, and The Shinoda Design Company has steadily gained prestige in the automotive capital of the world. Larry, as an independent designer, designs cars, trucks, snowmobiles, motor homes, land-speed–record cars, Can-Am racers and farm machinery. Few men so dominate the field of transportation design as Larry Shinoda.

Today, Larry's ethnic background is still something he sells along with himself. "But you have to have a sense of humor," he says. "Especially about your own language. Don't let it slip away—that's the best advice I can give to an ethnic person.

"Consider myself. I've made it pretty good, and at a time when Japanese seems to be 'in.' Everyone knows the names—Datsun, Sony, Honda, Toyota—and they're all gaining greater American acceptance. You'd think the demand for a guy like me would be pretty hot. Not so. The Japanese—and I've been to Tokyo now a couple of times—like to deal with Japanese designers who speak English, and American designers who speak Japanese. That last part lets me out."

So, here's what Lawrence Shinoda is doing now to sell his ethnic background along with himself: "Would you believe I'm taking concentration studies—crash courses—at Berlitz and other schools in order to learn my native tongue. One of these days this Japanese will learn how to speak Japanese—and then I'll do twice as good a job of selling myself."

Sell Yourself by Building Trust

My friend Anthony Rojas is the manager of Armando's, one of Detroit's most popular Mexican restaurants, located in the Little Mexico area on the near west side of the city. He is also a first-class bartender who boasts that he can make the best Margueritas this side of Acapulco. He also does a terrific job of selling himself and his ethnic background.

Although he works in a Hispanic neighborhood, largely populated by Mexicans, Puerto Ricans and Cubans, Tony lives on the east side of the city where he says his roots are. I've known him ever since we were punks in the ghetto.

"As a young kid I grew up with Greeks, Syrians, Lebanese, Arabs—nationality didn't mean a damn thing. Everybody else was just a kid. It wasn't until I was old enough to start looking for a job that I found out that being Mexican got in my way."

Tony learned quickly that he had to be a little streetwise. "In fact," he says, "I learned more on the street about how to make being Mexican work for me than anyplace else.

"You won't believe what a lot of non-Mexicans think about you. You haven't got any education. All you do is sit around in the sun under a mile-wide hat. You make junk jewelry. You fill your belly with nothing but tortillas and chili. None of you can be trusted."

It was that last "bunch of crap" as Tony puts it that got him down. The only way he figured for a guy to be trusted was to show everybody that he was absolutely honest. "If you trust Mexicans," Tony decided, "you'll buy Mexican, and if you trust me, you'll buy me.

"In a way some of the gringo ideas about Mexicans are right. It's true that some of the most beautiful silver jewelry you can buy is made by Mexicans. And, what's wrong with a good tortilla—with enchiladas and tacos?"

Nothing, judging by the way people come to Armando's. They come from miles away, from the north and east WASP suburbs of Detroit, and from Canada, happy to sit down with Mexicans and pleased when Tony greets them by their names.

It took a long time for Tony to find his spot and make a success at it, a long time before he learned not to hide his ethnic background but to use it in selling himself.

After service in World War II, from 1943 through 1945, Tony bummed around a bit. He learned a surprising thing. In California, much closer to Mexico, he found that people thought less of Mexicans and put them down more than they did in Detroit. When he tried to get a job in southern California people told him, "Sure, kid, but you can only go so far because you're Spic." So, what do the Mexicans do? "As soon as they began making a few bucks," Tony says, "they suddenly become Spanish. Madrid, Barcelona, you name it you got it. They think they're somebody—but, all they're doing is losing their pride. California wasn't for me. I headed back for Detroit.

"I always liked people. I wanted to be around people, talk to them, get to know them. I wanted to know all kinds of people. A friend said be a Mexican bartender. Nobody sells themselves like bartenders.

"I set out to get a job at one of the downtown taverns. I didn't know a damn thing about bartending. Most bartenders in Detroit were Irish anyway, not Mexican. But, I was honest. I admitted that I didn't know a gin and tonic from a Bloody Mary."

Tony didn't know if he could hack it either. Bartenders are always selling themselves to others, getting to know their customers by name, willing to lend an ear when somebody wants to bend it. But, before he could get the chance to work in a bar, he had to sell himself to the tavern management.

He was asked, "What's your nationality?" (In those days employers could get away with that.) Tony says, "I thought for a moment and remembered something I heard my old man say when I was a kid. It was a 100 percent honest answer. I said, 'I'm Mexican, what's yours?' Then I said, 'my ancestors were Indians, who were yours?' And then I said finally, 'who was here first?' The boss grinned. I got the job.

"I found out that if I was honest, my Mexican background took care of itself. I didn't have to hide it and I didn't have to push it. If a customer asked for a certain drink and I didn't know how to make it I told him so. Most of the time the guy just laughed and showed me. I think half of them liked to show off anyway."

Being honest with people came first according to Tony. If he was honest, then people would be honest with him. He refused to believe otherwise.

"I'm a human being first, then Mexican," Tony says, "but I know that being Mexican is part of what I am, a big part. For me, the best way I could let being Mexican help sell me to others was to work in a Mexican area where I'd be right at home, but deal with a lot of people who aren't Mexican but who wanted to buy a little 'south of the border' for an evening.

"When they buy that, they buy me first. I try to remember them all, their names, who they are and what they do, what they like to eat and what they like to drink.

"A customer came up to me the other day—been coming in for months—has his wife with him this time. He says, 'Tony, no menu. You know what I like—fix me up something special and the wife'll take what you recommend. I trust you.'

"I trust you. Those are words I like to hear. So I went into the kitchen, got together with the chef and fixed the guy and his wife up with a specialty from around La Paz. How could I sell myself any better—the guy trusts me? With him—I'll never hand him a menu again."

The way he's selling himself is sure working for Tony. He's managed Armando's for ten years now. In that time it has grown bigger to take care of the crowds. On an average day, Tony will take care of nearly three hundred people.

Sure, the food is outstanding, the nachos delicious, the tortillas plentiful, the refried beans just right. But, the food is also delicious at any number of other fine Mexican restaurants in our city (and in the Greek and Hungarian and Italian and Chinese restaurants, too). So, a lot of the success must be because of Tony, the kid who people said could only go so far "because you're Spic." Well, he's gone a long way.

As I see it, Tony's life and Tony's beliefs boil down to this advice: "Be honest about your ethnic background, don't hide it, make others want it. When they do, they'll want you, too."

You've Got to Have Love

I can speak Sicilian pretty good. I'm Sicilian and I tell people that. I'm proud of it. I don't care if people seem to think all Sicilians are Mafia; I don't have a godfather, how about that! The only offer I can make you that you shouldn't refuse is to study this book and learn how to do a better job of selling yourself.

Be proud of who you are. Hold your head up high and say, "I'm Polish!" (or, whatever) with a look and a smile on your face that says, "It's too bad you're not Polish, too."

All nationalities have a small percentage of people who have blackened the names of their countries or regions. But, I'm not going to take the blame for a few guys who have done something wrong.

If I were to have a hang-up about nationality, if I went through life thinking there was something bad about being Sicilian, then I would have started to believe that I wasn't as good a person as I could be. It would begin to show in my personality, and I wouldn't be sold on myself. And, then who would want to buy me?

I could tell you a lot about selling myself and my Sicilian background. But, I want to turn the job over to another Sicilian, Jimmy Vento. He's my barber and he probably knows more about where my head's at than anyone else. But, Jimmy was born in Sicily. I wasn't. He's a book in himself.

The little fishing village of Montallegro lies some sixty-five kilometers from Palermo. Here Jimmy, with his eight brothers and sisters, first learned the importance of love for family and fellow villagers as a means of selling oneself to others. His father, Jimmy says, had a great capacity for love for everyone and everyone loved him in return. Because of this, people were pleased to do things for him, and his influence in the village of Montallegro was great.

"Sicilians are very emotional," Jimmy says. "We don't just *like*, we *love*. We have a great love of life, of family, of friends, of good food and wine, of work, and of honor. I saw how much love my father had for those things and how it made him respected and loved in return in our village. I didn't know then how trying to be like him later on would be of so much help to me when I had to try to make people in the United States understand and accept my Sicilian background.

"I miss my father very much. Even today, now that I'm a grown man, when I think of him and the beautiful things he taught me, I cry.

"He taught me that if I want people to like me and accept me and come to my place of business, I must show them that I love them. I guess in America you would use the word *like*, but it's more than that. Anyway, my father's example has never let me down."

Jimmy Vento's father was a builder of houses, and by the age of ten Jimmy was working in a barbershop in his fishing village. He learned the trade quickly, but by the age of fifteen, Jimmy had lost his father. The only legacy left him was his father's burning desire to go to America. Jimmy made the desire his own dream. But the immigration quota was strict and coming to the United States was difficult. However, Canada welcomed him. Besides, Jimmy now had a sister who was living in Canada and so, with her help, and at the age of eighteen, Jimmy found himself in London, Ontario, unable to speak a word of English, but with the ability to give a first-class haircut.

He learned English, as Canadians speak it (saying *aboot* instead of *about*, for example) from his customers. He was one barber who couldn't talk their ears off; instead he let them do the talking and he learned.

Being a good dancer as well, Jimmy earned extra money as a ballroom dance instructor for an Arthur Murray studio in Toronto. With dancing, Jimmy let his feet do his ethnic talking and it was only natural that at a dance in London, he met a Ukrainian girl who had been born in Canada. He married her, began a family and then moved on to Detroit at the age of twenty-eight. That was seventeen years ago, and in those seventeen years he has achieved undreamed of success—financially, in his friendships, his marriage and his family.

Jimmy still gives his father the credit.

His first job was in the barbershop of the Greyhound Bus Station in Detroit, but within one year the ambitious young man had his own shop. In time he was to open four hair salons, each in one of Detroit's four finest hotels. Along the way he sold two of them to barbers who worked for him, and with the profits, moved another of his shops to the prestigious new Renaissance Center. There were many salons clamoring to get in this magnificent new complex, but it was Jimmy who "sold himself" and made it. He had help from others of influence, but he had sold himself to them, too. I asked Jimmy how he did it.

"I knew that here, just as in Canada, the answer was not in overcoming my ethnic background,"—and, by the way, Jimmy speaks excellent English now—"but in helping people understand it. I faced all the cracks Italians are used to and I decided to show people that Italians, Sicilians especially, are not all Mafia, or hot-blooded guys who carry stilletos, or guerrillas or gangsters or hit men. We're good people just like millions of others from other countries. I made up my mind I was going to become 100 percent American but still not stop being Sicilian.

"The first guy who gave me a job in his barber shop asked me what I was. My answer was, 'I'm Sicilian and I'm a hard worker.' He was buying both things when he gave me a chance.

"I remember the first person who sat down in my chair for a haircut. He asked me what I was. I said, 'I'm Sicilian. I don't speak English good. But I gave him a big smile instead of words. He bought the Sicilian because it came with a friendly smile. He always asked for me from then on."

To show people *who* he was was hard for Jimmy at first because he couldn't express himself in words. The feelings were there but the words weren't. They came later. Whenever I think of my friend Jimmy Vento however, I think about the words of that song from that movie about the King of Siam and the schoolteacher. "Getting to know you, getting to know all about you. . . ." According to Jimmy it's the only way to prove to people what you really are and not what they think you are.

In seeing that people "get to know you," Jimmy has also seen his business grow and prosper. His two salons are something to see. He employs eighteen people, female as well as male hair stylists. There are ten chairs in his large salon, and all are kept busy. But, as busy as Jimmy is himself he makes sure that he has plenty of time for his family, to show that love which is so much a part of his (and my) Sicilian background. He must sell that ethnic heritage to his four kids, too, because they are thoroughly Americanized. Beginning in Canada, with its emphasis on hockey, and continuing in the United States in a border city with Canada, his three sons have a kinship with hockey. Jimmy coaches a Little League hockey team yet devotes a good deal of his time, too, to his daughter whose interest runs to music. He is doing a great job of selling himself and his ethnic background to everyone, because he now cuts the hair of, and numbers among his friends, many top politicians in our area, as well as judges and other officials of the county. He is also a personal friend of the governor of our state, and his customers come from all over Michigan, many of them from great distances.

Not bad for a kid from a little fishing village near Palermo, who came to America as a teenager, who could not speak a word of English and who had only love, as Sicilians understand it, to offer.

Again and again Jimmy tells me, "The secret is to make sure people know you, really *know* you. Once they do, they can't help but love you."

Jimmy Vento's father would be proud.

To sum it up, these are the things I've learned from my five ethnic friends, as well as many others like them. They make good rules to follow whatever your ethnic background is. And, if you follow them you'll do a much finer job of selling that background along with yourself. After all, you've got something wonderful to sell.

1. Be proud of who you are. People like people who are proud of their heritage.

2. Hang on to your ethnic origin. Don't lose it by pretending to be something else.

3. Because you hate bigotry, make sure you wipe out any racial prejudices you may have about others. Show others where you stand.

4. Build your confidence, you *can* achieve your goal, whatever it may be (William Bailey).

5. Keep your rope tight, do all the things you're supposed to do and more (William Bailey).

6. Don't dwell on your blackness (or whatever your color); start controlling life by controlling your own head first (William Bailey).

7. Borrow from both your worlds, past and present, and use them both (Saul Wineman).

8. Find your Jewishness again (or whatever your national origin), find your own "market," a place to return to, and enjoy enjoy (Saul Wineman).

9. Show them who you are by what you can do (Lawrence Shinoda).

10. Keep a sense of humor. When the joke's on you, laugh (Lawrence Shinoda).

11. Hang on to your native language; if you're weak in it, learn it. It can work wonders for you in a shrinking world (Lawrence Shinoda).

12. Be absolutely honest; tie in honesty with your ethnic background. Sell yourself by building trust (Tony Rojas).

13. Never believe anyone who says you can only go so far because you're Chicano or Greek or whatever. Believe yourself instead (Tony Rojas).

14. Love, not just like, everybody (Jimmy Vento).

15. Do everything you can to help people get to know you and to understand you. Then they'll love you back (Jimmy Vento).

Fifteen "pieces of advice" to follow. They work. I know, because I know all of the people who have put their own advice to work and found success.

Things to Do NOW!

- Regardless of your race, color or national origin, put some or all of the fifteen guidelines to work in your life. Seek inspiration in rereading the stories I've told you about Bill, Saul, Larry, Tony and Jimmy. They shared them for a reason, to help you.
- Every morning when you get up think of those whom you'll meet that day, then say out loud: "I'm glad I'm Polish (or black or Chinese or Jewish or Indian or Eskimo or whatever)! Don't you wish you were, too?"

CHAPTER SEVENTEEN

Selling Yourself and Your Product

I WANT to move away for a moment—but not too far—from the world's best product, *you*. By now I hope you're firmly convinced that there's no one else like you in the world and that, when it comes to selling yourself, there is no other product in the world as good as you.

Selling oneself is something everybody must do in order to get along better with others, to influence others and to be more successful. This holds true, as we've pointed out many times, regardless of who you are or what you do. You may be a secretary, you may work on an assembly line. You may be a homemaker or you may be retired. Professions, vocations, jobs, relationships are as many, it often seems, as there are people.

This chapter is for those of you who actually sell a product to someone else, along with yourself, of course. This chapter is for salespeople specifically (but everything in it is of value to those who are in other walks of life as well).

You may sell at wholesale or you may sell at retail. You may sell door to door or you may sell through the mail or you may sell over the counter. In almost every line of selling a product you come in contact with people, with the possible exception of direct-mail selling, where advertising presells for you and you fill the orders. But even then the principles still apply.

In my book *How to Sell Anything to Anybody* I covered in detail how I became the world's number-one retail salesman by my special methods of selling automobiles. Some of the ways I used to prospect, qualify, demonstrate the car, answer objections and ask for the order, were well known to every car and truck salesman, *only I used them differently*, and some of the methods I used were my own and many of them were controversial. So? If they worked and made friends and built repeat business, who cared? A lot of head honchos cared, that's who, because even though a lot of companies love success, they're scared to death of rocking boats.

Well, I want you to rock boats. I hope you will.

Even though my book was about how I sold cars and filled "ferris wheel" seats with prospects, the way I did it would fit, basically, the sale of any product. That's why I called it *How to Sell Anything to Anybody*. However, I soon found myself getting very impatient with talk-show hosts who loved to put me on the spot with, "Okay, Joe Girard, sell me this pencil or this sports jacket or this wallet." (One such clever host went so far as to pull a rubber chicken—the kind magicians use in their acts—from a desk drawer and say, "Sell me this bird!" I felt like giving her the bird.) You see, none of these people were willing on air time to let me qualify him or her as to a *need* for the pencil or jacket or chicken, or to learn about buying motives or to discuss the customer benefits of the product. Each was chiefly interested in showing off.

Selling yourself *and* your product does not consist of magic, or showing off or luck. It consists of *home*work and *hard* work and *rewarding* work.

Let's talk about unchanging principles, how to use them and how to give them that little extra Girard touch which might just get you the order.

As salespeople, I'm assuming you know that selling strategy consists, basically, of these seven steps:

Basic Selling Strategy

1. *Prospecting.* (Finding people or organizations to which you wish to sell your product.)
2. *Qualifying.* (Learning what people *really* need versus what they *think* they need or want—and learning their ability to pay.
3. *Presenting.* (Showing your product off to its best advantage, wherever you sell it, and creating the desire to own.)
4. *Demonstrating.* (A first cousin to presenting, but now putting the product through its paces, showing what it *does* and further creating the desire to buy.)
5. *Answering objections.* (Overcoming any real or imagined resistance to the sale.)
6. *Closing.* (The moment of truth when you ask for the order.)
7. *Follow-up.* (Keeping the customer in the fold.)

Following those seven steps is what it takes to turn prospects into customers and *keep* them as customers.

Of course, the effectiveness of that selling strategy depends upon homework. I am also assuming that you *know* your product well, that you know all its features. Product knowledge is worth little without a selling strategy, and a sales strategy is almost worthless if you lack product knowledge. Get aboard your product fast and learn all about it top to bottom, inside out.

Now, there's a mile-wide difference between *selling strategy* and *salesmanship*. And, for the moment, it's not the basic seven steps we're interested in, but *salesmanship*.

The Joe Girard brand of salesmanship, some of which I developed myself and some of which I've gladly learned from others, goes right back to the selling philosophy I've always lived by: *I don't sell a thing, I sell me*. When I've sold *me* first, I don't have any trouble at all selling the product. We've talked a lot about selling yourself, but now let's relate it to a product. How do you relate *you* to the product so that you sell yourself first? Here are four good guidelines which have never failed to work for me:

1. Be your own best customer.
2. Put yourself in the customer's shoes.
3. Don't get behind a curtain.
4. Be bigger than your product.

Let's consider each.

First, *be your own best customer*. If you want your prospect to warm up to your product, you'd better show him or her that you're hot on it, too. How much confidence do you think a customer would have in the Plymouth you sell, for example, if he knew that "off the job" you drove a Fiat?

A General Electric appliance salesman ought to have a GE in his kitchen or laundry room and not a Sears Kenmore. And vice versa. Understand, I'm not endorsing either of those makes, or any other brands mentioned for that matter; I'm only making a point about salespeople's product loyalty.

A salesperson for a Schick or a Remington or a Norelco electric shaver is not much of a booster for his product if he shaves with lather and a Gillette safety razor.

Be your own best customer. To the extent possible, use, drive, wear, carry, display and talk up the product you sell.

Your prospects and customers will think, "If it's good enough for this salesman, that's a pretty strong recommendation."

There may be times, however, when you sell for a multiple-line dealership or shop. It may be quite impractical to use or wear or carry something of each line in your personal life. But, I know of a number of instances where salespeople have made a successful attempt to solve the problem. They sell with clear consciences.

A salesman I know who works in the home appliance section of one of Detroit's largest department stores handles the problem like this: He is expected to have product loyalty to a number of trademarks. So, he has a range of one brand and a refrigerator of another and an automatic dishwasher of still another. In his utility room are a washer and dryer, each of a different make. He has a clear conscience all right, but his wife complains that nothing matches.

A shoe salesman I know who works in one of our largest shopping malls has dress shoes of one brand, leisure shoes of another and slippers of still another. His store carries all three trademarks, plus others, but my friend says he's run out of closet space in his home. Brand loyalty to three is enough.

Again, to the extent possible, it just makes good sense to practice solid brand loyalty to the product line you're selling. If not, it simply might work to your disadvantage. Here's what one salesman told me about such a "backfire" because he goofed. In this case, it was loyalty to a customer's product.

"I was calling on a large electronics firm in the Philadelphia area, Joe, which sold at that time 'brown goods,' that is, stereo, television, radios and so forth. I had a preliminary meeting with one of their marketing executives for the purpose of picking up information to prepare a proposal.

"I needed a lot of facts and figures including a ball-park price range that would fit their budget. I decided to tape our conversation. I hadn't done my homework. I didn't know they also made a line of audio casette recorders. I pulled out my own tape recorder, a miniature model of Japanese make. My customer stared at it and at me and then told me pointedly that if I didn't know any more about his company's line than that, I had no business making a proposal to them. He ended our meeting abruptly. I never did get to first base with him for all the time he was with that firm.

"I learned a lesson, Joe. Don't get me wrong, my little Japanese tape job was a good machine, but it went over like a lead balloon with a guy who represented a competitive make."

The lesson here lies in the words *to the extent possible*. Be loyal to your own brand, the product you sell or represent, but be mindful of the fact that you may have to show visible loyalty at times to the product the other guy sells.

When in doubt, it's usually safe to follow that old bit of advice, "Go home with the girl you came with."

Second, *put yourself in the customer's shoes*. People do things for *their* reasons, not *ours*, and people *buy* things for *their* reasons, not *ours*.

So, look at the product you're selling from the customer's viewpoint. Walk around the car, or the tractor, or the icebox, or the dress and *mentally* look at it the way he does. You have to understand the customer's wants and needs. It's all part of fitting product to prospect. People buy your product really not because they understand all that much about it, but because they feel you have some kind of understanding about them.

However, you can't begin to understand them if you don't "walk a bit in their shoes" and look at things from their viewpoint. Maybe you even have to create a special viewpoint for them.

Here's one way a refrigerator salesman I know does this.

"I let my prospects look at the box, Joe, let him and his wife get a chance to appreciate the beauty and the color. I let them open the door and get dazzled a bit by the slide-out shelves and the crispers and maybe it's got an automatic ice-maker grinding out ice cubes which, face it, cuts down on freezer space. They're dazzled, I can tell. Hey, did you know that customers still get curious about the light that comes on when you open the door? Is it still on when you close the door? How about that, but they do.

"Then I walk 'em away from the product. That's right, walk 'em away. Once the refrigerator's out of view, I look at it from their mental viewpoint. I play back their first impressions. 'She's a beauty, isn't she?' I'll say. 'All porcelain inside, anodized aluminum shelves, nylon rollers, lots of space, right?'

"That lets me get on another tack—a chance to look at the box I'm selling from the *right* customer viewpoint, even though the customer doesn't know it yet that it's right. But, only the right viewpoint I may have to create for him is going to get me the order.

"I ask questions. Like, 'how many in the family, Mrs. Jones? How often do you shop for food, once a week, twice? Do you have any small children? What's the color of your kitchen? Do you entertain a lot? Do you freeze leftovers or take advantage of sales on meats or frozen foods?' I play back the answers. I get a picture of what they really need, not by what they're maybe dazzled by. That's the picture they now have, a *need* picture, and we're *both* seeing it from their viewpoint.

"What's it done for me, Joe? It's helped me step customers up. They really need more freezer space. If they don't entertain a lot who needs automatic ice cubes? I wind up selling maybe a side-by-side refrigerator/freezer, maybe even a separate food freezer. Seeing the product from the customers' viewpoint, and helping them get that right viewpoint to begin with, has been money in the bank."

Third, *don't get behind a curtain.* A curtain can be anything you've put up that gets in the way of a sale—something visible that makes you invisible. Whatever it is—your clothes, your jewelry, pictures on your closing-room wall, things on your desk—that curtains you from the customer's eyes can mean curtains for you as far as the sale goes.

For example, don't wear things that will turn a customer off.

He wants to buy your product, he doesn't want to pay your tailor for the new suit of threads you're wearing. So don't dazzle him with your three-piece suit. My friend, Ed Start, whom I told you about earlier, once told me, "Joe, if you sell in a blue-collar area, dress like the people you deal with. Your white shirt will get you exactly nowhere." Ed's right. The wrong clothes are a curtain, and without realizing it, that curtain is hiding you. How can a customer buy *you* along with your product, if he can't *see* you?

I always made it a practice to sit a customer in my closing room with his back to the window. Why? Because the view outdoors is a curtain. Several times I caught prospects looking over their shoulders to outside. As soon as I could, I had the window bricked up with opaque glass bricks.

An open door to the sales floor is a curtain if the customer can see past you and beyond to another area.

You might love that picture of geese flying south on your wall, but it's a curtain hiding you if the customer's mind goes south with the geese.

A woman I know who is very successful at selling in a large jewelry store in Cleveland told me about how she got rid of curtains.

"I was behind the earring counter, Mr. Girard, and doing very well. Each day I would wear a different pair of attractive earrings, my own, which I had bought at the employee's discount. Customers had a chance to see the line we carried on my own ears, and with my hair style. It really helped make sales.

"Then, one day, the management asked me to handle the frames for glasses in the optical department whenever I could until a new girl could be hired. We had a very special designers' line, Diane Von Furstenburg, Givenchy, you know. I enjoyed it. A customer would sit in front of me and I'd have them try on various frames and look at me so I could see how they fit. They looked at me all right but I soon found that their attention was on my earrings. It was taking far too long to agree on a selection of frames with those beauties dangling from my ears.

"I solved the problem this way. I stopped wearing earrings. When I was at the earring counter, I would clip on a pair to show to a customer, several pairs if necessary, and still was able to keep up my sales. When I stepped over to the optical department frames counter, my ears were earring-free. Nothing got in the way of those sales."

She had stopped hiding behind a curtain and when she did, things went smoothly again. Whatever may be a curtain for you, make it invisible, so the *selling you* is always in plain sight.

And, fourth, *be bigger than your product*. This is the best way to sell yourself first. Ever notice when you've had a picture taken out on a picnic or in your yard or on a camping trip perhaps, and you're close to the camera, how you completely cover a tree or bush or some other object behind you—even though the object may be three or four times bigger than you? That's because you're *in front* of it and closer to the camera. It's an optical illusion.

But, it's no optical illusion, it's reality, if you stand *in front* of your product. For the moment, you've become bigger than what you're selling. That's important, because the customer sees and buys you first.

Of course, I'm talking about standing in front of your product in a salesmanship sense. As I've mentioned elsewhere, I never used the expression, "I stand behind what I sell." Who can see me there? I've always said, "I stand in front of the product, too." People buy me and they know they can count on me from here on and they know my reputation is on the line.

For a sales-clinching moment I'm bigger than the product. So, too, must you be bigger than what you sell. That's the big difference between salesmanship and selling strategy. Too bad that it isn't taught more widely by all the "experts" who teach salespeople how to sell.

The fact is, when you have mastered the four simple rules I've just given you, you'll find the job of covering the seven basic steps to the sale of a product easier than you ever dreamed.

This is no idle promise. I've said it over and over. If I can do it, you can do it, too.

Now, let's cover a few other points in selling yourself and a product. They're principles tried and true but here is the way I've used them—and that's made all the difference. Again, they make a solid selling foursome:

Four Rules of Salesmanship

1. Let the customer in on your secret.
2. Let the customer into your act.
3. Let the customer use your broad shoulders to cry on.
4. Let the customer know you care.

Here's what it's all about.

First, *let the customer in on your secret*. Everybody likes a secret, to feel they know something nobody else does. They feel they're *on* to something, maybe they're even busting to tell it. They usually will if you tell them not to.

Now, one of the basic rules of selling is never to sell just a *product*, but to sell what the product *does*. The customer isn't interested as a rule in the *mechanics* of something, but rather how that something can make him happier through ownership or use.

Most salespeople know this rule by heart. They've been told so often not to forget it that they go to great lengths to make sure everything comes tumbling out. The poor customer is flooded not only with what the product does for him or her, but with a lot more history besides. It's that old story—some people when asked the time will tell you how the watch was made. Now, here's the successful way of practicing this first step.

Remember, the customer's main interest is "not in how it

came to be, but plenty of what it does for me." So, tell him—but hold *one* thing back as *your* secret. It doesn't have to be an important feature of your product, in fact, it can be minor. It's your air of secrecy that makes it important, and the fact that you just might share it with the customer. Nothing will get him or her more excited.

A sewing-machine salesman I know does it this way. He's learned all about his product and what it can do in the way of stitches, from buttonholes to plain to zigzag. His product has a dial which simply lets the user dial for the stitch she wants. When showing his product to a customer he'll say, "You can see, Mrs. Carleton, you can do a lot of different kinds of sewing with this machine. You can tackle any pattern in stride." Then he lowers his voice almost to a whisper. "But, let me tell you a little *secret* I've learned, that fashion designers in Paris, Rome and New York just hate to have get out. With this machine, you can do a *blind* stitch that looks exactly as if you did it carefully by hand, your personal touch."

Actually, Mrs. Carleton could learn everything about a blind stitch from the instruction book, but my friend makes it *his secret*, which he's sharing.

You can do this with your product, too, whatever it may be. I did it all the time. What happens is this. Through *your* air of secrecy, the customer is intrigued by *you* and what *you* do, and once again is buying *you* along with your product.

Second, *let the customer into your act.* Jimmy Durante, the comedian in films and on television, used to have a stock line: "Everybody wants ta get inta da act!" He was right. Everybody enjoys being part of something.

Every customer expects to be given a sales pitch in some way. He or she would be shocked if there wasn't any pitch. The customer expects to listen to you, watch you and be high-pressured by you. Give him a little of the first two, and avoid the high-pressure like it was a contagious disease.

Instead, pull a little surprise on the customer. Let him sell himself, or let her sell herself. Let them *say* and *do* what they expect to hear and see from you. Put *them* into your act. They'll be delighted to perform *with* you. Again, what they're doing is buying *you* along with your product. Here's how it works, as told to me by a friend who is a furniture salesman.

"I say to a customer, 'go ahead, Mrs. Foster, you open this sofa bed. Try it, make believe it's in your home.'

"She does this, slightly thrilled to be doing it, and then I ask, 'Mrs. Foster, tell me what it was like.'

"She'll no doubt reply, 'why, it was the easiest thing in the world, no effort at all. So simple. I'll have no trouble making things comfortable when we have guests.'

"What's happened, Joe, is that she sold herself because I let her get into my act. But, she'll always think of *me* when she opens that bed. Hey, wait a minute, Joe, I don't mean that like it sounds. Don't quote me."

Of course I'll quote him because he makes a good point. You try the same technique; I always did. Like with cars: "You take the wheel and drive it back to the dealership, Mr. Thompkins." Or with refrigerators: "You change the shelf arrangement with these removable shelves, Mrs. Galway." Or with sporting goods: "Let's step over here, Hal, you take this driver. I want you to get the feel, the swing, of the club."

There's nothing like letting the customer get into the act.

Third, *let the customer use your broad shoulders to cry on.* By crying, I mean all the objections he or she might have to the sale. The excuses, the real or imagined reasons, the stalls.

Every salesperson knows the importance of overcoming objections, those barriers to closing, and every salesperson tries his level best to overcome them. The Girard secret is to always overcome the objection with a bit of sympathy thrown in. Let him state his objection, offer your broad, understanding shoulders, then answer it. So many times answering an objection comes out like you were trumping your partner's ace. You've answered the objection, all right, but the customer feels you're just too slick, too all-knowing about it. That's why a little sympathy softens the blow.

A number of successful salesmen taught me this and I pass it on to you. For example: "I know the price seems a bit steep, and believe me, inflation sure has hit us all hard. I sympathize and understand your concern about how this hits your budget, but I'm sure we can work out easy payments that will take the sting out."

Use words such as "I sympathize," "I understand," "I see your point," "I feel the same way you do." Those are words that indicate you have understanding, that you care, that you recognize the objection (whether it be price, size, color, model, whatever) but that you're sure everything can be taken care of satisfactorily. You can dissolve more customer doubts, indecision, even hostility, with broad shoulders and sympathy than you ever can with cold, hard, indisputable facts.

Take it from me, I've been doing it for years.

And, fourth, *let the customer know you care*. That is, you care about him or her *now* and, even more important, you will continue to care for him or her, *after* the sale is made.

So many salespeople feel that once the order blank has been signed, the sale is over. Far from it, that's really the beginning because, unless you sell a product that will absolutely never wear out (show it to me!) your business success will come from selling that same customer again and again. *Repeat business* is the bottom line.

Again, every salesperson has been told the importance of follow-up. And most conscientious salespeople practice it faithfully. They follow up with a letter perhaps, or a call back, or the next time the customer comes into the store they ask how the product is working and if everything is satisfactory.

They go through the motions, but in my book that's not

enough. As sympathy goes hand in hand with overcoming objections, so does *caring* go hand in hand with follow-up.

A telephone call to a customer after you've sold him a product is follow-up; a personal visit to his home, if possible, which is something he doesn't expect, shows that you really care.

A "thank you" card after a sale is follow-up; a personal letter adds the element of *caring*. In fact, a letter every month shows that you not only care about the product you sold him, but that you care about him and that you want him to come back and often.

Most people do not like to be touched by casual acquaintances or salespeople, but there's nothing wrong with *mentally* putting an arm around the customer's shoulders when he's signed the order to let him know you care about him.

As one of my friends who sells used cars told me, "Joe, I look at the buyer. Often it's a young person's first set of wheels, and I say, 'I want you to know that you not only own a fine car that will give you years of good service if you take care of it, but you also now own *me*. You can count on me whenever you need me in the future. By the way, I'll get in touch with you in a week to see how everything's going."

Now, *that's* a salesman you *would* buy a used car from.

Follow up, sure, but make a CARE package out of yourself when you do. Believe me, it makes repeat business like nothing else.

Follow those Girard rules of salesmanship and you'll do a better job of selling yourself *and* a product.

I'm often asked, "What do you do, Joe, if the product you sell isn't any good?" It's a fair question. Often an item is a lousy product and the salesman faces a dilemma out in the real world of selling.

Okay, let's assume that you, as a salesman, become convinced that the product you sell is less than desirable. It doesn't matter here what the product is—it could be something sold across the counter at retail, or something sold wholesale. It could be a big-ticket item or a low-cost article. And it doesn't matter here where you sell it—a distributorship, a dealership, a department store, drug store, hardware store, lumber yard, discount house or classy boutique. You get the idea.

The main thing is that you think people who buy it are getting the short end of the stick. Let's also assume that your conclusions are valid. The product *is* no good. Period.

I've talked to a number of people in sales about this dilemma, and they've come up with some good answers. I pass them along to you.

A wholesale jobber salesman: "When you sell out of an independent distributorship, you're usually selling from a hefty catalog. The place carries a big inventory and probably is deep into multiple lines of whatever. Okay, your experience begins to tell you that Item NB-16332, for example, is from hunger. You've been getting complaints, you've tested it out as far as you can and other salesmen are getting negative feedback, too. The thing to do is to go to management and get them to drop the line. It's not just your reputation that depends on it; *his* will suffer, too.

"If you're backed up by the other guys on the sales force, you've got a pretty good chance to get it fingered out of the line."

A retail salesman who sells across the counter: "If complaints about a product are piling up and you begin to suspect it's from lemonville, you can go to the boss of the store or the department and show him or her that you can't give the thing away. Help get the price reduced, make it a special, but get it off the shelves. Urge the boss to tell the product sales rep that the store's going to push something else. It works at retail just as good as it does at wholesale."

A radio and stereo salesperson: "I sell a number of brands and I usually don't push for one if I see a customer is leaning towards another. But, if I know a certain brand isn't worth the money I don't care how much a customer likes it or thinks he likes it, I'll try to sell him off it. After all, if you've got six brands of clock radios on display, you've got a choice of five to sell if one of them is short on quality."

I've been in selling all my life. Selling a product. So, here's how Joe Girard sees it. You've really got four options:

1. Sell around the product.
2. Sell the product for what it is.
3. Try to get the product dropped from inventory.
4. Change jobs.

First, *sell around the product*. You may find this easiest to do when you work in a multiple-line outlet. Talk a customer off the lemon and on to something else. If a customer presses for a certain item that you think doesn't measure up, be frank about it and tell him or her. You may lose the commission on that one but you'll make it up on something else and your conscience will be clear.

Second, *sell the product for what it is*. For example, suppose you feel a product is bad because it's cheaply made, probably of short-term value and bargain priced. Remember, maybe that price is all some people can afford to pay. They have to settle for the amount of quality their budget can afford, perhaps only temporarily, but that's the way it is. Sell it then on the basis of, "You pay for what you get"—don't make any false claims, just help people buy what they can afford. Or, suppose you think a product is no good because it has a limited market. Solve that one by expanding your efforts in that market, even if it is a small one. A product which is "bad" because of market limitations has no faults of its own. Sell it to those to whom it appeals and do so with a clear conscience.

Third, *try to get the product dropped from inventory*. This might be quite a simple thing to do with your supervisor, sales manager or boss if the item is something like a tool in a hardware store or a brand of baking powder in a retail grocery outlet. It will be impossible to do in an automobile dealership. To the extent that you can, and depending on what you sell and where you sell it, urge that a product be given the deep six if it deserves it.

And, fourth, *change jobs*. Maybe not an easy thing to do, but maybe the best option for you. If you are a good salesman, you will be just as successful (perhaps more so) selling another product than the one you felt didn't measure up. A good conscience is far better than a good commission. Just make sure your feelings about the worthiness of the product are not just emotional but can be backed up by facts, experience, complaints, fallen-off sales and so forth. The rationale for changing jobs is really this: You aren't selling a product, you're selling yourself, and you *know* you're good.

Always remember, you may sell a product and the manufacturer may claim it is the finest product in the world, and it may well be, but even so, *you* are really the world's best product. So, sell yourself as if the bottom line depended on it. It does.

Things to Do NOW!

- Get aboard the product you sell, understand it and what it does. Learn its features, its advantages and its benefits. If you don't know *what* you're selling you have no business selling it.
- Review the seven basic steps of selling a product, then remember to put *you* in them through *salesmanship*.
- Learn and start practicing the four guidelines in selling *yourself* with the product: Be your own best customer,

put yourself in the customer's shoes, don't get behind a curtain and be bigger than your product.

Learn and start practicing the four rules of salesmanship: Let the customer in on your secret, let the customer into your act, let the customer use your broad shoulders to cry on and let the customer know you care.

CHAPTER EIGHTEEN

Selling Yourself and Your Service

PEOPLE WHO sell a service rather than a product are people who sell an *idea* about something, perhaps even something a product does, but not the product itself. Doctors sell no product; they sell their diagnostic or surgical skills, their specialization, their understanding, their medical (or dental or obstetric or psychiatric or other) knowledge and their experience. As such, everything they do in selling themselves and their services is wrapped up in an *idea*—the idea of overcoming or containing illnesses of whatever nature, or the idea of preventing illness before it happens.

Lawyers do what they do, idealistically, basically within the *idea* of justice; their services and the use of all their skills, experience and knowledge are focused on seeing that their clients are protected under the laws and statutes of our governments.

The services provided by a teacher are done within the *idea* of learning and developing. A technician or mechanic sells himself and the *idea* of keeping mechanical things doing the things they're supposed to do with as little down time as possible.

Insurance salesmen sell future freedom from want for loved ones; counselors sell guidance in all kinds of matters ranging from careers to marriage; a minister or priest or rabbi sells, basically, peace of soul; a travel agent sells, perhaps, romance and adventure; a police officer sells protection. Whatever the *idea* behind the service, there is the need to sell oneself as well.

People who sell a service of some type along with themselves, however, rarely think of what they do in terms of the *idea* or concept. When they learn to do so it becomes far easier to do a better job of selling themselves. It doesn't matter what the service is—the intangible. You might be a mailperson, a delivery person, an income tax auditor, a physician, a swimming coach, the leader of a scout troop, a city councilman or -woman, a professional snow remover, a waitress or waiter, a theater usher, a car-wash manager, a funeral director, a bank teller, the proprietor of a cleaning operation, a newspaper reporter or a performer on television, radio, stage or screen—whatever. You surely get the idea of what a "service" is.

It doesn't matter whether you are highly paid for your service or if you perform it for nothing: a skilled plastic surgeon who commands fees in the thousands, or a den mother in a Cub Scout pack who volunteers her time and service—

>*—All these people will do a better job*
>*of selling themselves along with their*
>*services if they learn to build the* IDEA
>*of that service into their lives.*

Bricks and Cathedrals

I can best tell you what I mean by retelling the famous and familiar story (author unknown at least by me) of the traveler who was passing through a city. He chanced to stop to watch a laborer patiently laying one stone brick upon another, performing a routine job skillfully and with loving care. Curious, the traveler asked the laborer, "Why are you taking such pains over the laying of some dirty bricks?"

"I am not laying bricks," the workman replied smiling. "I am building a cathedral."

You see, there was a great big beautiful *idea* behind that workman's service. In knowing this, he did a great big beautiful job of selling himself as well. The traveler moved on, impressed. "With workmen like that," he thought, "this building will stand a thousand years!"

This is a good example of substituting yourself when no physical product is involved. The one way to sell an *idea* rather than a *thing*, to influence others to buy that idea, is to express it as honestly and simply as the bricklayer did. This helps the person hearing your idea to understand it more readily. Then, usually, a great thing happens. He will usually strengthen the idea in your own mind, strengthen the worth of your service, sometimes to a far greater extent than a product salesperson might have in his or her product. Service sold along with oneself is always a great package to buy.

Service Selling Strategy

In the previous chapter I covered some of the selling strategy involved in selling a product: prospecting, qualifying, demonstrating, presenting, answering objections, closing and followup.

In most instances of selling a service rather than a product this same selling strategy applies. Your mastering the selling strategy as covered in the previous chapter will serve you equally well even though you sell a service along with yourself.

Also covered in the previous chapter was the subject of *salesmanship* as it differs from selling strategy. Remember, there were four guidelines: be your own best customer; put yourself in the customer's shoes; don't get behind a curtain; and be bigger than—in this case—your service. Those guidelines are as important in selling a service as they are in selling a product. Reread the previous chapter, master the selling strategy and the guidelines and put them to work.

However, there are services and services. If the service you sell is repair work or troubleshooting of any kind, or cleaning or landscaping or wrecking or drafting and designing—things of that nature—then the selling strategy applies. You must find customers by prospecting and you must cover most of the remaining steps right up through follow-up. This kind of service normally relates to *doing* something for some product a person owns—his or her car, appliances, house and property, clothing —you get the idea.

The other kind of service normally relates to *doing* something about the quality of a person's life. Doctors and dentists, for example, lawyers, teachers, counselors, law-enforcement officers, civic officials, waiters and waitresses—again you get the idea. Obviously, a waitress, who performs a very necessary service, does not prospect for customers (but the owner of the restaurant does); and she certainly doesn't close in the accepted sense of the word other than influencing a diner to try the chef's special rather than the regular items on the menu.

In fact, in this latter category of service, there are often strict rules governing the extent to which a doctor, lawyer or psychiatrist, for example, can prospect.

However, regardless of the kind of services you sell, regardless if some or all of the selling strategy steps apply, the guidelines of salesmanship still work for *all* types of service just as they do for all types of products.

To see them in action, let me tell you about four friends of mine. All of them are involved at "selling themselves" in professions that have no tangible product. One is in the field of insurance, another in education, another in communications and another in medicine. I have benefited personally from the services of two of them.

Regardless of their fields, they all do a fantastic job of selling themselves along with their services, as is proven by the success they enjoy.

(Incidentally, with reference to the chapter, Selling Yourself and Your Ethnic Background, all four of the people you'll read about have ethnic backgrounds—specifically, Jewish, Polish and Italian.)

Selling a Certain Future

My boyhood friend, John LoVasco, is an insurance salesman living in Grosse Pointe, Michigan. He was an identical twin, and when his brother, Eugene, died, the effect on him was shattering.

"It was a shock losing a twin," John tells me [of course, I knew his brother, Eugene, as well], "and I went into a deep depression. I was a young man, Eugene and I were very close—more so than regular brothers, I've been told—and I was left without any resources at all, nothing to fall back on. It was as if part of me had died as well.

"My wife, who I met just a year later, saved me. She helped me to grow up and she showed me how to go on. I had been working in the produce business, but I was no longer happy there. I wanted to do something that would help people. I figured that's the way Eugene would want it. Men or women who are left alone, or maybe with kids, after their wife or husband died, need help like I did when I lost my twin. I probably couldn't provide consolation but maybe I could lift their financial burden through insurance protection.

"So I got out of the produce business and went into the life insurance profession representing Metropolitan Life."

So out of John's pain came a resolve to help others, and the service he picked to sell was one that built a certain and secure future for those left behind. He probably didn't realize it at first, but the very reason for choosing the work that he did—the *idea*, you see, behind the service—was the beginnings of selling himself as well.

Not having much of a capital outlay he figured an insurance company, where he could develop his own clients, would be just the ticket for him. Metropolitan started him out on what John told me was "debits," that is, he went around from house to house collecting premiums on policies sold by others in the past. He lasted four months, perhaps a failure even quicker than he bargained for. "I wanted to start at the bottom," he said, "because if I failed I wouldn't have so far a drop."

While getting his start, he found it was tough going passing the state exams, and his manager at Metropolitan tried to be encouraging. "He told me," John says, "that I shouldn't be discouraged. A lot of people can pass a driving test, but that doesn't mean they can drive a car." John wasn't sure if the manager was telling him that even if he passed the state exams, he might not be very successful at selling insurance.

But, he didn't know John as I do. "I love a challenge," John will tell anybody, "and when I'm under pressure I rise to the occasion. And, I think you need a challenge even more when you sell something intangible."

So out of accepting a challenge as part of selling himself, John kept plugging away. He passed the state exams and he signed up with New England Life. Then, just as I had found my first customers for cars from the people I had known in the construction business, John found his first insurance customers from people he knew and worked with in the produce business.

Along the way in his career, John and his wife have raised ten children. A religious person, he says, "You've got to have faith in what you're doing, and that your service is profitable for people. I'd be less of a salesman if I didn't perform for myself the same service that I offer others. So, one of the first things I did was to take out a program of insurance for my own family. The greatest sermon you can preach is what your actions reveal rather than what you say."

Here's John LoVasco to tell the rest of the story. "It was a slow growth at first, but I wasn't on an ego trip. I figured other things came first, by that I mean my marriage and my family. I knew from the start that I wouldn't want to work on Sundays or holidays, and I always made sure to be home for the evening meal. My children knew they could count on me for that no matter what. You have to make sure your 'home' is working, know what I mean? I felt that if I wanted to portray a successful image to everybody else, in other words to sell myself to others, I had to start at home.

"If you're not doing a bang-up job there, you're going to be unsuccessful in the world of selling. You can't fool people. You may think you are, but you're not. Outward signs like a Mark-V that you might be driving can't really conceal your problems at home. Selling insurance is selling protection for loved ones. You'd better have some loved ones in your own life if you want to sell yourself and your insurance or whatever your service is.

"And you have to be willing to put in a lot of time and patience in selling a service—I think maybe even more than a salesman selling a product, but I wouldn't know. But, here's what I mean. I'd been trying to sell insurance to a prospect for the last fifteen years. No go, except small things now and then. There were times when I'd come home from his office almost in tears. He'd buy a million-dollar policy from one agent and he'd buy a quarter million from another. I'd say to him, 'save me the crumbs.' That's all I was getting anyway.

"Finally, in a recent recession, he fell on some really tough times. He had to let all his insurance go. It was then that all those other agents who sold him disappeared into the woods. It was almost like he hadn't existed. But, I hung in there, sending him notes, telling him to have confidence and not give up. One day I called him and asked him, 'how would you like $20,000? Could you use it?' He was incredulous. 'Where are you going to get it?' he asked. I told him that it was available in one of his life insurance policies that he didn't think he could touch because it was tied up in a trust. I went to work on it and I found a way to borrow the money out of the policy. I mailed him a twenty-grand check. It was almost like asking a person who was crawling in the desert if he could use an ice-cold drink.

"Well, times got better, and he appreciated what I had done for him so much that two years ago he bought a half-million-dollar policy from me and this year he bought a million. He said, 'I'll never forget what you did for me when I needed it. When the others did a disappearing act.' "

It was patience and caring and selling himself along with his service that got John, in the long run, a lot more than crumbs. How much more?

He belongs to the Million Dollar Roundtable and has been in that select group for the past twelve years. As John explains it, it's a club where insurance salesmen have to sell a certain amount of production. Out of the 250,000 life insurance salesmen in the United States, only about 5 percent belong. John has certainly exceeded that required amount of production. In the twenty-two years he has been with New England Life, he has averaged between two and three million dollars in sales each year.

"My concern," he says, "is to try to do a good job. That's all. You've got to give time and understanding. *You've got to put yourself in the sale*. I've always felt I'd rather have fewer clients and give them the service that they require, than have an abundance of clients and not be able to serve them well."

John's twin brother, Eugene, who passed away a long time ago, would have been proud.

By Your Pupils You Are Taught

Joel M. Wolfson is the founder and director of two of the most highly regarded summer youth camps in the east—Camp

Kirkland for boys and Camp Wingate for girls—both located in Yarmouth, Massachusetts.

I first met Joel in Miami, Florida, where I was on a promotion tour for the paperback of my book *How to Sell Anything to Anybody*. Actually, it was out by the pool of my hotel. Swimming trunks help to equalize.

There I was, a high school dropout.

There he was, with a Bachelor of Arts degree from Harvard, a Master of Education degree and an advanced graduate specialist in mathematics from Boston University.

All this, plus memberships in honorary societies that would make your head spin. He has taught elementary school, junior high, and special classes for the gifted child. He has worked on programmed instruction for teaching machines, preparation of school budgets and has chaired or served on committees ranging from the United Fund to mental health, from the Campfire Girls to vocational education. He is currently president of the Harvard Club of Cape Cod, Massachusetts, and, in the summer, he is the director of two youth camps (which he also founded)—one for boys and one for girls.

And, while he was piling up these impressive achievements in an area totally foreign to my background and experience, he also married and is now raising a family of four kids.

Believe me, I was impressed. Now, there is an old joke that you can always tell a Harvard man—but that you can't tell him much. It was probably started by a Yale man. Perhaps that's not true, but neither is the point of the joke. I found that Joel Wolfson was as interested in me telling him about myself as I was in listening to him. Here was a man who has been involved most of his life in selling a service to others, and at the same time selling himself in such an interesting and inspiring way, that my time with him in Miami hurled by with the speed of a Concorde.

How does he sell himself and his service? He does it by giving attention, being a good listener, showing concern and offering love. Here's what he later told me:

"I began my career, Joe, in college when, by chance, I took a job as a camp counselor. I found out that I was able to lead my group of fifth and sixth graders because they really wanted my attention in a positive way and my love."

As Joel points out, positive attention and love can never come from a product. A cooking range doesn't give *you* attention, and a home workshop band saw won't give you love. A product salesman certainly can give you attention, and he should, but he will rarely give you love—unless he's on the make for a female customer.

Joel continues: "As a young teacher, I found the same effect. I was able to teach more effectively because students wanted to please me. I am certain that before a person will imitate the behavior of another or change his attitudes and actions, he must have a desire to be like his teacher and have a true respect for his teacher's character. This belief demands a lot from one who has chosen to sell himself as an educator. There is no room for hypocrisy or negative feelings.

"As a public school administrator and a consultant to school superintendents, I spend the initial contact time in an attempt to sell my honesty and concern for quality education.

"As a summer-camp director my job is to inspire counselors to give everything they have to the camp community. And remember, such a degree of effort has less monetary rewards than most other summer jobs with less demanding requirements."

Joel points up here that, as I said earlier, some people who sell a service and really sell themselves along with it find that the paycheck may not be as big as the commissions of a product salesman. But the rewards and the satisfaction are beyond a pricetag. My friend, Joel, concludes:

"People in every role seem to respond to concern for themselves from their contacts. One way of selling your service is to be a good listener and to respond with compassion. So, selling yourself does not mean boasting about your accomplishments but rather demonstrating security in your goals and your life style so your 'customers' feel your success and want to emulate it."

In my book, if anyone wears a number-one pin it's Joel Wolfson.

The Problem Solver

My friend Dr. Sidney Lutz, a psychologist, is president of Sidney A. Lutz & Associates of Southfield, Michigan. If anyone sells an intangible it is he, which puts his service square in the *idea* ballpark.

His service is the sale of, basically, "problem solving." He sells a "fresh approach" toward defining (other people's or organizations') specific problems and coming up with alternatives.

A list of the things Dr. Lutz sells include, as he puts it, "consulting services to stimulate, create and put to work change; stating findings and conclusions clearly and simply; and helping customers for his services operate efficiently and profitably."

One way he succeeds in selling himself and his services is not to try to be all things to all people—not to spread himself too thin.

"True, but that is only one way I sell myself. Although I have a lot of skills in communication, especially in audio-visual techniques—in fact, I've operated my own videotape creative and production facilities down to and including handling the camera—I have a number of associates on call. They're my 'cadre of experts,' who are professionals in the fields of social work, law, engineering, education, medicine and psychology. I'll even sell my service in more than one language if that's needed."

Working with both individuals and businesses, with emphasis on business, Sid has been active in planning, researching, writing, designing, interviewing, advising, organizing and programming for organizations that range from nonprofit organizations to large manufacturing operations, from private corporations to government agencies.

"Here's how I approach it, Joe. I view all those organizations simply as a larger version of the family—just as the United Nations is a family of nations. They all need to air their feelings in family squabbles, they all need their strengths as a family reinforced, they all need family problems straightened out. So, how to do it?

"Well, selling yourself has a great deal to do with how you empathize with the people you're dealing with—all these business-family members. I think you simply have to put yourself in their shoes and try to think about how they might respond to the message you're giving them. That was the philosophy behind our associates' development of an in-depth training program for one of the major automotive companies. We had to think like this company, worry like it, have its expectations, and figure out its response to our services. You take on the customers' coloring.

"In fact, in many ways, when selling yourself and your services to customers, you have to be a chameleon. You must be able to change colors when the situation changes during your dealings with an organization or an individual.

"It's a question of having to be able to understand where your customers or clients are coming from and what their needs are, what their backgrounds are and what kind of life experiences they bring to you. Look, you've got to leave yourself wide open to a great number of experiences in order to relate to your customers."

Sid reminded me that this has been true in my own case. He recalls the picture I have on my office wall of myself, as a young kid shining shoes—a reminder, he points out, of who I am, a street kid who had to start to make a buck at a very early age. And, although I hadn't thought of it that way before, it helped me to relate to those coming into the dealership where I sold cars. It helped me to relate to them on a very down-to-earth level.

"The more experiences one has," Sid believes, "either in life or at work, the more able he or she is to sell his or her services effectively. The more people-relating you can do, the higher your batting average in selling yourself."

In essence, my friend Dr. Sid Lutz's advice is to increase your experiences in life, build on your past, especially as those experiences relate to people. It is the best way to sell an intangible. It is never too late to increase one's experience. But limiting one's experiences limits one's saleability of oneself and one's service. "In fact," Sid concludes, "I think that people who limit their experiences in life are taking an oatmeal approach to living. They have little contact with life and the world around them. An oatmeal person is bland, colorless, lifeless. So is an oatmeal organization. In fact, I have a rubber stamp which says *oatmeal*, and with which I stamp anything to do with an oatmeal concept of living. It goes in the oatmeal file under my desk."

I'll add my advice to my friend Sid's. Sell *yourself*, don't sell oatmeal. After all, you're selling a service, not a product.

Wrap It Up as Bedside Manner

My friend Dr. Arthur Seski is a very successful gynecologist in Detroit. I have known him for many years. His selling efforts are, of course, directed to women. He is not only a gynecologist, he is also an obstetrician. He delivered both of my kids.

I first met Dr. Seski (I've always called him that) in 1953, under frightening conditions. My wife, June, was suddenly taken deathly ill. The nature of her illness is unimportant here, except to say that it involved the services of a female specialist. I had rushed her to St. Francis Hospital and there I asked one of the Sisters, "Who is the best women's doctor I can get?" I was desperate. Without hesitation, the Sister replied, "Dr. Arthur Seski."

It was 3:00 A.M. when I called Dr. Seski and asked him would he please come to the hospital and check my wife. Now, he had never heard of me, it was an ungodly hour of the morning, he was sleeping and he could have thought of me as just another frantic husband wanting special attention. But, he didn't. I like to think that Dr. Seski is guided by the Hippocratic oath he took when he got his degree. In fact, I know he is. It's rare today to get a doctor to come to you, but it's not a sometime thing with Dr. Seski. Without hesitation he said to me that night, "I'll be right over." Before I could barely hang up, he was there.

He rushed my wife into the operating room for emergency surgery. Later, he came out and asked to see me. He showed me a huge syringe and needle filled with fluid. He was blunt. "Your wife wouldn't have lived the night if I hadn't gotten this, Mr. Girard."

Here was a man who had extended himself. A man who was concerned about a woman's life and my welfare. I thank God the Sister at the hospital recommended him (and you'll read more about that domino principle at work in an upcoming chapter). He saved my wife's life; if he hadn't, there would have been no Joe Jr. and Gracie.

I shall never forget another time when he sold himself by extending himself. In fact, it would be hard for me to forget because it was Memorial Day, May 30, 1954, my grandmother Vita Stabile's birthday (you read about her earlier), as well as Dr. Norman Vincent Peale's. This time I called Dr. Seski because my other grandmother, Grandma Girardi, was dying. "But, Mr. Girard, I'm a gynecologist," he said. Still, I begged him to come. He came immediately. He told me that all we could do would be to keep her comfortable. He couldn't heal her, but that isn't the point. The point is that he extended himself. And that's what selling yourself and your service is all about.

His work in gynecology and obstetrics means that his services include both giving and taking away. In gynecology he tries, perhaps, to improve a patient's ability to have a child, or through surgery remove something that may be life threatening. He must sell himself with equal success in each of those two overall areas. Shortly, Dr. Seski will tell you how he does it. But to go back to his beginnings.

"This is how I first sold myself," he says. "When I started out in practice I had a bunch of cards made up with my name and I would go to all the weddings I was invited to. I would hand out cards to young people and others—anyone who might appear to be a candidate for a baby, including the bride. Some of those people would come to my office later and I would treat them like members of the family. I think it's very important to do your best for people, in these cases my new patients. As a result they would respond, they would go out of my office saying that 'that doctor's all right.' "

In the area of obstetrics, Dr. Seski is involved in giving. It might even be said that there is an end product—a new baby.

"If you're an obstetrician," Dr. Seski says, "you really find yourself selling yourself in ways that you may least have expected. In pregnancies, you find yourself becoming a substitute of some sort during the entire prenatal care. I've found that the expectant mother uses the obstetrician as a substitute for everyone else, including her husband. Some patients become very attached to the doctor, although this dependency is usually temporary. Yet, it must be respected and used only for the patient's advantage.

"Then, too, during the postnatal care I find I must deal with patient depression. We call it the 'baby blues.' So, when the new mother leaves the hospital I say to her, 'Now you have two babies—and one is your husband. You must be sure to include him in the care of the new child.' "

Actually, what my friend Dr. Seski sells, along with himself, are reassurance, relaxation, trust, hope, confidence—all intangibles. These are doubly important when he steps from the field of delivering infants to the field of gynecology, which is concerned with the patient's entire reproductory system. Frequently surgery is involved. Here's how he handles that "service" and sells himself along with it.

"If I recommend any kind of special treatment—surgery, for example—I'll explain the procedures to the patient carefully, exactly what needs to be done and what to expect. In this way I also sell myself by showing that I am qualified, that I am on the faculty as a teaching professor at the medical school and that I am on the staffs of a number of hospitals. I want them to know that they're in safe hands.

"This is usually very reassuring to them. On top of that I send them home to think it over. I just don't grab the phone and schedule them in right away, unless, of course, it's an emergency. That, to me, is simply pushing the patient—losing maybe the sale of my services and even of myself.

"I find my patients appreciate that kind of treatment. That's because I soon learn that some of them are coming to me for a second opinion, which is correct and proper. Maybe they feel they were being hustled by another doctor; even if it isn't true they still may feel that way. So, I make sure my services have a built-in relaxing period, a think-about-it period. I feel that this lets people who are not buying a product from me be more comfortable. Often, then, if I suggest being scheduled into a hospital they'll let me do it, make the arrangements.

"But, selling myself goes beyond that first reassurance. I keep doing it in the hospital itself. I'll come in happy and smiling—it's the only way—and I'll do it very early in the morning."

(Incidentally, Dr. Seski enjoys the reputation of being one of the first doctors in the hospital each day.)

"If surgery is scheduled for that afternoon, I do everything I can to put the patient at her ease and to make sure she's relaxed. That includes having her family on hand if possible, and it certainly includes letting her husband be very near the operating room.

"In the operating room itself I do something that very few doctors do. I stay with the patient in the operating room before and after. Before surgery, I hold her hand while she's being put to sleep. The patient gets an additional sense of security out of that, knowing that you're right there. You know, many patients have a fear, a real anxiety, that someone else is going to do the surgery. But, if you're right there, reassuring them, they relax and go to sleep easily and without any difficulty with the anesthetic. All those little things really help me sell myself to them.

"Then, post-operatively, I see the patient at least a couple of times a day—morning and afternoon—even on my so-called days off. I come in with a cheerful 'good morning,' singing and whistling, and with a line that works for me, such as 'rise and shine, Buttercup, here comes sunshine himself!' "

Dr. Seski tells me that when the patients come in to the office afterwards for their checkups, they actually look forward to his singing.

I'll pass up the singing part, but I do know this. If I were to be the one to win that billion-dollar cash prize for the first guy to have a baby, I'd want Dr. Seski to deliver it.

Dr. Seski's services are for women, so I'd like to include the ladies in this chapter. Previously, in the chapter, Selling Yourself as a Woman, I told you about two women who were doing a terrific job with, not in spite of, their sex. Each is doing an equally terrific job in selling a service. One is Delvern Bell, a teller at a downtown, inner-city bank. The other is Maria Piacentini, who sells real estate.

Ms. Bell says, "I'm doing all kinds of bank transactions, cashing checks, posting, just all-around serving the bank's customers' needs. I find that if I do it with a smile, if I'm cheerful every time I assist a customer make a deposit or withdrawal, he feels good about that moment at the teller's window and I feel good. When I have that good feeling and I see it reflected back in the customer's face, then I know I've sold myself along with the bank's services."

Mrs. Piacentini says, "Sure, there is a product involved, a house, but I don't really see myself selling a building or a piece of land. I sell people. My service is seeing that people's expectations are met, whether I'm helping them to sell or helping them to buy. The way I sell myself along with it is to imagine always selling *with* them not *for* them, or that I'm buying *with* them not *for* them. I partnership with them instead of standing off working for them. They like it and I like it."

Things to Do NOW!

- No matter how lofty your service or how humble, start building cathedrals instead of laying bricks.
- Search for the *idea* behind your service; this is more than a customer benefit in a product, or even a service benefit, it is the *attitude* you have about your service.
- All you can *really* have is attitude; after all, you don't sell a product; there is rarely little you can lift, feel, touch, handle, operate or see.
- Follow the selling-strategy steps, some or all, if they apply.
- Follow the salesmanship guidelines in selling your service.

CHAPTER NINETEEN

Selling Yourself Without Selling Out

Now, WE want to cover some things that come under the heading of integrity. Integrity is a tremendous subject, but you can say a great deal about it in a very few words.

And, that's exactly what I intend to do. You don't need a lot of words to cover the ground. You are either honest with yourself or you aren't. You either know yourself or you don't. If you're not now honest with yourself it's time to get squared away. If you don't know yourself now it's time to discover who you really are.

Integrity is holding fast to what you, at your gut level, really are. If, at the gut level, you are not very much, or if you *believe* you're not very much, you still have integrity in that belief. But, where's the benefit? When you can know that you are a person of principle, that you can't be bought, even by yourself, and you hold fast to that knowledge and belief, then your integrity is something to be prized above all else.

Loss of integrity comes from selling out regardless of the reasons. Some people sell out for the big buck, some for prestige, some for glory, some for power, some for popularity and some out of fear.

When people talk about selling out they usually mean selling out to others: Benedict Arnold selling out America to the British; Judas selling out Christ for thirty pieces of silver. But, actually, whenever you sell out to others you are really *selling out yourself*. By the same token, if you start selling out yourself it won't be very long before you're selling out others. Remove the *out* from *selling out yourself* and you're back where you belong, *selling yourself*.

This chapter will cover briefly the positive effects that come from sticking to your principles and of not being willing to compromise them. And, I'll give you guidelines on how to do it, some arrived at by myself and some told to me by others.

What this chapter will not contain are examples of people I personally know now, or whom I have known, who have sold out. Why? Because I don't know any. You will remember I have advised you over and over to associate with winners, with number-one people, and to avoid hanging around losers. Losers are people who are constantly selling out. They sell themselves out by saying things like, "I'd put in an extra hour at prospecting, but I'm tired." Or, "I know I ought to handle so-and-so's problem, but I'd rather go out to lunch with the gang." Or, "There's more fun in the dope ring than there is giving a demo ride." Or, "There's no way I can get ahead in this company on ability, so I guess I'll have to apple-polish the boss."

You know those types. And you know me. I don't hang around with losers. I don't want to hear their "poor me," sad, sell-out songs. They all lack integrity.

Just what is integrity? Some people say integrity is represented by the way you *feel* about yourself at all times, in the fact that you know you have to live with yourself, and that you have to face yourself in the mirror every morning when you shave or put on your makeup, whatever the case may be. But listen you guys and listen you women, integrity is what you've got when you don't sell out to anybody else and especially to yourselves.

Let's look at some examples. What are some of the ways and where are some of the places that people sell out?

A great many sports figures have been accused of selling out in one way or another, sometimes proved, sometimes only suspected. There have been fighters suspected or known to have "lain down" in the ring to take the count. There have been football and basketball players suspected or known to have thrown the game. There have been jockeys known or suspected to have thrown the race. A lot of bets have been placed on the wrong guy, because the guy who should have won sold out. I won't name any names, but you, in your own mind, probably can and will. And, you know what I'm talking about.

There have been political figures on the world stage, or in national, state or local governments who have sold out their countries, their principles, their honor, their electorates. Only they can know and only history can judge. And, in judging, history is often pro and con. There are some people who feel that England's King Edward VII sold out the British Empire of that time when he abdicated in order to marry "the woman I love." There are just as many people who think that he didn't sell out. That he stuck by his principles and the empire be damned. There are some today who think we sold out Taiwan in order to recognize the People's Republic of China. There are probably more people who think that we didn't.

And it hasn't been long enough yet to forget the shock and disbelief of our country's citizens at seeing a president and a vice-president sell out the people's trust and be forced to resign. Losers. In fact, politicians often get away with selling out because of the public's attitude of "politics as usual."

Would you believe that a great many people simply expect a great many other people to sell out at one time or another? It's become that commonplace. A few weeks ago a friend of mine in the construction business placed a bid on the building of a series of culverts to provide drainage under a major highway. He told me, "Joe, I ain't gonna get the business."

"Why not?" I asked him.

"There are three other bidders besides me. And, I happen to know they're all lower. I've been underbid—a shortcut here a shortcut there. But I ain't gonna use cheap materials—hey, I gotta live with myself! This town's loaded with overpasses that are crumbling apart and that'll need to be fixed because the concrete's lousy. My bid on these culverts calls for the best materials—stuff that sand and salt won't eat away. I'll lose the bid."

He did, too. He lost because he wouldn't sell out. The sad part is that the people accepting the bids knew that was the game being played. They expected it. My friend lost, but he can still live with himself.

I was reminded of the joke I read once about an astronaut. The question was, "I wonder what the astronaut thinks as he's orbiting around in outer space, knowing that the space capsule he's in was built by the lowest bidder?" Fortunately, that's only a joke.

But there's hope for all those who decide not to sell out. Believe me, *you can win when you stick to your principles*. The *New York Times Magazine* of March 4, 1979, carried a great story about the late Edward R. Murrow by Joseph Wershba, who had been Murrow's associate back in the 1950s. It was during the time when the country was in the grip of "McCarthyism." Murrow was planning one of his "See it Now" programs on CBS television that would show up Senator Joseph McCarthy for what he was. CBS chairman, William S. Paley, gave Murrow his tacit support. And Murrow had absolute confidence that he would not have any trouble with the sponsor, the Aluminum Company of America. Why? Because Murrow had placed his principles on the line earlier. According to Joseph Wershba, "A few years before, when Alcoa had agreed to sponsor 'See it Now,' Murrow had met with executives of the powerful corporation. One of them asked him, 'tell me, Mr. Murrow, just what are your politics?'

" 'Gentlemen, that is none of your business,' Murrow replied.

"Far from being angered, the Alcoa executive reacted with an enthusiastic 'I *knew* that would be your answer!' Alcoa was sold on Murrow then and there and never tried to influence his program."

Whether in the field of entertainment, communications, sales, politics, sports, business, education, manufacturing or any other walk of life for that matter, you can *win* by sticking to your principles. You don't ever need to be a loser.

Here are some of the things that, if followed, cannot help but keep your integrity in good shape. Stick to these guidelines and you'll be in little danger of selling out:

How to Keep from Selling Out

1. Protect your good name.
2. Keep the right company.
3. Stick to your principles.
4. Beware of compromising.
5. Try saying *no*.

Let's look at each, one at a time.

First, *protect your good name*. Everyone in the world has the same gift given to him within a short time after he or she is born.

A name. Often several names. In time, a woman may change hers to a man's. Or, a man and woman may join their names together. Many people go through life known chiefly by a nickname. Some even go to court to have their names legally changed. And, some may be better known by a pen name or a name picked for stage or screen.

Regardless of what your name is, the value of your good

name is to be prized above all else. Your name and reputation should be spotless. It may start off that way and remain so all your life. Good. Or, it may have been spotted at one time or another and, if so, you need to bend every effort to remove the spots. Use elbow grease.

Your name should be recognized at once as standing for honesty and sincerity. It should be a name to be reckoned with. It is your very own trademark. It's important that you don't allow yourself to become Brand X. Your goal: Create a winning image just by the mere mention of your name.

Unfortunately, however, losing images can also be created by the mere mention of a name.

Consider some names in our recent history which have become associated with selling out. When Britain's Prime Minister Neville Chamberlain returned waving his umbrella from a meeting with Adolph Hitler in 1938 about the fate of Czechoslovakia, he thought he would be remembered for having brought "peace in our time." Instead, his name became forever associated with the word *appeasement*.

When Norway's Nazi party leader, Vidkun Quisling, betrayed his country to the enemy in World War II, and was rewarded with political power by Hitler for doing so, he gave up his good name. Then and now, to be a *quisling* means to be a traitor.

On the other hand, consider some names in our recent history which have become associated with *not* selling out.

During the missile crisis with Cuba, with America standing by ready to board Soviet vessels, Adlai Stevenson, in the Security Council of the United States, refusing to compromise a position which he knew to be right, quietly said, "Gentlemen, I'm prepared to stay here until hell freezes over, but we're not budging!" The entire nation watched on TV.

With the world's greatest automobile corporation hot on his tail, Ralph Nader refused to back down from his assertion that the Corvair automobile was unsafe at any speed. And, every consumer in the country was, or should have been, grateful.

Despite my world record of sales, I'm proud to say that, although it would have meant a boost to my income, I refused to sell a Corvair. I made every effort to steer my customers away.

You see, I, too, had to put my name on the sale. And, I was out to protect my good name.

A writer friend of mine tells me that he'll never forget the funeral of his grandfather. The old man, a farmer, died leaving virtually nothing. He had lost his land, his house and barns had burned down, his livestock was gone. All he had left was his good name. The eulogy was short and sweet. It consisted only of a few verses of Scripture: "There be of them that have left a name behind them. And some there be, which have no memorial. Their bodies are buried in peace; but their name liveth for evermore. A good name is rather to be chosen than great riches. How excellent is thy name in all the earth."

Whatever your name, Tom, Dick or Harry, don't let anything smudge it. Right down at the gut level, it's the best thing you've got going for you.

Just before the Declaration of Independence was signed, Benjamin Franklin said, "Gentlemen, we must all hang together or surely we will hang separately." Then, standing on principle, they all picked up their pens and signed. The signing not only gave us a free country, it gave us the expression, "Put your John Hancock on it."

Make sure your John Hancock is clean.

Second, *keep the right company*. You all know the expression, "People are known by the company they keep."

One of the most popular and best quarterbacks in professional football history was told he'd be suspended if he didn't get rid of his interests in certain bars or lounges. The NFL didn't like the company he was keeping. It was not consistent with the standards of professional football.

One of the most popular pitchers in the American League found his career on the skids for just about the same reasons.

One of the most well-known actors in films, famous for his

tough-guy, gangster roles, was forbidden to come into or work in England because of his suspected tie-in with gambling.

A very respected executive in the automotive industry was murdered not so long ago. After his death there was revealed a suspected association with a pretty messy list of companions which even his wife didn't know about.

For every such instance I could tell you, you probably could tell me one back. The fact is, your reputation—no matter how spotless it is—is often judged not by what you say and do, but whom you are seen with.

How can a schoolteacher, for example, maintain a reputation for integrity if, nightly, he or she is seen in a variety of "singles" pick-up bars. One real-life murder case came out of just such a situation, and later there was a book and movie about it called *Looking for Mr. Goodbar.*

A good rule to follow is *stay out of places you wouldn't be caught dead in.*

Avoid those situations you *wouldn't touch with a ten-foot pole.*

Don't go where *angels fear to tread.*

Sure, they're all trite expressions, but the fact remains that they're true.

Don't be seen socially or in business or in other situations with people you *know* to have a reputation that you want no part of. Sometimes it's not possible to know, but when you do know, split.

"Read the fine print" in life and seek out company which you know to be honest, truthful, reliable and trustworthy.

And don't be holier-than-thou about it. I guess my dad summed it up best for me. His advice was simply *keep your nose clean.* It was good advice.

Third, *stick to your principles.* Nobody is saying it's easy.

You have a set of beliefs you were brought up on. You carried them, hopefully, through your school years and into your work life and other adult activities. Trouble is, there's always somebody around trying to get you to give them up.

Don't. Because whenever the going gets tough or the road a little uncertain, the fundamentals are what you have left to fall back on. I have a friend who coaches a bunch of kids in basketball at a community center. They're a rough and tough gang. Sometimes in the enthusiasm of the game they begin to play basketball "their way." That's when my friend blows the whistle. "Okay, gang," he says, "let's get back to the fundamentals." A lot of times they don't like it—but they've found that that's what wins games.

Sticking to your principles is standing by what you know to be right. Even if it costs you the sale. Even if it costs you a student. Even if it gets you fired. Even if it costs you a friend. It's tough, right? But, it's the only way.

I know a woman who gives piano lessons. She is a skilled musician and an excellent teacher. Her living depends on her piano pupils. "You'd be amazed, Joe," she tells me, "at how many parents of kids with no talent want them to learn to play the piano. One session with the kid lets you know it's impossible. Even when you try to tell the parents, they don't want to believe it. I've had to take a stand. I will not teach someone who is unteachable, even though I would be paid well for it week after week. Friends say, 'Take the money and run.' But, I won't. My income could be a third bigger if I compromised. But, who's kidding who?"

Not everybody has the same set of principles—often young people have higher principles than their elders; they haven't had enough years yet in which others can get at them to sell out. And principles change to some degree depending upon time and period, national mood and value systems. I and those a few years older than I had strong feelings about the rightness of World War II and the importance of fighting fascism and Hitlerism in the world. A generation later, youth had just as strong feelings about the wrongness of Vietnam and American aggression. The situations were different, but sticking to one's principles hadn't changed.

Here's what you stick to: honesty, keeping your word, honoring commitments, respect for the other person's rights and your ideals.

Just as my old man had a word for me on keeping the right company, he also had another piece of advice when it came to principles. It was short and to the point: "Stick to your guns!"

Fourth, *beware of compromising.* Sticking to your principles is a positive thing to do toward selling yourself successfully. The greatest threat to standing by what you believe to be right is compromising. Compromising chips away until your stand is weakened.

Compromise is a situation in which you find yourself making concessions. You may feel there is nothing wrong in "giving up something" as long as the other person or persons give up something too. You may "explain it away" to yourself by saying, "Oh, well, I'm really making an adjustment in my life or at my work."

But all you're doing is kidding yourself and you certainly aren't selling yourself. I've learned, as have many others, that there are more pitfalls to compromise than there are advantages. My dictionary also warns that to compromise on an issue is to put yourself in danger of hurting your character and reputation. It can also expose you to risk and suspicion.

The best way to avoid compromising is to be your own man. You will not become the most popular person with those who wish you to lean their way or to "split the difference," or to "bend with the wind." But, then, selling yourself successfully does not necessarily mean winning popularity contests.

Two things happen when you compromise: *First*, you have put part of yourself in somebody else's debt. Never allow yourself to be in anybody's debt. If you do, it means the other person owns you or part of you. And, *second*, you have given an "inch or so" of yourself when you compromise.

There's an old saying, remember, that "if you give a person an inch, he'll take a mile." And, that's actually true. Compromise even just one "inch" and soon you'll be asked to compromise another inch and another. This is just as true if you compromise with yourself as it is when you compromise with others.

Compromising is not only selling out, but it is also selling yourself short. That simply means you are not being as successful a person as you can be. Perhaps most of your life you've been selling yourself short, letting people chip away at you, giving in to others when it meant giving up part of your principles, and worst of all not knowing why.

Perhaps you've known that you've been selling yourself short, compromising in your home life, your job life, your school life, and perhaps you haven't. Psychiatrists earn millions from people who have been selling themselves short in some way or another. I'm not knocking psychiatry—some of my best friends are shrinks. There are ways to come to know yourself better—there are many courses in awareness training, and you may want to consider them. I neither recommend them nor do I back off from them. I simply say, if it works for you, it's good.

But the better you know yourself the less likely you are to compromise. You are able to say, "Whoa, wait a minute, this person wants me to give in on something. Why?" Always remember, if someone wants you to yield your position a bit, it only means one thing. Your position is driving him up the wall and he won't be happy until you've eased off of it a bit. The minute you do, you're in his debt.

A friend of mine is a manufacturer of small castings used by the automotive business. His market is local and he uses trucks to make delivery. Here's what he told me over lunch a couple of months ago. "Joe, I've got a small fleet of wheels, you know that, maybe nine or ten. They don't give gas away and I've got to have drivers and swampers. But, it's my fleet and I can control it. If a shop says it needs something day before yesterday I can get it to him. When I say it'll be delivered, it'll be delivered."

"I know that," I told him. "So what's your point?"

"I been getting some pressure, some real pitches, from outside carting outfits that tell me I don't need this overhead, that I should liquidate the trucks, cut down to maybe twenty guys on the payroll, stop worrying about fuel—"

"And leave the driving to us?" I said.

"Right. They said I'll save money—I don't know how much, they're working on it. The thing is, I lose control. If I have an outside company make all my deliveries, I can only hope they'll deliver when I promise the stuff will be there. I don't think I care."

"About delivering on time?" I was surprised.

"No, no, about how much money I'll save. If I compromise on delivery, my reputation goes down the tube. I've never gone back on a promise to a customer yet. I don't want the damn trucking company owning me."

He was as good as his word. He didn't listen to the outside pitch (and it's true, it probably would have saved him money), and he still rolls his own small fleet. Compromising something he had built his company's reputation on just wasn't his way of doing business.

Let's make noncompromise your way of doing business, of living life, too.

And, fifth, *try saying no*. Such a little word. Only two letters that can work wonders for you. But, for many people the hardest thing in the world to do is to say *no*. Yet, saying *yes* to everybody can get you bogged down in more pitfalls than you can count, and those pitfalls stand in the way of selling yourself. Worse, many of them lead the way toward selling out.

It's harder to say *no* sometimes than it is to sell out. Selling out in this instance means selling yourself out—letting others eat up your time, letting others pick your brains, letting others talk you into carrying their load, letting others impose on you, in short—*letting others con you.*

Think about the times in your life when your automatic *yes,* or your *yes* because your arm was twisted or your *yes* because you didn't have the nerve to say *no* got you in over your head.

Would you serve on the refreshment committee? Well—uh —yes.

Would you mind taking charge of the parking? Well—I guess I could manage it. Okay.

Would you be a sport and give me your exam notes? I didn't get them all in class. Well—uh—sure.

Would you mind . . . would you do . . . would you serve . . . would you give . . . would you take . . . ? The questions like these, the impositions, are endless. When's the last time you said a good loud *no* to them.

No, I don't feel like joining your bowling league. I haven't got the time.

No, I won't promise to read the book. To tell you the truth, I'm not very interested.

No, I don't want to make something for the church bazaar. Why? The reasons are my own.

The first two or three times you try the *no* comeback you'll rock a few people back on their heels because they've been conditioned to your automatic *yes.* The *yes* that made you sell yourself out every time because you didn't have the guts to say *no.* But, don't worry that you'll be failing to sell yourself because you stop being a *yes*-man. Actually, nobody likes *yes*-men. In time, you'll be respected for your firm *no,* you'll be less imposed upon and when you do say *yes* to something it will carry far more force and meaning than it ever did before.

Does this mean you should stop being Mr. Good Guy? Of course not. There are times when you will want to say *yes* to something and when you should say *yes.* You don't abandon your civic duties, your friends, your church, your club, your neighbors. You've just stopped letting yourself be everybody's count-on-me buddy.

I've always said—especially when I was a salesman—that I never took *nc* for an answer. I liked to think so. The truth is, I took *no* for an answer a lot of times. It was good for me.

I like the story a young minister friend of mine tells. It's about prayer. "Joe," he said, "everybody says prayers, that is, most everybody, and they're usually asking for something. Get me a better job. Get my kid straightened out. God, help me to get well. God give me a break. And so on and so on. Then they'll come to me and say, hey, I prayed about that but God didn't answer my prayers. I'll smile and say that He probably did. The answer was no."

If God can say *no*, so can you.

There you have them—five simple guidelines to help you to keep yourself from selling out but still keep selling yourself. But, as usual, old Will Shakespeare said it just about the best way. You can keep from selling out and you can keep selling yourself to others. Here's his advice—and I can pass it on honestly. I've been to Shakespeare's plays.

> *This above all to thine own self be*
> *true, And it must follow, as the night*
> *the day, Thou canst not then be false*
> *to any man.*

Things to Do NOW!

- Resolve to put the five guidelines to work in your life starting today.
- Know that when you take the *out* from *selling out yourself*, what's left is *selling yourself*.
- Copy the quote from Shakespeare and put it on your bathroom mirror, in your office or shop, in your school locker, in your car, and carry it in your wallet or purse.

CHAPTER TWENTY

Girard's Chain Miracle

You ALL know what the domino principle is. Line up a row of dominoes, push the first one over and one after another they all fall down.

I once saw a remarkable demonstration of this on a nationally televised talk-show program. A young man, a guest on the program, had turned this principle into a feat of showmanship. Dominoes had been carefully set on their ends, hundreds and hundreds of them, in an amazing pattern. Loops, more hairpin curves than a mountain road and switchbacks. Walking over to the setup, the young man took charge of his hobby.

Using his finger to topple gently the first domino in the line, he grinned as the action started. Click, click, click, click. The momentum released by that first little white-dotted game piece increased and, one at a time, the force moved through the entire hundreds of pieces. Curves, corkscrew bends, row after row. It was fun, but it also demonstrated a principle that affects our successful ability to sell others in ways we probably never dreamed.

Chain reaction.

You've seen it on our roads and freeways in heavy traffic or in snow, ice, rain or sleet conditions. A car, tailgating perhaps, cannot stop in time when the vehicle in front of it brakes suddenly. The tailgaiting car rams into the rear of the braking car, which, in turn, is pushed into the rear of the car in front of it, which rams the car ahead of it, and so on and so on. You read about it the next day. A nine- or ten-car pileup. The tenth car ahead is not even aware what happened nine cars behind. And, the car that started it all is unaware of the momentum he created and the far-reaching results down the road in front.

Chain reaction.

It can be bad. But, the principle can also be positive and good. Nobody wants to fall down on the job of selling himself. Nobody wants to be in the lineup that gets fender-benders. Yet, it is not only possible but simple to have the dominoes in your life stay *up* instead of falling down, and to release force and momentum that bumps *out* the dents in life instead of putting them in.

The Law of 250

I've always called this principle the law of 250. In the past I warned only of the *negative* effects this law can have on sales. Now, I want to emphasize the *positive* effects it can have on your life and your ability to sell yourself.

We live in a world of cause and effect. Some one thing happens that causes an effect on something or someone. This, in turn, becomes a new cause which will produce its own effect or effects. Cause-effect-cause-effect—and, who knows where it will end?

A number of years ago, in an effort to get some idea as to where cause-effect could lead, I tagged the principle with the figure *250*. This number has a basis in fact. Those of you who have read my book *How to Sell Anything to Anybody*, or who have perhaps heard me mention the matter in a talk, will know that a funeral director originally gave me the insight. I'll repeat it briefly.

As a car salesman, selling from stock in inventory, and often finding we were short on one model or color or model with certain options, and long on another, I often wondered why nobody seemed to know just how many vehicles to order, as-suming that the dealership could get them even when they were ordered. I got no answers.

I asked a funeral director, a friend, how he knew how many of those little "In Memoriam" or mass cards to order, those that carry the name of the deceased and the dates of birth and death that are stacked alongside the visitors' register.

He told me that long experience and "averaging out" had taught him that 250 was the magic number, that with 250 such cards on hand, he was unlikely to run short or to have too many left over.

"It's a remarkable thing, Joe," he told me, "but each person, even though he's dead, represents 250 others."

I later double-checked this with a printer friend who told me much the same thing about weddings—whether he had print orders for invitations or announcements to be sent out after-wards.

"Over a long period of time, Joe, I discovered that the aver-age print order for wedding invitations, or for announcements after a secret marriage or elopement took place, was 250."

And, I recently had another indication of the truth of this magic number. I had just given a talk in Miami during which I mentioned my "law of 250." Shortly afterwards, at the Omni Hotel, I gave a copy of my book on selling to my friend Joel Wolfson from Massachusetts. Of course, the "law" is mentioned in it in some detail. When he finished my book he was staggered.

"Joe," he said, "I have recently worked along with others for months researching things to be done regarding the building of an addition to the synagogue where I'm president of the board of trustees. One of our main questions was how big should the social hall be? We needed space for receptions, confirmations, bar mitzvahs, you know. After a long look at our past experiences and our needs, we decided that what we required was space for twenty-five round tables each seating ten people."

His eyes sparkled with excitement as I waited to hear what I was sure he would tell me.

"Can you believe it, Joe? 250?"

I could believe it.

Have you ever noticed that when you enter many bars or lounges, or popular restaurants, that there will be a notice of some sort which says "seating capacity 250"? This is also true of the foyers in many movie theaters, where there'll be a small sign posted, usually by order of the fire department, that the standing room capacity is 250. I have a friend who is very active in community theater. One of the local auditoriums owned by an amateur group seats exactly 250. If the group oversells by as much as one seat, it must notify the fire marshal who will send around a representative to keep an eye on things. 250. Check it out yourself.

And the "law of 250" is what really lies behind the most successful advertising you can get, word of mouth. It's what sells movie tickets, good restaurants, books, doctors and dentists. Best of all, it sells people. *It sells you.*

As a salesman, I was always concerned with building up an owner file and a prospect file. I created one of the most valuable files in the country—how else could I have sold over 1,400 new cars at retail in one year?—and I have since turned it over to my son who is following in my footsteps. If anyone ever shoves me out of the Guinness Book of World Records it will be Joe, Jr. He's got the file to do it. It's up to him.

One day I sat down and looked at that file. It hit me like a truck barreling down the highway that every name in that file represented 250 others, and each of the 250 stood for 250 more. And on and on. It blew my mind. It was impossible for me to total up. And, when I did I first focused on the negative effects that this law could bring about. The reasons were sound.

Perhaps it's because most salespeople, myself included, have been brought up to believe they are bad-mouthed most of the time by others. "He's *just* a salesman," people will say. Or, "Watch out for old Mr. High-pressure!" So, at first I concentrated on the negative side of the "law of 250."

I said to myself, I counseled other salespeople and I wrote, "if you sell a person and he's *dissatisfied*, he's going to tell, eventually, through chain reaction, 250 others. And, many many more besides. Watch what you say to a customer," I warned. "It can backfire. If your deal isn't fair and the car customer thinks he's been had, he'll tell others. You can send 250 prospects down the drain if you treat a customer wrong."

All things *not* to do.

Accentuate the Positive

It was some time before that encounter with Wolfson, however, that I began to accentuate the positive and eliminate the negative. Before then, sometime in the '60s, I was still acting in terms of what *not* to do. You've noticed, certainly, that at the end of each of these chapters I have listed a number of *things to do*. Only rarely, when it makes a very solid point that can be put best that way, have I listed something *not* to do.

It was a good piece of advice that I received from my sales manager sometime around 1963 that pointed me in the opposite, the positive, direction. I listened to him because he did a terrific job of selling himself.

"Joe," he said, "think in terms of *good* results. It's a better way to go. If you sell a person, aim for his satisfaction button and don't worry about his bad-mouthing you. He'll have nothing to bad-mouth you about. If he's satisfied, he's going to tell everybody—your 250, if that's what you believe it is—plus a lot more besides. Say something *good* to a customer and it will backfire *good*. Make sure the deal you give a guy is fair and square and he'll tell others that you're a square guy. You can create 250 prospects for your product if you just treat the customer the way you like to be treated. Stop worrying about treating him wrong."

He was showing me a way to let the dominoes of my life stay *up*, not fall down. And, that's when I started calling the "law of 250" a chain miracle—Girard's chain miracle.

Think of it that way. Every person you look at, talk to, deal with, relate to—see the 250 other people standing behind him or her and put them to work. 250 pairs of hands miraculously working for you. 250 mouths ready and willing to help you sell yourself. Believe me, that's really plenty of pulling power.

Ninety percent of all the people who hear me speak, 90 percent of studio audiences at radio or TV talk shows, ask me questions about Girard's chain miracle, the "law of 250." I have repeated the story of my discovery of it until I am blue in the face. People never seem to tire of hearing it. "Joe," they'll say, "you know, that law of yours makes sense."

Recently, while readying for an appearance on the "Mike Douglas Show," aired in the spring of 1979, Mike said to me, "Joe, that 'law of 250' business is really something else!" And, he or one of his staff added, "You know, I never thought of people that way. I'm going to be really careful the next time I speak out of turn or do something wrong. Hey, it's a really strong point in your book." I told Mike and his staff, as I've told you, that it's not so much a question of doing something wrong, or speaking out of turn. What's important is doing something right and saying things that are positive and good.

What About the Payoff?

Since it's not easy to determine the down-the-road payoff in selling yourself, the best you can do is sell yourself to one person and let him or her take care of the other 250 for you. Long-range results are hard to measure when the jury's still out. No one can say to you with any degree of certainty that "because I gave my new car customer a fair deal, because I treated him right, I sold exactly seven new cars to people who heard about me through him." Nobody can say that "because I flashed my million-dollar smile one day at that chick at the skating rink, I gained fourteen in-laws." Who can tell?

But, here are some educated guesses told me by people who are doing a great job of selling themselves.

A new car salesman in Detroit: "In six months' time I sold sixty-five cars. Eleven of those were referrals, each one coming to me because a friend said he'd been treated right. I'm not sure, but there could be a twelfth. But, going back to the first of the eleven—he had bought from a guy I had sold to two months earlier. It hasn't ended yet."

A trainee in a training seminar: "Not long ago I signed up for a four-day training seminar. It was recommended to me as a mind-blowing experience by a friend of mine in California. In fact, that guy's been doing a great job of word-of-mouth on friends of his around the country. I took the course, and since then I've told four others who signed up for it. Now that they've taken it one of them has already passed the word on to two more who signed up. I don't know how much farther this'll stretch, but one thing about this training—it's sold only by one graduate telling another."

A mutual funds salesman in Detroit: "Our brokerage is a

member of the New York Stock Exchange. I spend a lot of time under the big board. I've got maybe fifty hard-core customers, guys I'm helping to build a portfolio. Each one came to me from one of the others. I've had a few house accounts, but my biggies all came because someone told them I'd take good care of them."

A manager of a large apartment house: "I almost got a ticket the other day coming into the office on the premises, but the cop let me off. I don't know why I lucked out but he waved me on with a smile a mile wide. Maybe his old lady had treated him right last night. Anyway, just because I felt lucky, I guess, I found myself passing that smile along to every tenant I dealt with that day. And, that ain't always easy. I get complaints. I could see the folks in the building soon were doing the same thing, like in the elevator. Someone's granddaughter was visiting that day and later, in the lobby, I heard her say, 'Grandma, I haven't seen you smile like that in a long time. Maybe your back doesn't hurt so much.' The kid was smiling, too. She carried it right out of the building to her mother who had come to pick her up. I saw her mother smile back. Hey, that cop never knew what he started."

A florist in Birmingham: "A little over a month ago a man came in to order a funeral spray. We're one of those flower-by-wire shops and have a big book which you can choose from. This guy didn't like any of the made-up stuff. So, he asked me if I could make up something nice and be sure to have it to the funeral home before that evening when there was going to be a rosary. I gave him my word, but I had a feeling when he walked out that he really didn't believe me. Maybe he's been taken before. But, I kept my promise. He called me up the next day, told me the flowers were great and they got there when I said they would. That's always nice to hear, but since then five customers have come in I've never seen before and everyone said they heard about me from that same guy. And one of them said it was because she heard I kept my promises."

Multiplying Yourself

Actually, those are all examples of ways to multiply yourself. Whether you like it or not, you're going to be multiplied. Here's one of the best examples I know of.

Much has been written about Ray Kroc, chairman of the board of McDonald's. The Big Mac. And these are some of the things I've read about Mr. Kroc. He used to sell malted milk machines to the former McDonald Brothers who were in the fast-food business, serving primarily hamburgers. In time, the ambitious and experienced Mr. Kroc took over the operation and he became McDonald's. When he did, he brought a particular philosophy with him that, whether he thought about it in these terms or not, was based on chain reaction. People come in and people go out and people talk. Cause-effect-cause-effect. So he made sure that what they'd talk about was good.

Kroc's philosophy was that every person would get a fair shake—and not just the one in the paper cup. He didn't want one person ever walking out who felt he hadn't got a fair shake. Or good food. The quality of the hamburgers had to be tops. The french fries had to be first rate. (I know a number of people who swear that the fries at McDonald's cannot be beaten anywhere.)

He made sure that every franchised outlet was policed constantly as to cleanliness. The place must be spotlessly clean, and it is. The windows must sparkle like diamonds, and they do. Everyone must abide by the rules. He wanted to be absolutely sure that there wouldn't be one person who'd walk away dissatisfied. More than that, really. He wanted to make sure every person who came in and out was pleased.

He's been successful in that goal. To my knowledge, McDonald's is one of the largest, most successful fast-food operations of its kind in the world.

Consider those signs out by the golden arches, telling passersby how many billions of McDonald's hamburgers have been sold to date. They tell you more than just sales figures. Those hamburgers weren't just sold by luck. They were sold by the domino principle: People knocking over one another trying to get in there.

Every time I drive by a McDonald's and I see the big *M* out in front, that big *M*, to me, stands for *multiplication*. What kind of multiplication? As an example, suppose you influence someone for good, that you really sell yourself strongly to a different prospect (or a friend, or a coworker, or an employee or a person with the munchies who wants a good hamburger) *just two times a week*. That's 104 people by the end of the year. With 250 others behind each one of those 104, you've influenced in some way 26,000 people. And behind each of those 26,000 are another 250. Mind-boggling, right? Imagine what it can be like when you're really selling yourself successfully to someone every day of the year.

No wonder Big Macs are numbered in the billions.

And, here's another way for you sports fans to look at it. My friend Augie Bergamo, who used to play sandlot baseball in the neighborhood where we grew up and who wound up playing with the St. Louis Cardinals, once put it to me this way when I told him about the "law of 250." "Joe, at 26,000 influenced-for-good people a year, you could in two year's time fill up Memorial Park, home of the Baltimore Orioles, or Riverfront Stadium, home of the Cincinnati Reds. And, you could almost pack Candlestick Park or Tiger Stadium or Yankee Stadium, the house that Babe Ruth built. It would have made Casey Stengel flip."

Throughout this book you've been told many times that confidence breeds confidence, that your positive attitudes are always showing, that enthusiasm is contagious, that honesty is always the best policy, that there is power in a promise, that a smile is a sensational thing, that youth or maturity or sex doesn't limit your sales power and that there is real appeal in your ethnic background.

But, until you add the factor of multiplication, Girard's chain miracle, you cannot realize just how far confidence can carry you and how far enthusiasm can spread, just how far the truth keeps working for you, just how powerful your promises can be and just how sensational your smile really is. It staggers the imagination.

To sum it all up, here's my advice, sweet and simple, to help you multiply yourself well and to keep those dominoes standing *up:*

Things to Do NOW!

- If you're enthusiastic, spread it.
- If you like someone, tell him or her.
- If you feel confident, show it.
- If you feel good, tell somebody.
- If you have a smile, share it.
- If you make a promise, keep it.
- If you can give someone a lift, give it.
- If you know it's the truth, say so.

CHAPTER TWENTY-ONE

The Payoff of Persistence

*"Nothing in the world can take the
place of persistence. Talent will not.
Nothing is more common than unsuccessful
men with talent. Genius will not; un-
rewarded genius is almost a proverb.
Education will not: the world is full
of educated derelicts. Persistence and
determination alone are omnipotent."*

I BELIEVE that. I do not know who said it; I will be happy to
acknowledge it when I do. But, it is another of the many signs,
mottos, quotations and "charges" that surround me on the walls
of my office. They may seem simple to some—a lot of plati-
tudes and schoolboy mottos like "If at first you don't succeed
try try again."

Well, if a motto works, I say use it. If it takes a sign on your office wall, or shop toolbox, or bathroom mirror or over the kitchen stove or inside your school or gym locker to get you charged up, use it. And keep using it. Keep doing the things that work.

That's what this final chapter is all about. Sticking with it. Hanging in there. The key words in the schoolboy motto are *try try again*. Key words in my own life are *keep doing it till you get it right*.

Ty Cobb, a baseball immortal and member of my own beloved Detroit Tigers, was American League batting champ for four years straight, 1912 through 1915. During that time he averaged over .410. Back in those days the clubs were different, the league was different, so-called spring training was different. Ty is reported to have told a baseball writer for one of the high school papers in Detroit, when asked how he got to be and stay a batting champ, that it was only through sticking to it. He had the strong arms, but muscles didn't mean anything if you couldn't control them, make them do what you wanted them to do. Ty is said to have gone out in the fields when he wasn't playing, and he would measure a distance from a big tree—a distance equal to that of home plate to the upper decks. Then he'd toss up baseballs and knock them out toward that tree. Over and over again. And the more he did it, the more often he'd send the pill over the treetop. Anybody can hit and most people can aim, Ty allowed, but only sticking at it over and over again will help you to hit the ball where you want it to go and how far you want it to go. A champ should know.

I once read an old clipping about Bobby Jones, one of the greatest golfers who ever set out over the links. He said practically the same thing as Ty Cobb.

But, sports don't provide the only examples. It was *persistence* that enabled Annie Sullivan Macy to teach the blind and deaf Helen Keller to enter into a world she couldn't see or hear.

It was *persistence* that lay behind Kettering's invention of the self-starter.

It was *persistence* that kept Thomas Edison going back to the drawing boards and his electric light until he got it right. He tried one thing after another in his search for the proper filament. Had "give up" been in his vocabulary you might be reading this book by a kerosene lamp.

And it was *persistence* that kept Bette Davis, one of the screen's most talented actresses, plugging away in her fight against her producers to win roles worthy of her. And, when she battled, she was battling for every star who felt "held down" by directors and producers who were afraid of their own shadows.

Does *persistence* always pay off? Of course not. We live in a realistic world. I was at a luncheon one day in Minneapolis and I sat next to a native son who was talking about another native son, who had been governor of the state, Harold Stassen. "Talk about persistence," he said, "its name is Harold. Stassen has been trying to be president of the United States for a hundred years and he hasn't made it and he won't make it."

"You're probably right," I told him, "but look at the fun he's had along the way."

The payoff of persistence can be great. Making it is great. Sure, we ought to keep our eye on the goal. But the value of persistence isn't always the goal. The value lies in the fact that you *tried*. How does that old saying go? "It is better to have loved and lost than never to have loved at all." Right on!

But, when the payoff does come—and it will more often than not, Harold Stassen to the contrary—the satisfaction is wonderful. But nobody has ever said persistence is easy.

The more you persist the more you may find yourself getting sand-trapped. That's why selling yourself successfully means overcoming obstacles; it's the same as selling a product or service means overcoming objections. Selling yourself can have more hazards than the Pine Valley Golf Course in New Jersey, which I'm told most golf pros in the country think is the toughest. One of its traps is the world's biggest—so big it's called Hell's Half-Acre. There are a lot of hell's half-acres in your goal of selling yourself. *But all traps are made to get out of.* It may take a lot of swings of the club, but eventually you will get out.

In selling yourself successfully, there will be scores of things that will suddenly get in your way just when you don't want them to. There will be people who will try to hold you back. It seems to be human nature. Ever notice that when you've gone on a diet, and you've been sticking to it and your exercise program, and the pounds are, thank God, melting off, there'll always be someone who'll say, "You're looking a little haggard, you know. Are you sure you want to keep losing?" If you're a salesman, I'll bet you can come up with a dozen examples of how just when you've made up your mind to make one more prospecting phone call, or to stay a half hour longer at your desk, there'll always be a good buddy coming along who'll urge you to knock it off and join the gang for a martini or a beer at the local watering hole. It seems to be human nature for people to be driven nuts when they see someone else being persistent.

So, when I tell you to hang in there, I'm also telling you that you'll be surprised, confused, often angry and frustrated at the number of obstacles raised against you. And, I'm also telling you that you can crawl under all the barbed wire in life and scale all the brick walls of discouragement without too many bruises and without tripping up as you run the race. You can keep going without falling down.

Life's a Marathon

A very good friend of mine has a son in his mid-twenties who recently ran a twenty-six-mile-plus marathon in Detroit. It was an international marathon because it included Canadians as well, and the course went back and forth across the Detroit River, our international boundary. The kid had trained for it a long time, but he had never run that far and wasn't sure that he could.

He ran a great deal of the race with a pain in his rib cage, cramps in his calves, and a blister on one foot that got as big as an egg. And, like most long-distance runners he told me of the "wall" that you seem to hit at a certain mile-mark, when you think you can't go a step farther, but that when you push on regardless you somehow manage to run through that wall and keep going. It happened to the son of this friend and he stuck it out to the finish line. He didn't win—as far as coming in first was concerned—and he didn't lose. Like with most things in life, the real race was against *himself* and time, and in that sense everyone who *finished the race*, no matter where he or she placed, was a winner.

Life is but a race. And, in selling yourself your main competition is *yourself*. Sticking to the job of selling yourself, your persistence, is what makes you a winner.

The Elevator Is Out of Order

The secret is to follow the old standby rule, "one step at a time." If you meet an obstacle or a problem along the way, tackle it, solve it, then move on to the next. That way problems don't become overwhelming. And, in clearing up one you may find that when you come to the next one it has already solved itself. Time solves an awful lot of problems. But, the best way to stick to it, to tell yourself that once is not enough, to get off the mat and come back for more, to develop the endurance you need to go the distance on your feet, is go by that "step at a time" rule.

You read earlier in this book that I have another one of those signs in my office that reads: "The elevator to success is out of order—you'll have to use the stairs—one step at a time." That still goes. If you take things one step at a time it doesn't even matter if there's an elevator in the building that's not working. As long as there are stairways or ladders leading to where you want to go, you're in good shape. Just keep climbing.

It's been said that those who are not busy, who are not struggling or striving—and that goes for success in selling yourself, too—are simply busy dying. Hard work and persistence, sticking to the task you've set out to do, the task of selling yourself in more and better ways, is healthy. Hard work never caused the death of anyone. But, boredom, sitting around, wasting time, daydreaming and failing to push on and take things a step at a time are deadly.

Persistence means being a leader in your own successful life, not a follower. Don't follow trails, blaze them. Of course, that means you've got to know where you're going. Another sign in my office (I told you they line my walls) reads: "The whole secret of life is to know what you want, to write it down and then commit yourself to accomplish it."

Now you know why there were so many items I listed in "things to do" at the end of each chapter that you were to write down. It strengthens your commitment to them. It gives you stay-power. And you need that stay-power when it comes to selling yourself successfully because if you don't stick to those "things to do" they won't work. How can they? Nothing will work for you if you don't program it into your program machine. I've had scores of people come up to me and tell me, "Joe, I've listened to you, I've read your articles, it all sounds good—but how can I be sure it's all going to work?"

My answer has always been, "How can you be sure it's *not* going to work? You won't know until you try—and stick to it."

Almost certain-sure, many of those same people will come up to me again, or write to me, and they'll say, "Joe, I'm glad I was persistent. That's really the thing that *made* it work."

That's the truth. A rule is no good unless it is followed. A guideline is no good unless you use it to guide you. A suggestion is worthless if you leave it pigeonholed in the suggestion box.

Persistence brings the payoff. It's what pushed back our frontiers, it's what explored our rivers, and mountains and forests, it's what built America. Think of life as if you are a person who is traveling a river in a canoe, just as our ancestors did in pioneer days. (Not mine, actually, we don't do much canoeing in Sicily.) But American pioneers, no matter where they came from, ventured into many rapids filled with "white water." As long as they paddled hard and fought against the current they made progress upstream. But, if they rested on their paddles, so to speak, they were swept back down the river. America wasn't built, fortunately, by people who let themselves be swept back downstream.

Or by people who let themselves be "talked" back downstream or "laughed" back downstream. Sure, you may see some smiles from others at your extra efforts in selling yourself, not smiles of encouragement but of slight ridicule. Sure you'll hear some snide remarks. Shut your ears. Those are the same people who say, "Are you sure you want to take off more weight? You looked better when you were heavier."

The hold-back people we talked about in an earlier chapter of this book are part of the risks we take. They are the play-it-safe people. Don't be one of those. Too many of us want to play it safe, don't want to get involved, don't want to have our boats rocked. Well, speaking as a former old-pro car salesman, I can tell you this: A car kept in a garage and off the street is safe. But, that's not what cars were built for. I read that someplace and whoever said it first I gladly give him or her credit, because it's true.

I learned a great lesson from a guy who knew what cars were built for and kept them moving out into the streets where they belonged. At the same time he told me that persistence really lay behind his success.

For years this salesman had the office next to me in the

dealership where I worked. He would amaze me with his ability to stay with it when it came to a sale. He always piled up an impressive record each year, and there's nothing I admire more than success when I see someone achieve it.

If a customer would start to get up and leave, this salesman would put a slight restraining touch on the guy's arm—no pressure, after all, most people don't care to be touched by strangers—just a gesture really that said, "Don't go, I want you for a customer." His face showed his stay-power, his eyes, his voice did the same thing. I never saw a guy who was so determined not to give up. One day I asked him what his secret was. I told him that I wanted to be like him, that I wanted to enjoy his stay-power.

"Joe," he said, "it's simple. I don't believe what people tell me about the word 'no.' To me, 'no' means 'maybe,' nothing else. And, 'maybe' means 'yes'—always. Get those meanings in your head, Joe, and they'll keep you hanging in there."

I never forgot his advice. I pass it on. When you're taking that "one step at a time" and your tired body and brain tells you "no" as you face the next step, tell your mind that "no" only means "maybe." Maybe you can take that step if you try. Maybe you can make it. Then, tell yourself that "maybe" only means "yes." The minute you say "yes, I can do it," you take that step and move on, just like my friend's kid, the marathon runner, who broke through the "wall."

The Three Rules for Being Persistent

1. Know what you want and commit yourself to getting it.
2. Since the elevator is out of order, get where you're going one step at a time.
3. Deep-six the word *no*. *No* only means *maybe* and *maybe* always means *yes*.

Readers, there you have it. I've shared as many of my experiences in selling myself successfully as I can. And, I've passed along tips and workable things to do that friends and business associates have shared with me. And I've cited things I've read and remembered.

You can't do them all at once, and you'd get bogged down if you tried. Take them a step at a time, stick to each of the rules, be persistent in following the guidelines and suggestions.

Soon you will begin to notice a change in yourself, a change for the better. Your enthusiasm machine, your confidence carburetor will be finely tuned. You'll feel good about yourself in ways you never felt before. You'll find yourself smiling more, losing or gaining weight if those are your goals, closing more sales if that's your bag, and getting along better with others no matter what the relationships. You'll find that you're no longer interested in singing "poor me" songs. You'll put on a happy face. And, you'll be surprised to find those things reflected in the faces and lives of others.

You'll appreciate and enjoy your maturity, and you'll stop being ruled by the impatience of youth. You'll take new pleasure in yourself as a woman, and, if you're a man, you'll feel less threatened by women who are making it in business.

And, maybe for the first time in your life, you'll be proud in new ways that you have a different ethnic background from others, that there is strength and power in that ethnic background that can work for you.

Promises will be easier to keep, truth will be easier to tell, and, like the boy Galileo who had a world widen for him when his father turned his telescope around, your own outlook on life will expand. And, so will your success.

How do I know this to be true? Because it's what has happened to me in the last fifteen years or so of my life. If these principles can pick me up, a failure at thirty-five or so, and turn me around 180 degrees, they can do the same for you. The principles, the guidelines, the rules, the suggestions are there for everybody. They're like a great, dazzling, tempting array of food along the cafeteria line of life. But, no one of them will do any good just sitting there. It's only when you reach out and take this one and that one and this one and put each on your tray that they really belong to you.

Help yourself!

Things To Do NOW!

- Sell . . .
    And Sell . . .
        And *Sell Yourself* . . .
            Successfully from now on.

Make the Most of Yourself

__HOW TO SELL ANYTHING TO ANYBODY
by Joe Girard with   *(K32-516, $3.95, U.S.A.)*
Stanley H. Brown   *(K32-517, $4.95, Canada)*
Also available in large-format paperback
         (K37-657, $5.95, U.S.A.)

Joe Girard has shown millions of men and women involved or interested in selling exactly how they can adapt the same selling techniques that lifted Girard to the top of his profession. He tells you: how to develop a personal and very effective direct-mail program; how to size up the customer's wants, needs and what he can afford; how to get the customer to trust you and to recommend other customers; how honesty can turn a "no" into a "yes"; how to turn customer complaints into orders; and how to make a lifelong customer from the very first sale.

__HOW TO SELL YOURSELF
by Joe Girard   *(K38-162, $8.95, U.S.A.)*
A large-format quality paperback   *(K38-163, $9.95, Canada)*
Includes: building self-confidence and courage; developing positive attitudes; learning to listen; managing your memory; exercising enthusiasm; selling yourself without selling out; the power of a promise; the sensation of a smile; and the payoff of persistence. With an introduction by Dr. Norman Vincent Peale, HOW TO SELL YOURSELF is the tool to a better, happier, more successful life for every reader.

WARNER BOOKS
P.O. Box 690
New York, N.Y. 10019

Please send me the books I have checked. I enclose a check or money order (not cash), plus 50¢ per order and 50¢ per copy to cover postage and handling.* (Allow 4 weeks for delivery.)

_____ Please send me your free mail order catalog. (If ordering only the catalog, include a large self-addressed, stamped envelope.)

Name _____

Address _____

City _____

State _____ Zip _____

*N.Y. State and California residents add applicable sales tax.   71